Strategic Party Government

Chicago Studies in American Politics

A SERIES EDITED BY BENJAMIN I. PAGE, SUSAN HERBST,
LAWRENCE R. JACOBS, AND ADAM J. BERINSKY

Also in the series:

Additional series titles follow index

Strategic Party Government

Why Winning Trumps Ideology

GREGORY KOGER

MATTHEW J. LEBO

THE UNIVERSITY OF CHICAGO PRESS   CHICAGO AND LONDON

The University of Chicago Press, Chicago 60637
The University of Chicago Press, Ltd., London
© 2017 by The University of Chicago
All rights reserved. Published 2017.
Printed in the United States of America

26 25 24 23 22 21 20 19 18 17   1 2 3 4 5

ISBN-13: 978-0-226-42457-6 (cloth)
ISBN-13: 978-0-226-42460-6 (paper)
ISBN-13: 978-0-226-42474-3 (e-book)
DOI: 10.7208/chicago/9780226424743.001.0001

Library of Congress Cataloging-in-Publication Data

Names: Koger, Gregory, author. | Lebo, Matthew J., author.
Title: Strategic party government : why winning trumps ideology / Gregory Koger and
    Matthew J. Lebo.
Other titles: Chicago studies in American politics.
Description: Chicago ; London : The University of Chicago Press, 2016. | Series: Chicago
    studies in American politics.
Identifiers: LCCN 2016024713 | ISBN 9780226424576 (cloth : alk. paper) | ISBN
    9780226424606 (pbk. : alk. paper) | ISBN 9780226424743 (e-book)
Subjects: LCSH: Political parties—United States. | United States—Politics and
    government—2009–
Classification: LCC JK2265 .K644 2016 | DDC 328.73/0769—dc23 LC record available at
    https://lccn.loc.gov/2016024713

TO OUR FATHERS, JOHN WILLIAM KOGER AND HERSCHEL WILFRED LEBO

Contents

Preface

This book provides a new chapter in a classic conversation. One of the very first political science books, Woodrow Wilson's *Congressional Government*, lamented the weak state of parties in the House and Senate compared to the British House of Commons. From 1885 to 2016, scholars have understood that legislators determine the role of parties in their chambers and that their choices vary over time and across chambers.

Over the last forty years, there has been a robust conversation about congressional parties as scholars have tried to understand the forces at work in Congress. This book builds on the work of "neoinstitutionalist" scholars like Barbara Sinclair, John Aldrich, David Rohde, Keith Krehbiel, Gary Cox, and Mat McCubbins. Like these leading scholars, we seek to provide an account of varying party influence grounded in legislators' goals and strategies. We emphasize the role of electoral competition and strategic interaction to explain why legislators will cooperate with their party leaders even when they disagree with each other on policy issues.

Our account benefits from our colleagues' research, but also from the last ten years of congressional partisanship. While scholars were debating whether parties "matter," the US Congress became increasingly partisan and an ever-increasing share of legislators' attention has been focused on helping their party succeed in the next election. This partisan competition is the game we set out to explain, but with an account that also explains how and why legislative parties change over time. Our initial insight was to apply new time series techniques to classic measures of congressional partisanship, which led to a new model of congressional parties and fresh ideas to test.

This project has had a long incubation period. Our partnership began over umbrella drinks at Trader Vic's in the Palmer House Hilton and has carried us across the country. Along the way, we have accumulated a vast number of debts. First, we appreciate the scholars who have coauthored chapters of this book: Jamie Carson, Ellen Key, and Everett Young. Our unindicted coauthor is Ben Bishin, who introduced us, has been a most generous commenter on this manuscript, and has been a great friend and colleague throughout the process. We also appreciate the research assistance of Marie Courtemanche, Justine D'Elia, Taylor Grant, April Johnson, Maxwell Mak, Adam McGlynn, Andrew O'Geen, David Perkins, Andrew Sidman, Claire Catotti, and Chris Weber. Among the many scholars who have provided comments, we especially appreciate Kathleen Bawn, Hans Noel, Gary Cox, Jeff Jenkins, Nate Monroe, Arthur Lupia, Chris den Hartog, Justin Buchler, Jeff Grynaviski, Gary Jacobson, Laurel Harbridge, Phil Paolino, Doug Roscoe, Stanley Feldman, and seminar audiences at Yale, Ohio State University, Washington University, the University of Georgia, Texas A&M, the University of Miami, Stony Brook University, and miniconferences hosted by UW–Wisconsin, Duke (Senate parties), and an Empirical Implications of Theoretical Models (EITM) miniconference at the June 2005 Canadian Political Science Association meeting in London, Ontario. We especially appreciate John Aldrich, David Rohde, and the Political Institutions and Public Choice Program at Duke University for hosting us for a seminar and book discussion. All remaining errors are our own, except for those attributable to Hans Noel.

In June 2005, we finished a full day at the EITM miniconference, and found our rental car sitting in an empty parking lot. With a dead battery. Before our conversation could devolve into assessing responsibility for the dead battery, another car entered the lot and parked right next to us. By Canadian custom, the driver had jumper cables and time to spare, and we were soon on our way. Had he not arrived just then, this book might not have been written. We would like to thank that guy and the friendly nation from which he comes.

We are grateful to Stony Brook University and the University of Miami for research support. The Dirksen Congressional Center provided a research grant for this study, and the National Science Foundation supported EITM and its travel grant program. We thank John Tryneski, Rodney Powell, Holly Smith, and the University of Chicago Press for their support and assistance through this process.

Most of all, we are grateful to our families for their support and love. Matthew thanks Pamela, Shoshana, Isaac, and Harrison for their love and patience. Greg thanks Brooke, Chase, and Camryn for their love, teamwork, and patience.

CHAPTER ONE

Worst. Congress. Ever. Why?

The current US Congress is divided into two competing parties that struggle to govern together. Since 2011, Republican and Democratic Party leaders have worked hard to make party positions clear and avoid embarrassing defeats, but they struggle to actually enact policy measures. As a result, Congress's job approval rating reached 9 percent in 2011, an all-time low, and experts dubbed the 112th Congress (2011–12) "the worst Congress *ever*" (Klein 2012; Ornstein 2011).

Then Congress's performance got even worse. After the 2012 presidential elections returned the same power balance (Democratic president and Senate majority party, Republican House majority party), the players resumed the game. The parties clashed over passing disaster relief after Superstorm Sandy hit the East Coast, and firearm background checks failed in the Senate. In September 2013, the Republicans refused to raise the national debt limit and attempted to withhold all government funding unless the Affordable Care Act, or "Obamacare," was repealed, leading to a government shutdown and fiscal crisis. By November 2013, the Senate Democrats' frustration at Republican obstruction of judicial and executive nominations culminated in a rare, highly partisan "nuclear option" reform to end filibustering against nominations. Congress passed zero of twelve appropriations bills before the October 1 deadline in both 2013 and 2014, while the 296 laws enacted barely edged the 284 enacted during the 112th Congress—the two lowest totals since World War II. Multiple pundits lamented that the 113th Congress was actually the worst Congress ever.[1]

Behind these criticisms and low job approval ratings is the sense that Congress is now primarily a forum for partisan competition. The majority parties in both chambers devote much of their time to crafting "message" bills that convey party positions but have little chance of enactment. By itself, this is not new; legislating-as-position-taking is as old as the Capitol itself. But these efforts are combined with a failure to complete basic tasks: developing a bicameral budget, passing appropriations bills, reauthorizing major laws, and maintaining the full faith and credit of the United States by raising the federal debt limit in a timely manner. To the extent Congress did act on these topics, it was frequently after a period of crisis bargaining with actors attempting to make take-it-or-leave-it proposals so they could win without compromise. In other cases, key measures were approved over the objection of most members of the House Republican majority, such as a partial extension of the Bush-era tax cuts (January 2013), the Hurricane Sandy relief bill (January 2013), a reauthorization of the Violence Against Women Act (February 2013), and funding for the Homeland Security Department (March 2015). These votes violated the "Hastert Rule," which dictates that bills should not reach the floor of the House without the support of most of the majority party.

Why is Congress stalemated by partisan disagreements? The conventional answer is that members of Congress (MCs) fundamentally disagree with each other along ideological lines. Republicans are conservative, Democrats are liberal, and even though their primary goal is to improve public policy, there is a decreasing set of policies that members of both parties can support. They represent constituents in increasingly party-aligned districts and states who embrace starkly different aspirations for national policy. While there is some truth to this view, there is a lot that it does not explain.

This book provides a different account of party influence in Congress. Like Lee (2009), we think the "ideological" account overstates the depth of constituency and policy disagreement as a driver of congressional polarization. We view congressional parties as fundamentally diverse, so even in our polarized era, there are real disagreements *within* each party on major policy questions. We also recognize that legislators represent complex constituencies with potentially conflicting policy views, so it is an oversimplification to portray legislators as advocates for a single ideological viewpoint when they are actually trying to satisfy a diverse set of donors, activists, interest groups, party loyalists, and average constituents (Fenno 2008). Despite intraparty diversity and complex constituencies, the *competition* between two parties for *electoral gain* is a driving force behind the partisanship we observe—legislators unite into parties to win elections in an arms race of partisanship. In our assessment, the prevailing view understates this critical component of competition in the congressional game. In order to avoid losing legislative battles, legislators may unite behind strong party leaders even when they have diverse policy views. They do so in the belief that party activists and voters will reward them for winning these contests, or at least trying to win.

Furthermore, even when legislators generally agree on matters of policy, they have an incentive to manufacture conflicts with the opposing party to diminish its reputation and slow its legislative progress. In several major policy areas, there are potential positive-sum compromises, so if legislators truly sought to maximize policy outcomes, they would gain by passing laws that codify significant areas of agreement while compromising on remaining issues.

As Norman Ornstein wrote, "Look what we have now: a long-term debt disaster with viable bipartisan solutions on the table but ignored or cast aside in Congress; an impasse over the usually perfunctory matter of raising the statutory debt limit placing the United States in jeopardy of its first-ever default; sniping and guerrilla warfare over ... health-care reform and financial regulation; no serious action or movement on climate change, jobs, or the continuing mortgage crisis; and major trade deals stalled yet again despite bipartisan and presidential support" (2011). On the other hand, the political credit for legislative success is zero-sum, so a party that helps its opposition pass its agenda is contributing to its own electoral disadvantage. We propose an account of congressional parties based on electoral competition to help explain this behavior.

1.1 Understanding Legislative Parties

From the beginning, political scientists have agreed on what congressional parties are *not*. Unlike European legislative parties, they are not consistently "strong," unified teams that vote as a bloc following the command of a dominating party leader. In the first political science work on Congress, Woodrow Wilson lamented that party organizations had little effect on the behavior of legislators or the policy output of the Congress: "At least there is within Congress no visible, and therefore no controllable party organization. The only bond of cohesion is the caucus, which occasionally whips a party together for cooperative action against the time for casting its vote upon some critical question. There is always a majority and a minority, indeed, but the legislation of a session does not represent the policy of either" (1885, 80). When Wilson wrote his famous book, both congressional parties held diverse and uncoordinated views on the key issues of the day: tariffs, monetary policy, railroad regulation, and liquor. When party leaders involved themselves in legislating, their greatest challenge was often overcoming the diversity of their own members' constituencies to achieve a result that advanced their party's general electoral interests.[2]

Within ten years, however, majority party leaders had become dominating figures in both the House and the Senate. In the House, the majority party suppressed filibustering and centralized control over the floor agenda (Binder 1997; Cox and McCubbins 2005; Koger 2010; Schickler 2001). In the Senate, a clique of Republican leaders provided direction to Senate Republicans, albeit without the immense procedural powers of the House Speaker (Rothman 1966).

By the mid-twentieth century, however, congressional parties were once again decried as too "weak" by scholars echoing Wilson's call for overt party government by urging electoral and legislative reforms to hold parties responsible for implementing their party platforms (APSA 1950). A coalition of interest groups and legislators sought to weaken the committee system, abolish or limit Senate filibustering, and increase party leaders' influence over individual members (Rohde 1991; Zelizer 2004).

It would appear that these efforts were successful. By a variety of measures, congressional partisanship has increased dramatically over the last fifty years (Sinclair 2006; Theriault 2008, 2013), giving rise to fears that partisanship makes Congress a less respected and productive institution (Binder 2003; Jones and McDermott 2010). The recent increase in congressional partisanship has given urgency to a classic question: Why does the influence of congressional parties rise and fall over time?

While there is no shortage of empirical research documenting congressional partisanship and identifying possible causes, what we most need is an updated *theory* of congressional partisanship. By a "theory," we mean a model that starts with clear assumptions about congressional actors, explains their strategies, and predicts their behavior with testable hypotheses. Since we are trying to explain behavior over time and across institutions, a useful theory will be flexible enough to explain how patterns of behavior shift as the political context changes and will help us explain past behavior so that we will understand why party influence has varied over time. It also will provide us with conceptual vocabulary we can use to interpret current events: What do the players want? Why do they behave as they do? And finally, a good theory will help us predict future behavior and understand the effects of institutional changes.[3]

As we explain below, we believe our model of legislative parties offers several comparative advantages over prior accounts. But this does not mean that we consider prior research on this topic to be *wrong* or fundamentally flawed. Over the last two decades, legislative scholars have been at the forefront of developing and testing *competing* models (e.g., Krehbiel 1991), in which empirical studies are intended to select a "winner" (e.g., Sinclair 1994). This is a "cage match" approach to theoretical development: two (or more) theories go into the data, but only one comes out. This is not our intent, and our work is not organized as such. Instead, a better analogy is that of a "software upgrade." We seek to build on the theoretical development and empirical insights of previous work on legislative parties. However, just as software may decline in usage if it remains static, a model of legislative parties may fade from use if it is not updated. Like a good software update, we seek to resolve "bugs" in existing theories, incorporate recent theoretical and empirical research, and add new features that we hope our readers find useful.

For example, our model includes familiar explanations for why partisanship varies with legislators' preferences over time and why a majority party values the ability to keep issues off the chamber agenda. But our account goes further to explain how competition between parties leads to symmetric partisanship, why partisanship varies with party size, how parties select issues for the chamber agenda and ensure their passage ("positive agenda power"), and how and why partisanship in the legislature is tied to voters' evaluations and election outcomes. Our empirical tests cover a wide range from experimental studies of individual voters to historical patterns of legislative outcomes, partisanship, and elections in both the US House and Senate. While there has been ample empirical research on congressional parties, this work is unique in its effort to trace the connections between electoral politics and governing.

1.2 Toward a Theory of Congressional Parties

For the first eight decades of research on Congress, scholars were mostly interested in describing the activities of congressional parties, measuring their strength, and lamenting their "weakness" relative to European parties. One early effort to explain legislative party strategy was Froman and

Ripley's "Conditions for Party Leadership" (1965), based on analysis of votes and their observation of the House Democrats' whip system during the Eighty-Eighth Congress (1963–64). They found that partisanship varied with leadership involvement, whether the vote was procedural or substantive, visibility, constituency pressure, and the role of state delegations. This work helped explain why partisanship can vary from issue to issue, from vote to vote, during a two-year Congress.

Why, though, does partisanship vary over long periods of time? A classic answer is, "because congressional constituencies vary over time." Cooper and Brady (1981) develop this thesis with a comparison of party organization in the US House at the beginning and middle of the twentieth century. They attribute the declining power of House party leadership over this time span to the increased diversity of congressional districts; over time, the Democrats represented a broader range of economic interests, which made it difficult for the party to unify its members around a coherent economic program.

1.2.1 Conditional Party Government

John Aldrich (1995) and David Rohde (1991) have refined the simple constituency model with their theory of *conditional party government* (CPG; Aldrich and Rohde 1997–98, 2000a, 2000b, 2001; Aldrich et al. 2007; Rohde 2013). Rohde (1991) attributes the recent increase in congressional partisanship to both constituency change *and* internal party innovation. The realignment of conservative Southern whites from the Democratic Party, the full enfranchisement of Southern blacks loyal to the Democratic Party, and the realignment of the Northeast from Republican to Democratic dominance all contributed to making congressional Republicans more conservative and Democrats more liberal. However, Rohde notes that partisanship is also endogenous: pro-party reforms of the 1970s contributed to the resurgence of congressional partisanship in the 1980s.

Stated in general terms, the central claim of the CPG theory is when the two parties are *internally homogenous* (the members of each party tend to agree with each other) and there exists *interparty disagreement* (the two parties tend to disagree on major issues), we should observe three patterns: (a) increased delegation of resources to party leaders, (b) increased use of party leadership powers, and (c) increased influence of parties on policy outcomes. In the US House of Representatives (the primary focus of this work), increased party influence should result in patterns of policy outcomes that favor the majority party. When these conditions are met on a particular issue, we should expect to see party leaders actively striving to win. Over time, parties will grow stronger during eras when we observe internal homogeneity and interparty disagreement.

The CPG framework does not explicitly predict any relationship between legislative parties and electoral outcomes. Legislators' preferences will be influenced by the way in which they are recruited for office, are selected as the candidate of a party, and win their general election (Aldrich et al. 2007), but the focus of the theory is on the *legislative* role of party organizations and their leaders. In CPG, the party is a machine that focuses on *altering* policy outcomes on a subset of issues that divide the two parties from each other and unite them internally.

In response, Krehbiel (1993) questions whether the efforts of parties and their leaders have a significant net effect on policy outcomes. Party labels may be correlated with members' preferences in this view, but parties do not alter legislative behavior. This challenge provoked a torrent of research demonstrating significant "party effects" in voting, agenda setting, and outcomes.[4] Collectively, this work suggests that parties can influence legislators' votes, but party leaders minimize the extent to which members vote against their own electoral interests. Instead, House majority leaders carefully structure debates to minimize difficult choices between collective party interests and the induced preferences of party members. When difficult votes are inescapable, majority party leaders convert just enough votes to carry the day. Party leaders are thus most active when the majority party is internally divided and extra effort is necessary to overcome intraparty disagreement.

The evidence of "party effects," however, amplified the need for a more explicit theory of legislative parties, leading to Krehbiel's (1999) second critique of the CPG model. If members already agree on a given issue, Krehbiel asks, what is the marginal influence of party effort? If party members disagree on a policy issue, how do they gain by empowering a party leader to induce some of them to vote against their own personal views and electoral interests? He argues, "When the condition for CPG is met, behavior of partisans and nonpartisans is observationally equivalent" (35). Krehbiel concludes by calling for a simple, clearly stated model of legislative parties. Hill (2012, 919) echoes this request, noting that "the theory surrounding [CPG] has not been systematically articulated in the ways that science conventionally expects for a general theory," which results in confusion about exactly what the CPG model is and is not (921).

Furthermore, there is simply a great deal of party behavior that is outside the scope of the CPG model. Modern party leaders are highly involved in the reelection efforts of their members by raising funds and helping them develop their legislative resumés. Party leaders often schedule legislation that has great political value but little chance of surviving the legislative process—for example, the Republicans' attempts in 2011, 2013, and 2015 to overturn the Democratic health reform law of 2010. Party leaders often invest great effort in issues that divide their parties— for example, civil rights legislation in the mid-twentieth century (Caro 2002; Mann 1996), which is often cited as a salient example of an issue that parties should keep off the chamber agenda and party leaders should abstain from. And Smith (2007) stresses that CPG does not incorporate the relative size of the two parties into its calculus and that any theory of legislative parties originating in the US Congress should be tested on *both* the House and the Senate.[5] Finally, the temporal sequence of the recent partisan era suggests that congressional polarization precedes any change in mass partisanship. Congressional partisanship began to increase after 1970, long before voters became more loyal to their parties (Bartels 2000; Hetherington 2001; see also chapter 6). Collectively, these questions suggest that an expanded model of legislative parties could be quite useful for explaining the behavior of contemporary parties.

1.2.2 Legislative Cartels and Agenda Control

A second model of legislative parties is the cartel model (Cox and McCubbins 2005, 2007). In the cartel model, legislators form teams with the ultimate goal of promoting their shared reelection. Toward this end, they empower leaders to maximize the collective reputation, or "brand," of their party. One important tactic of party leaders is to avoid legislation that splits their party coalition; presumably, such legislation will detract from the party brand when the party gets "rolled" by a subset of their party and the bulk of the opposing party. To avoid being "rolled," parties seek to dominate the procedural power of their chamber by dictating the rules, choosing the leaders, and setting the agenda. If the majority party succeeds in maintaining procedural control of the chamber, it can suppress legislation that would divide the majority party.[6]

Our *strategic party government* (SPG) model shares several of the basic claims of the cartel model: the focus on electoral success, collective delegation to leaders to maximize electoral success, concern for the party image, and a key role for parties in the agenda setting process. Our focus is much more expansive, however. We consider other tactics that party leaders might use to advance their parties' interests and how their efforts to promote (or oppose) a positive agenda can create tensions between the collective interests of political parties and the individual interests of their members. In particular, we emphasize the arms race competition between the strategies of the majority and minority parties, while in the cartel model the minority party plays a passive role. And since our account makes the primacy of electoral interests clear, we provide an explanation for why a majority party with agenda control would allow itself to be rolled: the majority party will "release" blocked proposals when doing so advances its public reputation or coalition-building strategy. Last, while the cartel model has been extensively tested in the legislative realm, we expand our empirical scope to test for relationships between legislative behavior and election results.

1.2.3 Vote Buying

A third model of legislative parties focuses on a single but critical stage of the legislative process: winning key votes. Early models were not explicitly focused on party leadership (Groseclose and Snyder 1996; Snyder 1991), but more recent work has provided insight on the logic of partisan voting. Patty (2008) provides an insightful model in which legislators care about both policy outcomes and their public positions, and each party chooses a level of party pressure to conform to the party's position.

1.2.4 The Case for a New Model

This review of the main strands of research on legislative parties highlights the need for a model of parties that is comprehensive in scope, spanning both elections and legislative behavior. Any such model should include an explicit set of propositions about who the main actors are, their goals, the structure of the game they are playing, and the strategies they pursue.

As the next section (and chapter 2) explains, we seek to provide such a theory. Our approach preserves the core question of CPG: why does congressional partisanship vary? And we retain its key insight: legislative partisanship is linked to the similarity of the constituencies of each party's members. To this we add a central role for strategic competition as an explanation for partisanship.

One key break with recent research is our focus on the electoral purpose of legislative parties. While individual legislators may have complex goals, including career ambition and making good public policy, we assume that parties focus on providing the necessary condition for their members' primary individual goal: reelection. Reelection requires legislators to satisfy a diverse set of constituencies and requires legislative parties to maintain a brand name and to satisfy and expand the segments of the national party coalition.

Consequently, we avoid the use of a very common set of assumptions, which we call the "legislative spatial model." Following Duncan Black (1948), there has been a set of formal models assuming that legislators are policy seekers. They seek to minimize the difference between their ideal policy and the policy choice resulting from the legislative game. While early social choice studies questioned whether such legislators could make any stable decisions using majority rule when there are multiple issues at stake (Arrow 1950; McKelvey 1976; Plott 1967), subsequent works assumed a set of rules that limited debate to a single issue at a time and thus stable outcomes (Krehbiel 1998; Shepsle 1979).

We share Frances Lee's (2009) concern that legislative scholars have overemphasized the role of ideology in legislative decision making and Barbara Sinclair's (2002a) concern that the assumptions of the spatial model may cloud our understanding of what parties do and how they influence the legislative process. The legislative spatial model does not assume that legislators are disinterested in reelection but rather that any electoral interests are folded into the selection of an "induced" ideal point. However, the legislative spatial model distorts MCs' electoral incentives in two ways. First, it ignores the complexity of legislators' constituencies. Richard Fenno (1978) famously noted that legislators serve multiple constituencies of varying importance: personal, primary, reelection, and geographic (later he added "campaign contributors" as a distinct constituency; Fenno 2000). On top of this, legislators may have their own views that influence their actions and their estimations of constituent views (Miller and Stokes 1963). Rather than representing a single "ideal point," legislators must balance the views of multiple constituencies (Arnold 1990) and may seek help from party leaders and institutional rules to mitigate the tensions between competing constituencies.

Second, legislators do not *act* as if their rewards are tied to policy outcomes. As Mayhew (1974) suggests, a great deal of their behavior—including their votes—can be described as *position taking*. For MCs, the vote itself is the important thing, while the outcome is often simply a by-product of legislators choosing the position that best satisfies their multiple constituencies. Legislative parties may be more attentive to winning votes, but even so, they are motivated not by policy outcomes per se but by the effect of collective positions and outcomes on their reputations, their coalitions, and their individual members. Consequently, parties often invest effort in legislation that fails to alter public policy, such as Democrats' efforts as the Senate minority party to extend funding of Planned Parenthood in 2015. These attempts were doomed to fail, so in the legislative spatial model, they are a waste of time and effort. In the real world, the Democratic attempts served the political purpose of highlighting opposition among Republican senators in precarious states. Model assumptions should reflect this kind of political reality.

Similarly, we minimize our use of "ideology" scores such as NOMINATE. These scores are typically generated using the assumptions of the legislative spatial model and item response theory to estimate each legislator's ideal policy preference. While the scholars who create these scores often acknowledge the central role that political parties and constituencies play in shaping and influencing these "preferences," in practice, congressional scholars often treat them as if they measure something independent of—or prior to—party or electoral factors. Furthermore, if the estimated preferences are calculated without any independent information about the proposals under consideration, they will understate the number of issue dimensions (Londregan 2000) and can overstate the influence of "preferences" in cases of clear party influence. If all the members of each party vote together and in opposition to the other party but alternate between supporting liberal and conservative measures, item response models that are agnostic about the content of proposals will misclassify this behavior as ideological— as perfectly explained by policy preferences—rather than the strategic partisanship it actually is.[7]

Therefore, we focus our analysis on direct measures of legislative behavior: outcomes and party unity in roll call voting. The classic party unity measure captures the percentage of votes on which a legislator sides with his or her party when most of his or her party votes against most of the other party, so it is a descriptive statistic.

1.3 Strategic Party Government: An Overview

Our story begins with a simple claim: the primary purpose of a congressional party is to win elections. However, this simple goal requires complex trade-offs between the interests of the collective party and those of individual members. Parties base their strategies on the preferences of their own members but also on the strength of the opposing party. This framework provides a rich set of propositions that we investigate in this book.

1.3.1 Just Win, Baby: Legislative Parties as Election-Maximizing Cartels

We assume that parties try to maximize their share of the seats in each chamber of Congress. This does not imply that individual *legislators* are solely motivated by election. Indeed, it is likely that most modern politicians seek (re)election so they can advance their own notions of good public policy or to pursue their career interests. We contend, however, that party organizations do not cater to all of their members' personal goals. Instead, parties and their leaders focus on the "lowest common denominator" of providing the necessary condition for a successful legislative career—a job.[8] The activities of parties and their leaders can be classified into three categories: helping members as individuals, maintaining party coalitions, and promoting a positive collective image.

HELPING PARTY MEMBERS GET ELECTED   Legislators govern together, but they campaign alone. Parties, however, can help individual members develop a marketable legislative resume and raise the funds to wage vigorous campaigns. First, legislators often desire some sort of accomplishment for which they can claim credit with their constituents—for example passing their own bills, funding a local pork project, or obtaining jobs and government benefits for individual citizens (Lazarus et al. 2012; Lazarus and Reilly 2010; Mayhew 1974b). Party leaders may possess enough influence in the legislative process to help their members pass their pet bills or get their priorities incorporated into larger bills, provided these bills do not impose excessive costs on other party members (Crespin and Finocchiaro 2008; Hasecke and Mycoff 2007; Lazarus 2009).

Second, parties may help members obtain committee assignments that confer extra influence on policies that are important to their constituents or that help members raise campaign funds. For most of congressional history, parties have dominated committee assignments in both chambers. Current research suggests that party leaders use committee assignments as a reward for party loyalty, as a mechanism for setting the chamber agenda, and as a way to help party members obtain reelection (Coker and Crain 1994; Cox and McCubbins 1993, ch. 7; Frisch and Kelly 2006; Heberlig 2003; Kiewiet and McCubbins 1991; Leigton and Lopez 2002; Rohde 1991, 77–79; Rohde and Shepsle 1973; Smith and Ray 1983).

Third, parties can help individual legislators raise campaign funds. In the modern era, this aid takes several forms. Party leaders appear at fundraisers for members and challengers of their party, and they raise and redistribute funds through their own "leadership" political action committees. Each congressional party has a formal campaign "committee" that coordinates electoral effort, including raising and redistributing campaign funds. These campaign committees also provide MCs with telephones, donor lists, and training to help them raise their own funds. Recently, leaders have also begun to identify their weakest incumbents so that donors who want to help the party retain seats know to whom they should give funds.

Fourth, individual legislators prefer a voting record they can defend to their constituents against the attacks of critical opponents. Ideally, this means that each legislator casts votes that are consistent with the preferences of his or her primary and general constituency. In practice, voting is an inherently risky activity because legislators are often uncertain about the policy consequences of their actions. Thus they seek to avoid specific votes that could be fodder for an opponent's campaign. In addition, they seek to avoid overall voting records that are inconsistent with their constituents' views (e.g., a high party unity score in a district that is moderate or leaning to the opposing party).

These efforts are consistent with the SPG model's claim that the primary purpose of parties is to promote the reelection of their members. Consequently, legislators have an incentive to select leaders who will be effective at providing resources, responsive to requests for committee assignments and assistance on their personal legislative goals, and providers of campaign aid. Regardless of their policy cohesion, members of a party have an incentive to delegate power to leaders so that their leaders can help members build their individual reputations.

MAINTAINING A PARTY COALITION   Congressional parties and their leaders may also strive to sustain and increase their party's coalition. American political parties are best understood as coalitions of interest groups and activists whose appeal varies widely across demographic groups. Congressional parties may advance proposals and hold roll call votes to keep groups allied with their party satisfied and to appeal to potential new members of their party coalition (Karol 2009).[9] For example, in September 2010, the US Senate held a cloture vote on a defense authorization bill to limit the floor debate to three issues critical to Democratic constituencies: a repeal of the military's "Don't Ask Don't Tell" policy for homosexuals, a proposal to allow some undocumented aliens who came to the country as children to become permanent residents, and a bid to streamline the Senate's process for approving judicial nominations. The Senate Democrats lost this vote 56–43, but the failed effort helped demonstrate the majority party's interest in these issues (Donnelly 2010).

For the sake of coalition management, party leaders may work to promote legislative proposals that divide their congressional members. In doing so, most of the members of a party may vote against a proposal that passes—the technical definition of a "roll"—but their party coalition may nonetheless be strengthened. This occurs when the gains from assuaging affiliated groups or bringing in new allies outweigh the cost in lost seats, party switches, or diminished support from offended party backers. For example, during the 1950s and 1960s, Democratic Party leaders were heavily involved in organizing the passage of civil rights legislation that starkly divided the Democratic coalition (Caro 2002; Mann 1996; Valeo 1999). Bawn (1998) provides a formal model explaining why party leaders may side with intense minorities within a legislative party, while Scott James (2000) provides historical examples of how party leaders engineered the passage of regulatory legislation that appealed to critical electoral groups rather than their own party members. In each case, intraparty consensus was *not* a necessary condition for the involvement of congressional party leaders; instead, the critical factor was the collective electoral interest of the party.

ADVANCING COLLECTIVE PARTY REPUTATION   Parties and their leaders have a second goal: promoting the collective image of the party. For years, public opinion scholars have argued that citizens have general ideas and memories about parties per se (e.g., Box-Steffensmeier and Smith 1996; Campbell et al. 1960; Erikson et al. 2002; but see Green et al. 2002) that influence their party affiliations and voting behavior (Cox and McCubbins 1993). The "brand names" of parties are based on cumulative and constantly updating memories, so they are both somewhat stable *and* responsive to politicians' actions (Erikson et al. 2002; Grynaviski 2010; Pope and Woon 2009; Snyder and Ting 2002; Woon and Pope 2008).

Legislative parties seek to manipulate their collective image. One function of parties—today embodied in their "conference" leadership—is articulating a unified media strategy. That is, party leaders help select and disseminate the talking points they want members to use to explain party behavior, and leaders often act as spokespersons for their parties.

A second tactic is enacting legislation that enhances the party brand. This includes landmark legislation like the creation of Medicare in 1965 that a party can hold up as a historic achievement. Of course, the linkage between major bills and party reputation also implies that credit-claiming is part of the legislative process; parties compete for their share of the credit for passing popular legislation, or they seek to make it clear which party is responsible for controversial legislation like the 1993 Omnibus Budget Reconciliation Act, the 2003 Medicare Modernization Act, or the 2010 Affordable Care Act. Also, parties must pass "maintenance" bills like appropriations bills and budget legislation, as well as those that reauthorize farm and highway programs, raise the debt limit, and pay for military deployments and other emergencies. Failure to do so could make a party seem incompetent (Adler and Wilkerson 2013). Responsibility for addressing major issues and passing maintenance bills falls primarily on the majority party, so the majority party probably feels greater urgency to enact legislation to satisfy public expectations.

Third, each party may seek to highlight clear issue contrasts that can be used in the next campaign. By bringing up bills and offering amendments that separate the parties on major issues, party leaders may seek to portray the opposing party as (for example) profligate spenders, antidefense weaklings, tax increasers, corrupt scoundrels, or generally resistant to popular majorities on key issues. The roll call votes on these "message" issues may provide ammunition for challengers against incumbents of the opposing party and may provide themes for incumbents to use in their own campaigns.

For some issues, the predictions of the CPG framework are equivalent to those of SPG's electoral reputation-based model. If a party conference is united behind a proposal that will improve the party's reputation, then both theories would predict that party leaders will invest any necessary effort to ensure its passage. But they also diverge to the extent that party leaders prioritize issues that divide their membership to advance the collective interests of the party or suppress proposals that are supported by most of their membership but detract from the electoral interests of the broader political party. In order to achieve policy success and create partisan contrasts, party leaders must often ask their members to cooperate and to vote as a team. This creates a tension that is a key feature of congressional parties: the tension between diverse individual interests and the incentives to cooperate as a team.

1.3.2 Madison's Joke: Local Interests, Collective Action

It is well known that the authors of the US Constitution did not expect durable political parties to persist in the republic they designed (Hofstadter 1969). Nonetheless, parties soon developed and, under various names, have persisted to the present day. Politicians in the new republic soon found that their new institutions essentially required parties to function well but found that it was difficult to be both a local representative *and* a loyal team player.

The classic explanation for why America has almost always had two major parties is Duverger's law: if we elect representatives in single-member districts by plurality vote, a two-party system is likely to emerge, as additional parties will be unable to compete electorally (Duverger 1951). In the American case, parties solidified as the desire to coordinate on candidates for president (McCormick 1982) and Speaker of the House (Jenkins and Nokken 2000; Jenkins and Stewart 2012) led to the development of national party organizations. And within Congress, parties developed and persisted to increase efficiency and avoid chaos (Aldrich 2011).

However, American political culture has long undermined legislative party cohesion. In Federalist 10, James Madison predicts that the new nation would be so politically diverse that no single, passionate segment of society could command a majority in Congress. For example, modern American society is cleaved and subdivided by class, race, religion, gender, ideology, profession, state, sexual preference, ideology, and age.[10] Moreover, the geographic segmentation of America into states and districts permits the demographic composition of districts to vary wildly, so the dominant faction in one district may be near-absent in another district. States and districts may also vary by primary industry or urban-rural composition, and they may have their own unique political history and culture. The consequence of this political diversity, Madison hopes, is that no nefarious schemes to benefit a particular group at the expense of another group or the public interest could succeed. No one faction would have the numbers to accomplish this feat, *and any coalition of factions would struggle to implement its schemes in the public eye.*

The inherent diversity of American society makes it challenging for "strong" parties to survive. While it is possible for legislative parties to unite on some issues without coercion, complete voting cohesion on every question in the European style would require a typical legislator to side with his party over his local constituency some of the time. In practice, legislative parties do sometimes call on their members to support the "team" rather than follow their consciences or vote with their constituents' preferences, but the members may pay a price for their loyalty at the ballot box.

This is *Madison's joke*. As a nation, we need political parties to help choose our leaders, to make Congress work effectively, and to hold a governing faction jointly responsible for collective decisions. As citizens scattered across a diverse quilt of states and districts, however, we may be influenced by party labels when we vote, but we also consider legislators' individual votes, accomplishments, promises, and behavior. Consequently, our legislators must often balance the benefits of collective action with the costs of taking positions that are unpopular with their constituents. Our model of congressional parties is grounded in this tension between collective action and individual accountability.

1.3.3 The Strategic Balancing Act

So far, we have shown that a party is an organization striving to retain and win seats while minimizing the number of unpopular votes its members have to cast. The members and leaders of a party decide how much they wish to cooperate as a party. A crucial element of this choice is *interparty competition*. Each party, after all, is striving for *relative* advantage: a better reputation, more pork projects, more policy achievements, a better issue agenda to campaign on, and more votes for its positions *than the opposing side*. As each party balances the costs and benefits of party influence, it makes sense for a party to look across the aisle and try to anticipate the strategies of the opposing party so it can make their best response.

In the next chapter, we explain why competition induces partially symmetric strategies: parties tend to adopt similar (but not identical) strategies over time in an arms race competition. Just as a nation allocates resources to military competition against a peer competitor while saving the rest for domestic consumption, parties strive to be strong enough to win the fights they can win while avoiding the unnecessary electoral costs of excess partisanship. This is why congressional parties can be quite influential even when their members do not vote in perfect unison on every issue.

1.3.4 Testing the Theory

By laying a broad foundation for our theory of legislative parties, we are able to incorporate the results of the recent torrent of research on parties into a cohesive framework. The SPG model also makes several unique predictions, which we test in the chapters to come.

In the electoral sphere, we expect that, at the margin, voters will punish politicians who are excessively partisan. This is easiest to observe in the presidential elections, where a candidate promises to be "a uniter, not a divider" (George W. Bush) or "change the tone in Washington" (Barack Obama) despite the long odds against bipartisanship in the current era. We test this claim in chapters 3 and 4. This would also help explain why quality challengers are more likely to emerge against incumbents with a partisan voting record (Carson 2005). We also expect that party leaders will allocate campaign funds and fundraising assistance to help marginal incumbents and the challengers who are closest to victory (Jacobson 2008). Finally, in chapter 5 we show that, collectively, parties *lose* seats as their partisanship increases but *gain* seats as their success rate increases.

In the legislative arena, we expect (as noted above) that parties will strive to help members develop their individual résumés by assigning them to favorable committees as well as helping them to pass their own bills and obtain funds and benefits targeted at their districts. We also expect that the majority party will attempt to bring up and pass "signature" legislation that enhances its reputation, and both parties will attempt to force roll call votes on issues that pit the opposing party against the preferences of most voters (or of critical voting blocs). One example of this is "blame-game politics," in which Congress sends bills to a president of the opposing party to force a very public conflict on an issue (Gilmour 1995; Groseclose and McCarty 2001).

On critical votes that pit parties against each other, we expect the majority party to allow members to defect as long as it has enough votes to win (King and Zeckhauser 2003). At the same time, the minority party is likely to encourage its members to vote against the majority party if it has a chance to win the vote—thereby embarrassing the majority party—or if the conflicted majority party members would have to pay a greater electoral penalty for backing their party than the conflicted members of the minority party would. For this reason, we expect to see parties mirroring each other's voting cohesion on individual votes and over time. As we highlight in chapters 6 and 7, the majority party's vote counting is linked to the relative size of the majority and minority parties: larger majorities can afford to be less cohesive because they can afford more defections without risking defeat (see also Patty 2008).

Unlike the CPG model, the SPG model specifies when we might observe a strong party even though its members are ideologically heterogeneous: competition with the opposing party can induce party members to overcome their differences. We also expect that majority parties may invest great effort to pass legislation on issues that divide the majority caucus if doing so is in the interest of their party's reputation or would aid in party coalition building. Furthermore, the SPG model incorporates several features of congressional parties that CPG theory does not explicitly explain, such as the dynamics of close votes, the influence of party size, and the efforts of party leaders to promote the public image of their parties and to help their members win elections. Finally, like cartel theory, SPG explains the importance of procedural partisanship as both parties seek to promote their "message" issues and shield their members from votes that force tough choices.

1.4 Plan of the Book

We begin our account of congressional parties in earnest in the next chapter, which explains our theory of strategic party government with greater precision. The rest of the book is devoted to testing our theory's assumptions and predictions. In chapter 3 we present the results of an experiment that tests the assumption that voters disapprove of partisanship per se and finds that citizens in the study disapprove of partisan behavior but not ideological extremism. Chapter 4 extends this question to the results of congressional elections from 1952 to 2004; we find that individual legislators pay an electoral penalty for voting with their parties.

Chapter 5 conducts a macrolevel study of congressional elections from 1789 to 2006. At the aggregate level, we find that parties pay an electoral price for their party unity. However, legislative victories are an electoral boon, which explains why parties seek to win important votes with a minimum level of party unity. Moreover, the US Senate provides a valuable natural experiment to demonstrate that these patterns are driven by campaigns and voters. The US Constitution initially allowed state legislatures to choose the members of the US Senate, but starting in 1914, the Seventeenth Amendment to the Constitution formally required that senators be directly elected by the voters of their states. Before 1914, we observe very little relationship between party unity and election outcomes (as measured by the share of the chamber controlled by each party). After 1914—and especially after 1930—this pattern changes dramatically so that the negative relationship between party unity and seat share is stronger in the Senate than the House.

Chapter 6 begins the institutional side of our analysis by analyzing macrolevel patterns of partisan voting in the House and Senate from 1789 to 2006. We test the central claims of our theory: in both chambers of Congress, parties are less unified as they grow in size and parties respond to each other's partisanship. The results are consistent with our expectations. Additionally, we find that the ideological cohesion of the parties has a limited role in explaining party unity. This chapter then goes on to apply this framework to the development of congressional parties over the last fifty years.

Chapter 7 begins by explaining the whip system in Congress, using the 2005 passage of the Central American Free Trade Act as a case study. We then apply the strategic party framework to individual roll call votes in Congress. Not surprisingly, we find that party cohesion in voting is directly linked to party success: parties that vote together are more likely to win. We also find that party influence is symmetric across votes; when one party bands together on an issue, the opposing party is likely to unite as well.

Chapter 8 concludes the book with a discussion of today's "polarized" Congress. Our framework provides a fresh interpretation of modern party politics. A key source of the polarization we observe in the modern Congress is interparty competition for power. Regardless of the extent to which party members agree with one another, each modern congressional party is polarized because the opposing party does an increasingly good job of presenting a united front. Anyone hoping to "cure" congressional polarization should consider the role of competition as an engine of polarization.

A Theory of Strategic Parties

The only defense against organization is counterorganization.—E. E. Schattschneider, Party Government: American Government in Action, 1942

This chapter presents a theory of legislative party strategy. Ultimately, we seek to understand why legislators delegate authority to their parties and why this delegation varies over time. As discussed in chapter 1, we believe that our framework can help tie together previous research and help explain the political behavior we observe every day. The basic elements of our theory are a description of the main actors, their goals, the rules that constrain or incentivize their actions, the strategies actors adopt, and predictions for the behavior we expect to see. We are interested in the actions of parties as groups, but we ground our theory in the goals and behavior of individual legislators. In particular, we assume that legislators have several goals, but the primary reason legislators delegate to parties is to promote their own electoral fortunes.

Our theory has several steps. We begin with a <u>model of citizen voting</u>. What do voters want? What do they reward? Then we discuss how <u>political parties help their candidates win elections</u> given the preferences of voters. Third, we explain when and why parties seek to influence <u>legislative voting</u>. Our exposition begins with party tactics on individual roll call votes. On which votes do party leaders attempt to influence individual legislators' votes to affect the outcome? How do they make this calculation? A key claim from this discussion is that as a party's share of the chamber increases, observed party unity is likely to decrease. Subsequently, we explain how parties set the legislative agenda and thereby influence which roll call votes occur and which ones do not. This is the second level of party strategy: deciding what to decide.

Finally, we turn to <u>institutional choices</u>. We explain how legislators decide how much power to delegate to party leadership. We also explain how this choice is made in response to the partisanship of the opposing party, leading to arms race competition between the two parties.

As discussed in chapter 1, this framework builds upon decades of research on congressional parties. We see our primary contributions as (a) making a more explicit connection between electoral incentives and party organization than previous works; (b) explaining the role of reciprocal partisanship, in which the members of a heterogeneous party might unite in opposition to the partisanship of an opposing party; and (c) integrating separate strands of research on parties into a coherent whole.

2.1 Previous Models of Legislative Parties

In section 1.3, we provided an overview of recent models of legislative parties. In this section, we discuss in greater detail a diverse set of recent theoretical work that the SPG model draws upon. In doing so, we highlight the assumptions and implications of each framework, clarifying what we incorporate from these studies and how we innovate.

2.1.1 Conditional Party Government

In its simplest form, the conditional party government (CPG) model has been influential since Froman and Ripley's article "Conditions for Party Leadership: The Case of the House Democrats" (1965), but its influence increased after the publication of books by David Rohde (1991) and John Aldrich (1995). In its original form, the CPG model holds the following:

1. Legislators are the key actors.
2. Legislators have multiple goals that influence their induced policy preferences. Having selected a set of policy goals, they seek to change public policy to conform to their views.
3. Legislators delegate power to party leaders to promote the party's policy agenda.
4. Majority party leaders use this power to advance legislation on which there is broad consensus within the majority party (Rohde 1991, 31–33, 105–18).

In recent work, David Rohde (2013) has added majority control as a goal for party leaders to pursue. This provides a rationale for leaders' fundraising and media relations, which have been important parts of their jobs since the 1980s (Rohde 1991, 92). However, as an addition to a pre-existing model, this raises a fresh set of questions. How do parties make trade-offs between achieving policy change and winning reelection? Under what conditions would we expect parties to settle for a bipartisan compromise rather than maintain the status quo to preserve an issue advantage? Are legislators indifferent between a one-vote majority and a sizable majority, or between holding a quarter of a legislature's seats and holding 49.9 percent? Fowler and Smirnov (2007) find that there are significant payoffs for legislators as the *size* of their party increases, while empirical research finds that larger majorities are able to afford more defections among majority party members (Lebo et al. 2007; Patty 2008).

Most critically, the defining feature of CPG is its "conditions": delegation to party leaders occurs if (a) policy preferences are homogenous within each party and (b) there is a significant difference between the policy preferences of the two major parties. If we layer a new goal into the CPG framework, do these conditions still apply? Or would we also expect diverse, overlapping parties to centralize power if delegating power advanced their electoral interests? While some imprecision should be expected from any model of legislative parties, in its current form, it is difficult to specify or test the logic and predictions of CPG. One of our goals in framing the SPG model is to provide this additional clarity.

2.1.2 Agenda-Setting Cartels

A second model of legislative parties highlights the role of political parties in manipulating the rules and agenda of legislatures to advance the electoral interests of the majority party (Cox and McCubbins 1993, 2005). In this "cartel" model, the members of a party face a collective action dilemma: they have a shared interest in promoting the brand image of their parties, since their electoral fortunes depend in part on the value of this brand. However, each legislator may have incentives to deviate from the collective action required to promote the party brand.

Cox and McCubbins (1993) posit that legislators solve this problem by choosing party leaders and empowering them to punish and reward legislators in the pursuit of collective goals.[1] The critical duty of each party member is to support the party on procedural issues: selection of chamber leaders, defining chamber rules, and setting the chamber agenda. In *Setting the Agenda* (2005), they extend this argument by focusing on the role of "negative agenda-setting": the majority party's ability to keep issues off the chamber agenda. Specifically, Cox and McCubbins use a spatial model to identify which status quo policies will be protected: those in the "block-out zone" between the majority party median and the chamber median.

The spatial model helps explain how negative agenda setting works but introduces a distinct and potentially contradictory set of assumptions. The cartel framework is grounded in *electoral* interest, while the spatial model they utilize assumes that legislators' payoffs are tied to the extent to which public policy conforms to their policy preferences. These are not the same thing. The tension between these goals is minimized if the majority party brand is hurt when the majority party is "rolled" (bills pass over the opposition of most of the majority party) or if they are "disappointed" (bills supported by most of one party fail). If, on the other hand, the majority party's electoral interests are sometimes served by allowing itself to be rolled, then electoral interests and policy maximization lead to different outcomes. As it happens, the majority party in the House was "rolled" several times on major legislation during John Boehner's (R-OH) tenure as Speaker from 2011 to 2015. In most of these cases, these policy defeats gave the Republican Party a face-saving escape from the hard bargaining stances preferred by a majority of the Republican Party on budgetary and gender issues.

Overall, the cartel framework offers several keen insights: the claim that parties have a collective reputation that leads to partisan tides in congressional elections, that parties exist to promote this reputation, that a great deal of their power stems from setting the legislative agenda, and that one of the greatest sources of party influence is the power to *do nothing*. The authors intentionally leave subjects for subsequent research, such as the development and promotion of each party's positive agenda (that is, the proposals it attempts to pass), the connections between legislative actions and electoral outcomes,[2] and how competition between parties can affect both parties' voting strategies.

The SPG framework we develop in this chapter builds on the cartel model by explaining how legislative action ties to electoral outcomes, how parties delegate power to their leaders, and how leaders use that power to promote a positive agenda.

2.1.3 Party Brands and Logrolls

There are two strands of research on how legislative parties maximize their electoral fortunes. One strand, following Cox and McCubbins

(1993), develops the notion that political parties cultivate the reputation of their brand name. Much of this work focuses on the electoral implications of brand names (Grynaviski 2010; Snyder and Ting 2002, 2003), but some research also traces the relationship between legislative action and election outcomes (Woon and Pope 2008).

Another strand (e.g., Aldrich 1995, 29–45; Bawn 1998; Dixit and Londregan 1996) conceives of parties as strategic logrolls in which legislators provide payoffs to a set of constituencies, interests, or regions to maintain and expand their party coalition.[3] This can include "divide-the-dollar" games in which legislative leaders allocate pork barrel spending to their members, or a multidimensional coalition in which party members support the diverse policy priorities of party-aligned groups.

These are not necessarily competing visions of party strategy, but they are conceptually and practically distinct from each other and also distinct from a model in which legislators simply vote their preferences. As discussed below, each of these strategies may pit the interests of a legislator's geographic constituency against those of his or her party and potentially force legislators to make difficult choices.

2.1.4 Equilibrium Party Government

A final formal study we wish to discuss is the equilibrium party government (EPG) model developed by John Patty (2008). Like Patty, we seek to add elements missing in existing theories: a focus on the tension between individual and collective interests (2008, 639) and the expectation that party strength will vary with the *size* of the party as well as the preferences of party members. We follow Patty (2008, 642–43) in positing that legislators have preferences over party strength and that each party chooses the level preferred by the median member of the party. Below, we characterize this decision as the selection of a "budget" for party leaders to allocate instead of the "bond" each member posts in the EPG model, but this is a slender distinction.[4]

While there are similarities between SPG and Patty's equilibrium party government, our framework adds two major components: competition between parties as an incentive to strengthen party leadership and an empirical investigation of the relationship between legislative partisanship and electoral outcomes. Likewise, there are similarities between SPG and the CPG and cartel models; in our effort to craft the best possible framework, we have incorporated a great deal of the wisdom from these models. The strategic party government framework, however, adds value to this conversation by highlighting the role of interaction between majority and minority parties and by more explicitly tying legislative actions to the electoral fortunes of incumbents and parties.

2.2 Legislative Elections and Legislative Parties

How do legislative parties and their leaders influence elections? How do electoral incentives constrain legislative parties? This section begins by summarizing the components of electoral success, including the direct effect of party affiliation and the indirect effects of legislative power and success obtained by and through legislative parties. The benefits of parties, however, are constrained by the electoral costs of deviating from local constituents' preferences, which we label "Madison's Joke."

2.2.1 The Calculus of Voting in Elections

We begin our story with the decisions of individual voters. We expect that voters who choose between candidates (as they do in the American context) base their decisions on five factors: any generic preference for the incumbent, candidate valence, party reputation, and evaluations of the incumbent's policy and partisanship. The *incumbency advantage* measures the electoral benefits of holding office, including the ability to deter potential challengers by amassing campaign funds (Box-Steffensmeier 1996; Cox and Katz 1996; Leavitt and Wolfram 1997). By *valence*, we mean factors other than party, ideology, and incumbency that distinguish candidates.[5]

The remaining three terms are more central to this study. *Party reputation* represents a voter's generic preference for one party over the other, as discussed above. *Policy* represents the voter's sense that a candidate's policy views correspond to his or her own.[6] While party affiliation can signal a great deal about a candidate's policy views (Krehbiel 2000; Snyder and Ting 2002), in this equation, *Partisanship* represents the extent to which legislators act as loyal members of their party. As discussed in chapter 3, voters may perceive that candidates prioritize the national party over their local constituency. This variable reflects the voter's evaluation of the perceived loyalty of the candidates.[7]

We can express this claim as a voting formula with voter i choosing between candidates j and k of different parties (P_j, P_k) with x_i, x_j, and x_k

representing the single-peaked and symmetric policy preferences of the voter and candidates along a unidimensional policy spectrum, candidate j as the incumbent, and each candidate possessing valence attributes v_j and v_k. Vote choice V is the probability that voter i chooses candidate j and thus is bounded between 0 and 1.

$$\text{(Valence)} \qquad\qquad \text{(Policy)}$$
$$V_{ijk} = \beta_0 + \beta_1(v_j - v_k) + \beta_2(P_j - P_k) + \beta_3(|x_i - x_j| - |x_i - x_k|) + \beta_4(PL_j - PL_k) \;\; (2.1)$$
$$\text{(Incumbency)} \quad \text{(Party Brand)} \qquad\qquad\qquad\qquad\qquad \text{(Party Loyalty)}$$

When averaged across voters, the β terms represent the influence of each factor on electoral outcomes. For example, in the 2008 presidential election, some voters chose between Barack Obama and John McCain on the basis of party affiliations; for others, a comparison of the policy differences between the candidates; and for others, differences in race, age, military background, and home state(s) loomed large. When we analyze voters' choices in the aggregate, we estimate the typical effect of each factor relative to other factors.

Of course, voters are not machines; both their perceptions of candidates and their priorities are malleable. We assume that voters begin with beliefs about their incumbents' traits and behavior, based in part on their party affiliation. Over the course of a campaign, both candidates (and other organizations) seek to influence the parameter values for party reputation, ideology, valence, and party loyalty while also trying to influence the weights attached to each. Campaign resources—money, volunteers, and media coverage—are essential to this effort. We assume that challengers allocate their campaign resources to highlight the contrast that is most favorable to their campaigns, so some challengers will focus on valence, some on policy, some on partisanship.

2.2.2 The Role of Parties in Election

While the ultimate electoral choice is made by voters in distinct constituencies across a diverse country, there are several ways that political party organizations and party leaders can influence elections. First, party organizations can aid candidates by <u>directly campaigning on their behalf or providing resources to their candidates</u>. Party organizations may campaign directly by providing generic pro-party advertising, coordinating voter turnout efforts, or paying for television ads promoting candidates or attacking their opponents. Party organizations (like the congressional campaign committees; Kolodny 1998) can also make donations directly to candidates, as can party leaders; modern party leaders (or aspiring party leaders) are likely to establish leadership PACs to collect and redistribute campaign contributions (Cann 2008; Currinder 2003; Heberlig and Larson 2005; Kanthak 2007). Party leaders can also help coordinate donations from party-loyal donors to the races where their money will have the greatest marginal effect (Herrnson 2009). Finally, to the extent that some donors are interested in building ties with the party in power, legislators may find it easier to raise funds when they are members of the majority party (Cox and Magar 1999), although this may be conditional upon the relative influence of the majority party.

Second, party reputation is a significant component of voters' choices, and these reputations depend on an accumulation of previous actions and statements. By "reputation," we mean the positive and negative attributes voters will associate with each party.[8] Reputations are important to understanding both the attachments people make to candidates and parties as well as voters' willingness to support them in elections.

What do we know about party reputations? First, we know that both reputations and the importance that voters place on them can change over time. Studying the United Kingdom, Gary Cox (1987) reports that party labels became the primary factor in voters' decisions after parties became the dominant actors in the House of Commons. Recent congressional elections have also varied in the extent to which they are "nationalized" by political parties instead of "localized" by individual candidates (Abramowitz 2010). In the United States, the tendency of party-affiliated voters to vote for the candidate of their party has varied over time (Bartels 2000) in response to elite behavior (Hetherington 2001). Also, party reputations can vary by issue. Polls commonly give Republicans the edge on national security and taxes and give Democrats an advantage on social welfare and the environment. But these issue advantages vary significantly over time (Pope and Woon 2009) and can be affected by economic conditions and political events (Erikson et al. 2002, 109–51). Candidates often play to these issue advantages by highlighting the importance of issues "owned" by their parties—for example, Democrats holding campaign events at homeless shelters (Egan 2013; Petrocik 1996).[9] While presidents have a significant effect on party reputations, congressional behavior also shapes citizens' evaluations of political parties. As discussed below, the electoral importance of party reputations motivates the development of party organization (e.g., choosing formal leaders) and party involvement in legislative agenda setting.

Third, parties can use their legislative power to develop incumbents' personal reputations and to emphasize and clarify specific issue positions. For example, parties can provide incumbents with committee assignments that relate to the interests of their constituents. Furthermore, party leaders can use their agenda-setting powers to help their members claim credit for legislation, amend bills, and obtain targeted spending projects ("pork") for their constituents. As discussed below, parties may use their agenda-setting powers to manipulate which questions are decided by roll call votes, thereby creating a clear record on some issues while leaving others ambiguous.

2.2.3 Madison's Joke

As voters evaluate both individual legislators and the collective reputations of parties, legislators may be able to survive on an "incumbency advantage" even when voters may prefer the opposing party (Carson and Roberts 2013; Gelman and King 1990; Mayhew 1974b). The accumulation of an incumbent's service can prove powerful in the minds of voters, even when Congress and her political party are out of favor. On the other hand, legislators depend on parties for their nominations, for campaign resources, and for the electoral advantages gained through legislative cooperation.

As long as party policies coincide with the preferences of a member of Congress's (MC's) constituency, she can more easily advance her electoral interests by going along. But in practice, party agendas often clash with the local preferences for some portion of a congressional party. For example, even during this "polarized" era, significant portions of the House Democratic Party were conflicted by some provisions of their party's agenda for the 111th Congress (2009–10): some thought that the emergency stimulus bill was too expensive, that the health care reform too expansive (or not ambitious enough!), and that the "cap-and-trade" climate change legislation would raise taxes and impose costs on regions of the country that mined and consumed coal—including many districts represented by Democrats. To some extent, this reflects the fact that they represented districts that were inhospitable to Democrats—Democrats captured forty-nine House seats in 2008 in districts that John McCain won. But it also reflects the inherit diversity of this "patchwork nation" (Chinni and Gimpel 2011; Gimpel and Schuknecht 2004) so that voters in districts that had long elected Democrats disliked elements of the Democratic agenda.

The tension between collective action and local interests was fore-shadowed by James Madison in two of the best-known *Federalist Papers*. Federalist 51 describes the elaborate "checks and balances" between the branches of the federal government that complicate efforts to enact policy change. Political parties help reduce this friction: within years of the US Congress's founding, politicians organized political parties to facilitate coordination within and across the branches of government (Aldrich 2011, ch. 3). Federalist 10, on the other hand, extols the fact that a large republic will "take in a greater variety of parties and interests," so it would be unlikely that an indivisible majority would dominate political decision making. Instead, any coalition that emerges will be an artificial union of diverse interests. The coalition will succeed as long as it acts in the general interest of the country but fracture when it seeks to implement the selfish schemes of party members to the disadvantage of the nation or some other group of citizens.[10] This is Madison's joke: politicians must cooperate as durable coalitions to make policy in this lawmaking system, but their constituencies are often too diverse to sustain the cooperation necessary for governance.

As suggested by Cox and McCubbins (1993), this sets up a *collective action dilemma* for members of a legislative party. Cox and McCubbins focus on the static implications of this dilemma: legislators have an incentive to select and empower party leaders (1993), including the power to censor legislation that would divide the party membership (2005). In the succeeding sections, we develop the dynamic side of the story: what conditions motivate legislators to increase or decrease the role of parties and party leaders in the legislative process over time?

2.3 Parties and Floor Voting

We begin our account of legislative party organization with roll call voting on the "floor," or plenary, of a legislature. Traditionally, voting has been treated as the defining act of legislative parties, with a "strong" party being synonymous with cohesive roll call voting (Lowell 1902; Wilson 1885). Like many more contemporary scholars, we take a broader view of party influence to include influence on the policy agenda, public debate, and elections. In order to understand this broader notion of party influence, however, we begin with floor voting to understand when and why party leaders may try to convince their members to vote together and which votes they would prefer to avoid altogether.

2.3.1 Legislative Voting: Actions versus Outcomes

We begin with a simple claim about roll call voting: legislators may care about both the *collective choice* of their chambers—whether measures pass or fail—and the *individual position* they take. A legislator may value outcomes that improve the reputation of his or her party or that, from his or her perspective, improve public policy. Additionally, legislators are judged for the positions they take. Citizens, the media, interest groups, donors, and party officials evaluate the roll call votes cast by individual legislators and reward or punish them accordingly.

There are several reasons for external actors to focus on individual vote positions when evaluating legislators. First, citizens and other actors may find that roll call votes provide a more concrete basis for evaluation than ordinary campaign rhetoric, as promises and general positions are translated into decisions on specific legislation. Second, roll call votes help illustrate the *relative* priorities of legislators; candidates for office might easily embrace both environmental protection and lower gasoline prices, or balanced budgets and a strong national defense, but roll calls are especially informative because they reflect *choices* between competing priorities. As such, they can provide a lot of information on legislators' future behavior even if the same exact decision never occurs again. Finally, organized groups and parties may use information gleaned from roll call votes in one session of Congress to win future votes on the same issue.

Following Arnold (1990, especially 60–87) and Bishin (2000, 2009), we assume that legislators have a nuanced understanding of how vote positions affect their reelection prospects by swaying the behavior of subsets of constituents known as "subconstituencies." They estimate (a) the likelihood that each subconstituency group becomes aware of their actions and (b) the effect of this information on a subconstituency's support for their reelection. Some votes pose particularly difficult choices such that either vote position yields a negative position payoff.[11]

Using the two dimensions of actions and outcomes, we can generate a typology of legislative preferences. The grid in figure 2.1 maps legislators' preferences regarding a single proposal with action payoffs on the verti-

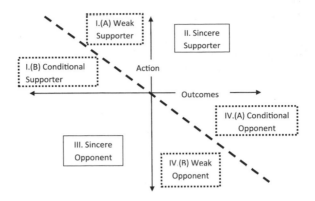

FIGURE 2.1. A typology of legislators' action and outcome payoffs

cal axis and outcome benefits on the horizontal axis. We can categorize legislators by their (policy, position) pair, so a legislator who wants a bill to succeed *and* benefits from voting for the bill is a (YY); other types are (NN), (YN), and (NY).

The first and most important point this figure illustrates is that wanting a proposal to pass and wanting to vote for a proposal are two distinct desires. Obviously, these two goals can coincide. An MC in quadrant II (YY) benefits from voting for the measure and also from its passage, so he or she is unconflicted and will support the measure absent extraordinary party influence. Conversely, MCs in quadrant III find the proposal both costly to vote for and a negative policy outcome (NN), so voting against these proposals is simple.

But position and outcome preferences also diverge. For legislators in quadrant I, *supporting* the proposal is beneficial, but *implementing* it provides negative payoffs (NY). These legislators may prefer to publicly support the proposal while privately undermining its likelihood of success. These legislators can be further divided[12] into "weak supporters" (section I.A), whose political interest in supporting the bill trumps their opposition to its passage (NYa), and "conditional supporters" (section I.B), whose political interest in supporting the bill is trumped by their opposition to its passage (NYb). While both weak and conditional supporters can be persuaded to oppose the measure, conditional supporters will prefer to oppose the measure if their choice determines whether it succeeds or fails, whereas weak supporters would rather vote for a bill they oppose than endure the slings and arrows of outraged constituents.

The same logic applies to quadrant IV, but in reverse. Legislators in this quadrant prefer that these proposals succeed while publicly opposing them (YN).[13] "Conditional opponents" have outcome payoffs that exceed their political stakes (YNa), while "weak opponents" face political costs that exceed their interest in the proposal's success (YNb). We use the general term "conflicted" for legislators with divergent policy and position payoffs (YN and NY).

The distinction between rewards for actions and outcomes is critical to understanding legislative party strategy. Party leaders can help legislators realize the gains from position taking without the pains of policy enactment for proposals in quadrant I. And especially, leaders help pass proposals in quadrant IV: expensive to vote for but beneficial if they pass. To understand how they manage these conflicts, we must take a closer look at how leaders approach floor voting.

2.3.2 A Typology of Votes

Let us assume, for now, that party leaders have full information about the political and policy preferences of every member of the chamber. If so, for any given proposal, they know the number of sincere supporters, sincere opponents, and conflicted legislators (quadrants I and IV in figure 2.1). Based on this information, one can parse proposals into three categories based on their level of support:

- *Simple success:* There are enough unconflicted supporters to assure passage.
- *Simple defeat:* There are enough unconflicted opponents to assure defeat.
- *Contested vote:* The outcome depends on the votes of conflicted legislators.

There are some party agenda items that fit into one of the first two categories. It is common during periods of divided government, for example, for the majority party of a chamber to bring up the president's budget proposal for a vote with the expectation that the president's party will not bother to support it, leading to a simple defeat. The majority party prefers bills that are popular and unite its members, and these proposals will often yield simple victories. However, many proposals with great impact on party reputation are decided by contested votes. Over the last ten years, this has been the case with landmark bills like the addition of a prescription drug plan to Medicare in 2003, the 2008 financial bailout, the 2010 health care reform law, and the 2011 debt limit increase. Despite the

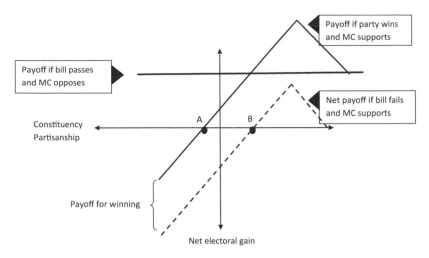

FIGURE 2.2. Voting payoffs

costs to individual party members, party leaders decided that it was in the collective interest (and, perhaps, the national interest) to invest maximum effort into enacting these laws. In such cases, party leaders can play an important role corralling members of their own party and wooing members of the opposing party.[14] The next two sections explain party strategies on contested votes.

2.3.3 Contested Votes: Majority Party Strategy

We begin with the strategy of the majority party, which *usually* (a) enjoys agenda-setting prerogatives, (b) wins, and (c) bears most of the blame if measures fail and receives credit if they succeed. In practice, each of these expectations is sometimes violated, but there is enough truth in them to justify our two-stage presentation.[15]

We are interested in contested votes, and so it would help to illustrate what a contested vote looks like. Figure 2.2 does so, showing the payoffs for a range of legislators within a hypothetical (Republican) party. The *x*-axis measures the Democratic (left side) versus Republican (right side) tendency of each MC's constituency.[16] The *y*-axis measures the total utility for each legislator based on his or her individual vote and the collective outcome. There are two possible payoffs for party members, both shown as single-peaked lines. The upper line depicts the payoff for MCs if the measure passes, while the lower line depicts the payoff if it fails. This particular example assumes a uniform positive payoff for winning and vote-based payoffs that peak around the party median and decrease symmetrically. This is one of many scenarios; in practice, some MCs may benefit more from winning than others, payoffs may be asymmetric, and the peak payoffs might go to MCs representing more centrist or partisan districts.

Of particular interest in this case are the MCs with moderate districts lying between points A, where an MC is indifferent between "aye" and "nay" if the proposal wins and she is the decisive vote, and point B, where an MC is indifferent between "aye" and "nay" if the proposal loses and she votes for the proposal. For these MCs, their preferred strategy would be to vote against the proposal while other legislators vote to pass the measure. That would allow them to reap the uniform payoff for the measure's success while avoiding the "loss" for opposing the measure. However, if all conflicted members follow this strategy and there are not enough unconflicted members to pass the proposal, it will fail. These conflicted legislators thus face a *collective action dilemma*; if the bill passes, they are better off, but it is costly to them as individuals to support the party's proposal.

If there are just enough conflicted MCs and supporters to form a winning coalition, the conflicted MCs will all vote with their party. If there are more conflicted members than are necessary to win the vote, party leaders and conflicted members may decide which members must cast an unpopular vote to help their parties. In such situations, party leaders may engage in *vote buying*, in which leaders provide compensation to MCs for switching their votes. In practice, it is likely that most vote buying takes the form of implicit logrolling within a party—that is, legislators agree to vote with their parties on occasion when they are conflicted with the expectation that other legislators will do the same so that over time they will all be better off. John Aldrich (2011, ch. 2) portrays coordination of logrolls across votes as a solution to a collective action problem. In our framework, when legislators participate in such logrolls, they are granting power to their party leaders, and this behavior counts as part of the *budget* delegated to party leaders. However, logrolling is not always sufficient to win. Leaders may need to make additional promises to win important votes, and these may include legislative favors such as promising MCs to schedule their legislation, electoral favors such as fundraising assistance, or both.[17] Collectively, the implicit logrolling and explicit quid pro quo contracts compose the price to the majority party for winning the vote.

Party leaders do not necessarily compete to win every contested vote. There are two conditions for party leaders' investment in a particular vote:

- The net payoff across all members must exceed the price of the vote. If the costs exceed the gain, party leaders will not buy votes and let members vote independently.
- The net gain from the investment of party effort on one issue offers a better return on investment than on any alternative vote. As we discuss below, we assume that party leaders have a limited "budget" of powers they can use to influence outcomes, and they allocate this budget to conflicted votes that offer the most reward.

Consequently, we expect to observe these empirical patterns:

Hypothesis 2.1: Party leadership investment of party effort—and hence the unity of parties in roll call votes—is higher on issues that have the greatest impact on the majority party's electoral fortunes.

Hypothesis 2.2: Party leaders invest party resources in legislators who are conflicted.

Hypothesis 2.3: Assuming an agenda that includes some contested votes, majority party unity should decrease as its share of the chamber's seats increases.

2.2.4 Contested Votes: Minority Party Voting

The preceding discussion ignores the efforts of the opposing party, yet the minority party has its own strategic calculations. First, we survey minority party tactics and then explain how majority tactics depend on the cohesion of the majority party.

The minority party (or "opposition" party) can adopt three basic strategies:

- *Free voting*, in which all minority party members vote with their constituents' preferences with little effort at coordination
- *Defeating* the majority proposal and thereby denying the majority any boost in its collective reputation from a victory

- *Pain maximization*, in which minority party members vote against the majority party proposal as long as the electoral costs incurred by conflicted majority party members exceed those of conflicted minority party members

The minority party's choice of a strategy depends on the cohesion of the majority party. First, if there are enough unconflicted votes between the majority party and the opposition for a simple success or simple defeat, the minority party's default strategy will be *free voting*, since the outcome and the vote choices of majority party members are not in doubt.[18]

There are two scenarios for contested votes. First, a *determined majority* has enough votes between the unconflicted votes for its position (YY, assuming a majority party proposal), weak supporters who will vote for a bill even if they don't want it to pass (NYa), and conditional opponents who can be "bought" by the majority party (YNa). In the end, a determined majority party can always buy enough votes to win, but the minority party can make it expensive for the majority party via a strategy of *pain maximization*, in which conflicted members of the minority party vote against a proposal (even if it is in their personal political interests to support it) in order to force conflicted members of the majority party to vote for a measure they consider politically costly. This also forces the majority party leadership to expend some of its leadership budget so it has less to use on other disputes.

Of course, a strategy of pain maximization only makes sense if the minority party gains more (in electoral risk incurred by conflicted majority party members) than it loses (in electoral risk incurred by its own members). Otherwise, the minority party would be better off with a strategy of free voting.

On the other hand, there may be a *weak majority* that lacks the votes to pass its own proposal, even when conflicted members and any YY minority party members are counted. At first, the minority's response must seem obvious: defeat the measure and deny the majority party any credit for success. However, such measures can be very popular or critical to the national interest (such as the Troubled Asset Relief Program [TARP] legislation in October 2008), so aiding their defeat would harm the minority party's reputation as well.

Obviously, blocking is preferable if the benefits outweigh the costs. Thus if the minority party would make a relative gain in reputation if the bill failed and there are low costs to rallying votes against the measure, the minority will kill the majority's proposal. Less obvious, however, is that the minority might choose not to kill the bill if the gains from a strategy of pain maximization (the majority converts all its conflicted members, joined by some conflicted minority party members) are greater than outright victory—particularly since if the minority party has the votes to kill the bill, the majority party's conflicted members will likely desert and vote against their party's proposals.

One implication of this discussion is that there should be an asymmetric pattern of vote margins on contested votes. We concur with King and Zeckhauser (2003) that the majority party will "win by a little or lose by a lot" on key votes—that is, the majority party will either buy enough votes to eke out a narrow victory (perhaps over a minority party that is also buying votes to drive up the majority's cost) or invest no effort in a vote that it cannot win, so only true supporters will vote for the majority party's position while all others will vote with the minority party.

2.3.5 Agenda Setting

While the succeeding chapters do not directly analyze House or Senate agenda setting, a few comments are necessary to explain how the selection of issues fits into our framework.

First, we generally expect that both the majority and minority parties seek to maximize political returns by manipulating the bills, nominations, and issues that are debated on the chamber floor. In doing so, each party seeks to improve the relative reputations of its own party, influence the coalition of supporters of the two parties, and distribute policy benefits to the districts of its individual members. This is not incompatible with the claim that legislators often work on routine bills to fund the government or reauthorize expiring laws (Adler and Wilkerson 2013), since neither party wants a reputation for incompetence. But it does mean that agenda setters will often bring up legislation that is unlikely to become law but does help reinforce the "brand" of the agenda-setting party and that a majority party will allow itself to be "rolled" for the greater purpose of avoiding criticism for blocking popular or necessary legislation.[19]

More relevant to this chapter, the agenda-setting process is constrained by the formal and informal resources available to party leaders. Even today, party leaders and their staff can only focus on a few big issues per Congress (Koger 2003, 228). Thus a critical task for legislative parties is to effectively allocate this "budget" of party resources across a bundle of issues. Obviously, the larger a party's budget, the more ambitious its agenda can be. We also expect that party leaders will sequence legislation to minimize the price of tough votes by staging them early in a Congress (Lindstädt and Vander Wielen 2014) or when the general public is otherwise distracted—for example, late on a Saturday night during football season.

Finally, it bears emphasis that one means of buying votes is to promise agenda space for other issues. Party leaders can promise to bring up bills favored by individual legislators in exchange for a vote and to hold a party coalition together by credibly promising a sequence of proposals that satisfy different factions within a party.

2.4 The Partisan Arms Race

The next step is to explain variance in party influence and the role of party leaders. This is a classic case of *collective action* facilitated by *delegation*. Legislative parties do not necessarily need formal leaders to cooperate; in the early years of Congress, when there were few members in either chamber, legislators cooperated as parties without much formal organization. But as chambers grew larger and the legislative process became more complex, legislators found they needed formal leaders to coordinate their actions and provided them with a "budget" to accomplish their goals.

2.4.1 Party Budgets

There are several components of a party budget. First, the tangible elements are a budget, offices, and staff. Second, some members may agree to serve on a party whip team to collect information about legislators' preferences. Third, parties may delegate authority within the party caucus, such as the ability to make committee assignments, or may revise the rules and practices of their chambers to grant authority to party leaders.[20] Most important, however, is legislators' informal contribution of cooperation: a willingness to agree to intraparty compromises, take a fair share of electoral risks, refrain from offering amendments that divide or embarrass one's party, and conform with the party's "talking points" for floor debate and media interviews. Combined, these formal and informal delegations compose the "budget" that party leaders can invest in their party's interest.

2.4.2 Preferences over Party Budgets

The next question is, why do legislators' desired levels of party influence vary across members and over time? The classic answer is that party strength varies with members' preferences, conceived as the similarity of their constituencies (Cooper and Brady 1981) or of their preferred policy outcomes (Aldrich 1995; Rohde 1991), which are a function of legislators' individual views, donors and activists, primary election voters, *and* the mass of voters in their districts. Our theory accommodates this view. Recall the model of electoral success from section 2.1: legislators expect that their reelections depend on the party brand differential, their personal policy positions, and their personal reputations. A stronger party leadership will presumably improve the party brand at the cost of members' personal policy positions, while having a mixed effect on legislators' legislative entrepreneurship. For the latter term, party leaders can help legislators pursue their own priorities but may also crowd out the opportunity for legislators to act as policy entrepreneurs on their own.[21] The classic view posits that as the trade-off between collective party positions and legislators' constituencies eases, the costs of increasing the party budget decrease, and so legislators' preferences shift toward desiring stronger parties.

But this is not the *only* factor that influences legislators' support for party influence. Legislators may also increase the role of party leaders as the legislative process and party cooperation become more complex. Steven Smith (1989) explains the emergence of stronger congressional parties in the 1980s as a response to the institutional reforms of the 1970s, which made it more complex for legislators to navigate the committee, chamber, and conference stages, and they sought the aid of party leaders to coordinate the confusion. A third factor is the size of the legislature and hence the party caucus; as James Madison states in Federalist 58, "In all legislative assemblies the greater the number composing them may be, the fewer will be the men who will in fact direct their proceedings." The larger size of the US House helps explain the centralization of parliamentary powers in chamber leaders relative to the Senate, while we also observe much more internal party structure in the US House than in the Senate.

Fourth, legislators' support for party influence may vary with their party's share of the chamber.[22] All else equal, the members of a very large majority party may find it relatively easier to pass legislation without a great deal of party influence simply because there are more unconflicted members who may find it in their own interest to support the party's position without extra persuasion. Members of a narrow majority party, on the other hand, may need to empower leaders to win close votes with a united party. For the minority party, there may be little gain in empowering party leaders when their party holds few seats, while they are much more likely to win votes when the party chamber shares are near parity.

Fifth, and most critical to our account, *the legislators of one party may prefer a stronger (or weaker) party in response to the efforts of the opposing party*. Our intuition is that legislators improve their electoral situations if they can win votes (especially for the majority party) or force the members of the opposing party to cast votes that cost them electoral support in their districts (especially for the minority party). If members of a party with a small party budget find themselves losing legislative votes by close margins to a well-organized party and losing electoral support as a result, then they have a strong incentive to increase their party budgets enough to win more legislative votes. We elaborate on this view in the next section.

The members of each legislative party make ongoing decisions about how much power to delegate to their leaders. How do they choose the size of the leadership budget? We assume legislators will prefer to delegate more influence to party leaders as long as the benefits exceed the costs and will most prefer the budget level where the benefits of an additional increment of leader power equal the costs—and if all delegation is costly, then legislators will oppose any delegation to party leaders. In theory, this should result in each party choosing the level of party influence preferred by the median member of the party.[23]

2.4.3 Party Budgets as an Arms Race

Since party influence offers both benefits and costs, the straightforward implication is that each party chooses a level of party power that balances the *marginal costs* and *marginal benefits* of additional party unity. The "marginal costs" are the negative impact of the nth unit of party unity on a party's share of the chamber's seats. Similarly, "marginal benefits" are the electoral gains that accrue from the increased legislative success provided by the nth unit of party unity. Party members choose a level of party influence by deciding how much vote-buying and agenda-setting power to delegate to their leaders and by selecting leaders who are more or less inclined to use their powers to advance the electoral interests of party members.

We make the weak assumption that the benefits exceed the costs up to some level of party unity, after which the costs exceed the benefits for additional increments of party unity. If this assumption was not true, we would observe either zero party influence (costs always exceed benefits) or absolute party influence (benefits always exceed costs).[24] Congressional parties typically exert some influence but do not control every choice, suggesting that the equilibrium lies in between the extremes of zero and absolute influence.

What is the optimal level of party influence? For inspiration, we turn to a classic model of an *arms race* from international relations. The classic notion of an arms race is that two countries must decide how much to invest in armed forces and do so in response to the investment of the opposing country (Kydd 2000, 229). We think legislative parties follow a similar dynamic: each party chooses a "budget" of party influence, which is its best response to the opposing party's budget. Like a military arms race, partisan competition does not necessarily escalate to maximum investment, but it usually leads to investments higher than they would be in the absence of competition. One key difference is that military arms races do not necessarily lead to actual conflict, while legislative "arms races" manifest themselves in constant conflict on roll call votes, agenda setting, fundraising, and media relations.

We can adapt the classic Richardson arms race model (Richardson 1960) to encapsulate the key features of strategic party government in a simple set of expressions:[25]

$$\dot{PU}_D = \alpha_1 PU_R - \alpha_2 PU_D + \alpha_3 \qquad (2.2)$$

$$\dot{PU}_R = \beta_1 PU_D - \beta_2 PU_R + \beta_3 \qquad (2.3)$$

where $\alpha_1, \alpha_2, \beta_1, \beta_2 > 0$ and $1 \geq PU_D, PU_R, \alpha_3, \beta_3 \geq 0$.

The $\dot{PU}_D$ and $\dot{PU}_R$ terms are the instantaneous rates of change for Democratic and Republican Party unity—the tendency of each party to shift its cohesion at a given point in time. The α_1 and β_1 represent each party's *response* to the party unity of the other party, the α_2 and β_2 represent each party's *fatigue* level (its decreasing enthusiasm for additional cohesion), and α_3 and β_3 capture each party's *grievance* level (its support for party unity independent of other considerations).

At equilibrium, a party does not wish to change, so PU_D and PU_R are zero and we can express PU_D and PU_R in terms of the other variables:

$$\dot{PU}_D = (\alpha_1 / \alpha_2)PU_R + (\alpha_3 / \alpha_2) \qquad (2.4)$$

$$\dot{PU}_R = (\beta_1 / \beta_2)PU_D + (\beta_3 / \beta_2) \qquad (2.5)$$

The key implication is that each party's responsiveness to its opponent, and to popular demand for more partisanship, is constrained by "fatigue," or the extent to which legislators believe that additional party influence would be costly. We are also interested in some of the straightforward dynamic implications of equations 2.2 to 2.5.

First, we should attach some substantive meaning to the α and β terms. The <u>response</u> terms (α_1 and β_1) indicate the extent to which a party matches the investment of the opposing team. As discussed in chapters 5 and 6, we expect these parameters to increase (a) as the rewards for winning legislative contests increase, (b) as the procedural advantages of the majority party *decrease*, and (c) as policy views of the two parties' members differ (the CPG claim).[26] We also expect α_1 to increase as the size of the Democratic Party's chamber share decreases, while we expect β_1 to increase as the size of the Republican Party's chamber share decreases. The <u>fatigue</u> terms (α_2 and β_2) should increase (a) to the extent that constituents disapprove of partisanship, (b) as the constituencies represented by a party become more diverse (the CPG claim), (c) for the majority party, and (d) as legislative power becomes centralized in party leaders.[27] The <u>grievance</u> term should increase as the party "base" of local organizations, interest groups, donors, and primary voters actually rewards partisanship. It should also vary with major events such as the terror attack on the United States on September 11, 2001, or especially controversial elections like the 2000 presidential election that contribute to an atmosphere of antagonism or consensus.

We illustrate the interaction between the costs and benefits of party influence in figure 2.3. Figure 2.3 depicts the strategic choice faced by the Democratic Party as it chooses its level of party unity (the vertical axis), resulting in a distribution of legislative success (the horizontal axis) between the Democrats (left side) and Republicans (right side); below we explain how these figures incorporate Republican strategy. The diagonal lines represent the marginal costs and benefits of each unit of party unity. The marginal electoral costs line represents party "fatigue": the di-

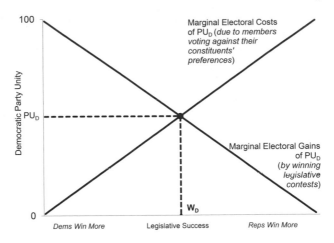

FIGURE 2.3. Strategic party calculus of Democrats

rect and negative effects of having additional party unity pull legislators away from their districts' preferences. The marginal electoral gains line represents the "response" and "grievance" terms: the indirect and positive effect of having additional party unity lead to legislative victories that help the party win seats, as well as any direct positive payoffs for partisanship. These are portrayed as 45° lines, but they may also be concave or convex, may be tilted at different angles, or may shift over time; the key feature is that their intersection represents the optimal strategy. Each choice along the vertical axis represents a marginal payoff on the cost and benefit lines. In figure 2.3, the Democrats choose the equilibrium value, PU_D*. By choosing the level of party unity such that the marginal costs match the marginal benefits, the Democrats maximize their net gain from the legislative game.[28] Any level of Democratic Party unity higher than PU_D* costs the Democrats more than it benefits them, while party unity lower than PU_D* would mean that the Democrats are settling for less than the ideal combination of party unity and winning.[29]

Most important, we expect that a change in the party unity of one party will affect the strategy of the opposing party. An increase in one party's unity will be partially mirrored by an increase in the opposing party's unity. The logic of this claim is displayed in figure 2.4.

An increase in the Republicans' Party unity is portrayed as a rightward shift in the Democrats' marginal gain line from T_1 to T_2. If the Democrats maintained their T_1 level of party unity, then the win distribution would

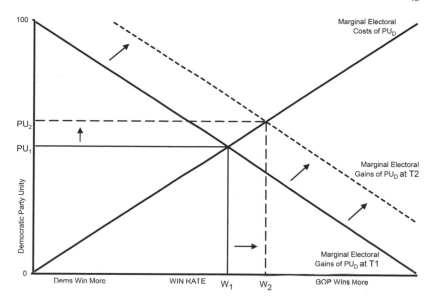

FIGURE 2.4. Strategic party calculus: Democrats respond to a shift in Republican unity

shift markedly in the Republicans' favor. If, on the other hand, Democrats sought to maintain their win share from T_1, they would have to dramatically increase their party unity. Both these responses are more costly than a "partial" matching strategy, in which Democrats shift from PU_1 to PU_2 and allow their win share to decline from W_1 to W_2; this is the Democrats' new equilibrium strategy.

> *Hypothesis 2.4*: Party influence will vary with the effort level of the opposing party. Thus Democratic Party unity should increase as Republican Party unity increases.

2.4.4 Uncertainty and Party Competition

The preceding section specifies how much power legislators should delegate to party leaders given the weights attached to their response, fatigue, and grievance parameters and the strategy of the opposing party. In theory, this formula yields a specific best strategy for each party, and the members of each party choose that strategy. In practice, there is a great deal of uncertainty about these decisions, so there is no guarantee that each party will choose its optimal level of party influence. Furthermore, several of the components of the party "budget"—leaders, party rules, and chamber rules—may be inflexible and thus difficult to update quickly. This section explains this uncertainty and its effect on party strategy.

A major source of uncertainty is the opaque meaning of democratic elections. One reason is that it is hard to evaluate the signal(s) that voters intend to send. As E. E. Schattschneider says, "The people are a sovereign whose vocabulary is limited to two words, 'Yes' and 'No.'" (2003, 52). Politicians observe the results of elections, such as the change in chamber share, who won and lost, and changes in election margins. They also know what they said during the campaign and may infer that elections outcomes were attributable to their "message." And in the modern era, politicians can read exit polls to divine the intent of voters. It is hard to know how these signals should be translated into party strategy for the *next* election. Elections are, to a large extent, a retrospective evaluation of previous strategy. They help politicians understand what they should have done in the past, but election results do not tell politicians what they should do going forward. Indeed, a strategy that led to losses in one election might be the best strategy for the following election. There is often a discussion within each party about what the results mean, and different factions may use the results to urge the rest of the party to embrace their views.[30]

A second source of uncertainty is that multiple parameters change at the same time. During the transition from one Congress to the next, a party chooses its party budget at the same time that chamber margins and chamber control may have changed, there may be a new president to work with, and new issues may arise on the policy agenda. To some extent, this selection is an ongoing decision,[31] but it is common to select leaders and choose party and chamber rules before each Congress, so party budgets are partially determined during a period of uncertainty.

A final source of uncertainty is the opposing party. Again, each party attempts to adopt its best response to the opposition, but the opposing party often keeps its strategy secret. The opposition strategy is partially revealed as it chooses its leaders and rules, but its overall commitment to a united front is revealed on a case-by-case basis—that is, for a given bill, the strategies of the two parties may be unknown, and over the course of a Congress, the general partisanship of the opposing party gradually becomes clear.

Thus we expect that party strategies will partially reflect the party competition seen in previous time periods. If the parties' choices result in a significant gap in party unity, we expect the parties to correct for it in the next period. This implies that we should observe the following:

> *Hypothesis 2.5*: Parties will correct differences in party influence. Thus parties will reduce differences in party unity seen in the previous period.

2.5 Summary and Conclusion

This chapter summarizes the logic of strategic party government—the competition for power between legislative parties. We begin with voters and candidates to understand how parties can help legislators in elections. Since American voters weigh the individual behavior and traits of candidates heavily, legislators face a trade-off between the benefits of party cooperation and the costs of conforming to party leadership. Party leaders take these tensions into account as they compete to win votes and select the issues considered by the chamber, while party members balance the benefits of cooperation and autonomy when deciding how much power to delegate to party leaders. The result is an arms race competition: each party's strength is chosen based on its own characteristics but also as a response to the opposing party's strength.

We test our multistage theory in a series of chapters. We begin this testing with the preferences of individual voters.

CHAPTER THREE

Microlevel Foundations

Do Citizens Dislike Partisanship or Extremism?

Coauthored with Everett Young

W e begin our empirical study with individual voters. Our theory assumes that legislators often pay a price for cooperating with legislative parties. This chapter tests whether voters punish legislators for their
partisanship or ideology and explains why. We use an experiment in which
subjects are presented with legislators who vote in lockstep with a party
and with legislators who vote consistently as liberals or conservatives. In
the role of voters, subjects *penalize* those legislators voting as loyal partisans but slightly *favor* legislators who vote as consistent ideologues.

The next section clarifies our expectations for citizens' evaluations of
legislative behavior and then explains our experimental design and presents our initial results. Our main finding in this first stage is that voters
punish partisanship while tolerating—and even admiring—strong ideological views. The remaining sections then seek to explain why citizens
might react this way. We find that much of the punishment is imposed by
voters affiliated with the party opposed to the legislator's party. Voters are
more likely to sanction legislators of the opposite party to the extent that
the voters personally identify with their own party. Beyond that, however,
subjects generally dislike the use of partisanship and think poorly of legislators who display too much of it. These findings support our claim that
legislators often pay a price for partisanship, and this tends to reduce the
influence of party organizations in response to legislators' "fatigue" with
strong parties.

3.1 Partisanship and Ideology

In the previous chapter, we proposed a simple formulation of the calculus of voters' preferences: if voter i chooses between candidates j and k from different parties (P_j, P_k) and x_i, x_j, and x_k represent the single-peaked and symmetric policy preferences of the voter and candidates along a unidimensional policy spectrum, with candidate j as the incumbent, and vote choice V is the probability that voter i chooses candidate j.

$$\underset{\text{(Incumbency)}}{\phantom{V_{ijk} = \beta_0 + \beta_1(v_j - v_k)}} \overset{\text{(Valence)}}{} \overset{\text{(Policy)}}{}$$

$$V_{ijk} = \beta_0 + \underset{}{\beta_1(v_j - v_k)} + \underset{\text{(Party Brand)}}{\beta_2(P_j - P_k)} + \beta_3(|x_i - x_j| - |x_i - x_k|) + \underset{\text{(Party Loyalty)}}{\beta_4(PL_j - PL_k)} \ (2.1)$$

Each of the β terms reflects a distinct way of thinking about legislative elections. The β_0 term reflects the power of incumbency due to name recognition and the institutional benefits of office holding, such as personal staff, franked mail, casework, and committee seniority (e.g., Carson and Roberts 2013; Cox and Katz 2002; Jacobson 1987; Mayhew 1974a). The β_1 term reflects a range of research on the effects of candidates' personal traits—such as personal background, race and gender, celebrity status, and so on—as well as their campaigning skill (Canon 1990; Carter and Patty 2015; Fenno 2008; Fulton 2012; Lawless and Pearson 2008; Stone and Simas 2010). The β_2 term reflects the overall differential between party "brands" due to issue positions and past performance. The classic *The American Voter* (Campbell et al. 1960) argues that most voters hew to long-term party loyalties, and mountains of subsequent research has elaborated on systematic variation in party reputations and voter partisanship—all sharing the premise that party labels are important drivers of vote choice. The β_3 term, on the other hand, reflects a vast literature based on the assumption that voters are primarily ideological—they choose the candidate who best fits their governing philosophy. Often this approach further assumes that the various public policy issues debated during campaigns can be summarized in one or two ideological dimensions (Downs 1957; Enelow and Hinich 1984).[1] Finally, the β_4 term is an addition to the traditional conception of voting. As this chapter elaborates, it measures the extent to which voters perceive a candidate (especially the incumbent) as subordinating the preferences of his or her constituents to the interests of a political party. While there is often an element of policy disagreement in this judgment, there is also a betrayed expectation that legislators will prioritize their own constituents over their party affiliation.

While our model of voting *can* accommodate these diverse influences on vote choice, the actual influence of these factors varies from voter to voter, race to race, and year to year. For this study, it is particularly important to understand the role of party labels and partisan behavior in the electoral process and to compare these factors to the role of ideological proximity.

A great deal of prior research casts doubt on the ability of voters to punish legislators for their ideology or, more broadly, their voting record. In the decades since Campbell, Converse, Miller, and Stokes (1960) documented the average citizen's lack of knowledge about politics, scholars have struggled to reconcile the political ignorance of the average voter with the expectation that they will evaluate the complex actions of their representatives. Among institutional scholars, a central research focus examines whether voters penalize elected officials who act contrary to their preferences, suggesting at least some level of voter attentiveness (Erikson 1971). Some research examining legislator behavior on highly visible issues finds little or no penalty for voting contrary to constituents' preferences on, for example, pay raises (e.g., Kingdon 1989; but see Theriault 2005) or even generally (Bernstein 1989).

Others find substantial penalties for voting contrary to citizens' ideological preferences (Canes-Wrone et al. 2002) or views on a single issue like health care (Jacobson 2011; Koger and Lebo 2012; Nyhan et al. 2012) or for a pattern of partisanship in legislative voting (Carson et al. 2010; Harbridge 2015; Koger and Lebo 2012; Lebo et al. 2007). These studies are, explicitly or implicitly, based on theories of voting behavior. For example, if Canes-Wrone et al. (2002) are correct that ideologically extreme legislators suffer in their bids for reelection, it necessarily implies that voters both can recognize such behavior and tend to punish it.

In fact, much of the political psychology literature finds that voters, especially the less politically interested, neither understand ideological concepts like liberalism and conservatism very well, nor do they have an easy time placing political events in ideological terms. Instead, voters are more comfortable identifying themselves as Democrats and Republicans than they are as liberals or conservatives. Campbell et al.'s *The American Voter* (1960) and especially Converse's "The Nature of Belief Systems in Mass Publics" (1964), found that Americans were largely unable to make much use of ideological concepts or even the terms *liberal* and *conservative* to organize their political world. In contrast, Campbell and colleagues (1960) wrote, "Few factors are of greater importance for our national elections than the lasting attachment of tens of millions of Americans to one of the parties" (121). Partisanship reflects an affective duty that speaks to who people are rather than simply a summary of which issue positions they prefer. And in the current era of partisan polarization, voters may form stronger attachments to their parties than to their ideological cohort, so voters may have a much stronger reaction to legislative actions contrary to their partisan preferences than those contrary to their ideological views.

In contemporary politics, partisanship has been shown to be a stronger determinant of political behavior—especially vote choice (Bartels 2000)—than ideology. Goren (2005) shows that partisan identity is more stable than core ideological principles and that partisanship constrains ideas about equal opportunity, limited government, and moral tolerance, while the opposite does not hold—that is, partisanship shapes ideology; ideology does not shape partisanship. Partisan identification is so strong that it can cause people to alter their views of other issues through motivated reasoning (Taber and Lodge 2006) or even cause them to endorse policies that directly contradict their party's ideological commitments (Lavine et al. 2012).

Partisanship is deeply ingrained and begins early. Work on political socialization has found that party attachment develops before ideology (Campbell et al. 1960; Greenstein 1965; Hess and Torney 1965; Hyman 1959; Sears 1975; Sears and Valentino 1997), and while a "revisionist" view (Franklin 1984) holds that partisanship can change in response to political events, evidence for the power and stability of partisan attitudes in shaping citizens' views of politics continues to grow (Green and Palmquist 1990; Green et al. 2002; Hetherington 2001).

In contrast, much classic research on ideology finds that only those with significant expertise make effective use of the concepts of *liberalism* and *conservatism* to structure their political attitudes or to guide their political behavior (Bennett 1988; Judd and Krosnick 1989; Zaller 1992; but see Achen 1975 and Nie et al. 1978). Even political experts appear to need high chronic levels of special motivation—the "need to evaluate"—to fully use ideology to guide their opinion formation (Federico and Schneider 2007).

One way to discuss this contrast is as a choice between competing heuristics. Heuristics are mental shortcuts that help voters make political decisions and potentially allow them to approximate the rational, information-driven voting behavior that democratic theory presupposes (Huckfeldt et al. 1999). Thus they are commonly presented as a potential solution to the problem besetting democratic theory: that voters are not very knowledgeable or competent, but they ought to be for a democracy to function (Erikson et al. 2002; Huckfeldt et al. 1999; Lau and Redlawsk 2001; Lupia 1994; Lupia and McCubbins 1998; Popkin 1991; Popkin and Dimock 2000; Rahn 1993; Sniderman et al. 1991; but see Kuklinski and Quirk 2000).[2]

The study of political heuristics has identified numerous shortcuts that help both more *and* less politically sophisticated citizens make use of politics (Lau and Redlawsk 2001), including a "likability" heuristic, a "deservingness" heuristic (Peterson et al. 2011), and an "endorsement" heuristic (Lupia 1994). Lau and Redlawsk (2001) test five heuristics, with the politician's party and his ideology as two of the five (endorsements, viability, and appearance are the other three). In comparing ideology and partisanship, they suggest that the party is "simpler to grasp and noticeably more prevalent on the American scene" (958).[3]

If we think of our question as asking which shortcut—the partisan cue or the ideological cue—voters are more likely to use to gauge legislators' type, our research extends this literature by comparing the relative effects of partisan and ideological heuristics on candidate preference. We designed experiments, first, to establish the differences in the way people respond to partisan versus ideological information about legislators and, second, to try to clarify the reasons for any differences we might find in these reactions.

3.2 Experimental Design

We begin with an experiment on two separate samples: 142 undergraduate students in political science classes at Stony Brook University located on Long Island, New York, and 104 adults—54 from Long Island and 50 from Tallahassee, Florida.[4] Participants first answered a battery of questions about themselves, including their ideological and partisan self-placement on 7-point Likert-style items ranging from strong conservative or strong Republican to strong liberal or strong Democrat. They also indicated their level of "partisan social identity" (Greene 1999) and "ideological social identity," as discussed below.

Each participant then read an explanation of what roll call votes are and learned that these votes, by members of the US House of Representatives, are public knowledge. Participants would shortly thereafter learn about certain legislators' roll call votes.

Participants were told that these votes could be characterized in either partisan terms or ideological terms. A vote "with the Republicans [or Democrats] and against the Democrats [or Republicans]" was easy enough to discern just by looking at roll call votes and the party membership of the representatives who voted. Whether a vote was "on the liberal side of the issue" or "on the conservative side" could be determined by reference to "ratings by Americans for Democratic Action (ADA)," an actual organization that rates legislators as to their degree of liberalism or conservatism. We made the claim that the ADA had rated each fictitious roll call vote as liberal or conservative and that this was the information the participants would soon see.

Each participant was next exposed to two different fictitious legislators, said to be members of the US House standing for reelection. For each representative, participants underwent the same procedure:

1. Participants were introduced to the representative by name and received bland, nondiagnostic or barely diagnostic information.[5]
2. Participants were asked to estimate on a 7-point scale, from "strongly support" to "strongly oppose," their willingness to support the representative's reelection with the expressed understanding that they had very little to go on. This was our first measure of "electoral support."
3. Participants were exposed to a page displaying ten separate fictitious roll call votes the representative cast while in office. For each roll call vote, the issue covered by the bill was briefly summarized, and then the vote was characterized in either partisan terms or ideological terms—as will be explained further below.
4. Participants answered three distracter questions, such as self-judged personality or political knowledge questions.
5. Finally, participants answered a battery of questions about the representative, indicating the participant's estimation of him on a number of traits, such as independent-mindedness, toughness, and so forth, and were again asked to rate their willingness to support his reelection using the same scale as in step 2. This was a second, post-issue exposure measure of electoral support.[6]

Each subject saw two separate pages: The first described ten positions of one representative in partisan terms and the second described ten positions of a different representative in ideological terms. On the partisan pages, votes were described as with the Democrats (or Republicans) and against the Republicans (or Democrats). On the ideological pages, legislators were reported as voting on the liberal or conservative side of an issue. The substance of the vote itself—for example, that the representative supported rather than opposed abortion rights, opposed rather than supported building a weapons system, and so on—was not given. For example, "On the issue of whether states should be allowed to permit their residents access to marijuana for medicinal purposes, Rep. Allen was rated by ADA as casting his vote on the *liberal* side of the issue."[7] The representative's votes could be 60 percent, 70 percent, 80 percent, 90 percent, or 100 percent aligned either with a party or with an ideology (with the remainder of the votes obviously on the other side).[8] This, of course, created variation in the amount of "lockstep voting," either partisan or ideological, displayed by a representative, which became our primary independent variable of interest.[9]

After exposure to roll call votes and distracter questions, participants expressed support as part of the battery of questions outlined in step 5, which also included seven perceived traits of the politician.[10] The key variables were as follows:

- The participant's self-placement on a 7-point Republican-Democratic Party identification scale and a 7-point liberal-conservative ideological identification scale, recoded to range from 0 to 1
- Liberal, conservative, Republican, and Democratic *social* identity (discussed in more detail below), recoded to range from 0 to 1
- The participant's electoral support for each of the politicians based on preliminary bland information, measured on a 7-point scale—the "pre–roll call vote" electoral support
- The amount of legislative lockstep voting (distance from 50 percent to 50 percent) of each politician to whom a participant was exposed, from −5 (100 percent liberal or Democratic) through 0 (nonpartisan or nonideological) to 5 (100 percent conservative or Republican)
- The participant's post–roll call vote electoral support for each of the four politicians, measured on a 7-point scale
- The participant's general impression of the politician on several separate traits

3.3 Results

Result 1: Respondents Punish Partisanship, Not Ideological Extremism

The first step was to see, at the broadest level, the extent to which partisan loyalty and ideological extremity hurt politicians in voters' eyes. The main dependent variable for this analysis, then, is the difference between the preexposure and postexposure levels of electoral support. This variable ranged theoretically from −6 (where a participant went from indicating "7" for strong support to indicating "1" for strong opposition) to +6 (where the opposite occurred). As it happens, changes in electoral support ranged from −4 to 4 (with a mean of −0.26 and a standard deviation of 1.61) for ideology-described politicians and from −5 to 3 (mean −.60, sd 1.76) for partisan-described politicians. The main explanatory variable is the amount of partisan loyalty or ideological voting of the legislator. This variable was coded so that a participant's exposure to a legislator voting with one side 6 or 7 out of 10 times was coded 0, and exposure to a legislator voting with one side 8, 9, or 10 out of 10 times was coded 1.[11]

We include in our first analysis a single control variable: the extent to which the voter's party identification or ideological self-identification opposed the incumbent's party. This is coded to range from 0 to 1, with 0 being a voter-incumbent match and 1 being a mismatch.[12] This covariate controls for the tendency of voters to evaluate incumbents' partisanship or ideology from their own perspectives. We also want to minimize the possibility that our findings are the result of the characteristics of our participants rather than of the fictional incumbents.

The initial findings are shown in table 3.1 and figure 3.1 with results from the full, combined sample of students and adults in column A, followed by the separate student (column B) and adult samples (column C).[13] Column A shows that in the full, combined sample, the results are strong, and this holds when we move to either subsample. When the dependent variable is the change in support after seeing the incumbent's positions portrayed as partisan, lockstep voting has a strong negative effect on support. For the full sample, extreme legislators suffer a decline of 0.71 scale-points (on the 7-point scale) for being lockstep or near-lockstep roll call voters above and beyond the expected penalty (2.32 points) exacted when the voter's party identification changes from maximally for to maximally against the legislator's preferred party.

On the other hand, the effect of ideological extremity is noticeably *positive*, though not quite statistically significant. A penalty still exists (2.04 points for a minimal to maximal change) for a legislator being opposite the participant's ideological self-ID, but the consistency of ideological voting is not in itself punished. Finally, the coefficients for partisan and ideological extremity are significantly different from each other ($p <$ .001), establishing that partisan lockstep voting yields electoral sanctions, while ideological extremity does not.[14]

TABLE 3.1. **Changes in intent to support legislator after partisan lockstep roll call voting versus ideologically monotonous roll call voting**

	A. Full sample		B. Student sample		C. Adult sample	
DV: change in support before/after seeing legislator's positions in partisan terms						
	Coefficient (se)	*p*-value 2-tailed	Coefficient (se)	*p*-value 2-tailed	Coefficient (se)	*p*-value 2-tailed
Legislator was very partisan	−0.71 (0.20)	0.000	−0.64 (0.24)	0.007	−0.83 (0.34)	0.016
Voter's party ID opposite of legislator	−2.32 (0.27)	0.000	−2.67 (0.33)	0.000	−1.94 (0.44)	0.000
Constant	0.92 (0.21)	0.000	1.18 (0.26)	0.000	0.65 (0.33)	0.051
DV: change in support before/after seeing legislator's positions in ideological terms						
Legislator was ideologically extreme	0.34 (0.21)	0.109	0.39 (0.25)	0.123	0.22 (0.34)	0.516
Voter's ideological ID opposite of legislator	−2.04 (0.31)	0.000	−1.20 (0.42)	0.004	−2.95 (0.46)	0.000
Constant	0.49 (0.24)	0.038	0.05 (0.30)	0.862	0.96 (0.37)	0.009
Wald test of H_0: effect of hyperpartisanship = effect of ideological extremity	$\chi^2 = 12.9, p = 0.0003$		$\chi^2 = 8.80, p = 0.003$		$\chi^2 = 4.61, p = 0.032$	
N	241		137		104	

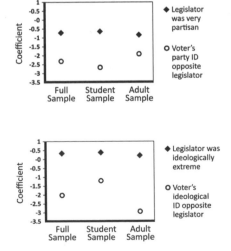

FIGURE 3.1. Changes in support, lockstep voting versus ideological voting
Top panel, Change in support before/after seeing legislator in partisan terms. *Bottom panel*, Change in support before/after seeing legislator in ideological terms.

To assure that these results are not the effect of an overly liberal sample, we reran the analysis with *only* the fifty-nine self-identified Republicans in the sample. For them, the coefficient for partisan extremity is −0.62, while the coefficient for ideological extremity is again positive (0.48). Using only the seventy self-identified conservatives, we obtained the same results: the coefficient for partisan extremity is −0.83, while the coefficient for ideological extremity is 0.40.

To be sure, the key findings that partisan lockstep voting damages electoral support at the individual level while ideological extremity does not are robust regardless of how the sample is divided. Using the combined sample and then partitioning by various demographic and other variables, the coefficient for partisan lockstep voting was between −0.5 and −1.0 and significant at $p < .05$ whether we look at only liberals or conservatives, only Republicans or Democrats, only the higher- or the lower-educated, only males or females, only the strongly religious or the less so, only those in the upper half or those in the lower half of incomes, or only the more or the less politically knowledgeable.[15] Also, for every one of these subsamples, the coefficient for ideological extremity was positive. Below we show that even for people evaluating members of Congress (MCs) of their own party or ideology, the tendency (not quite statistically significant) is to reward ideological extremity and to punish the party hack.

In sum, the results are unambiguous: When an incumbent is known to have voted with one particular party a great majority of the time, voters of various demographic stripes withdraw electoral support.[16] And when an incumbent's roll call votes are ideologically consistent, voters do not appear to exact electoral punishment for this fact alone and might even reward such behavior. Given this result, it remains to be explained *why* this difference occurs.

WHO PUNISHES PARTISANSHIP, AND WHY?   In addition to generally comparing the importance of partisan and ideological cues for voters, we also seek to understand <u>why</u> voters react to these cues and which voters are more likely to be affected by them. We contrast the "identity threat" explanation with the "principled agent vs. party hack" explanations and we seek to determine whether independent voters or opposite-party voters are more likely to punish partisan legislators.

We have already mentioned the first possible mechanism: partisanship, not ideology, triggers and possibly threatens voters' <u>sense of identity</u>. When a legislator votes in lockstep with a voter's less-preferred party, that voter may feel this as a more personal affront than when the legislator votes consistently against the voter's ideological group. The rival explanation is that voters may decline to punish ideologically extreme voting because they consider it a sign of strong principles and of a coherent vision for the future of the country. Voters may actually gain respect for a representative with a consistent voting record along ideological lines. Excessive partisanship, however, is a favorite target for politicians, the media, and voters when explaining what is wrong with politics. Simply, voters might give credit for independence to a "maverick" MC who votes consistently liberal or conservative while labeling an MC who consistently votes with his or her party as a "party hack," loyal to party above constituency.

Of course, voters' reactions to partisan loyalty may differ across subgroups of voters (Harbridge and Malholtra 2011). Thus aside from demonstrating that, on balance, incumbents pay an electoral price for legislative partisanship, we consider two possibilities. The first explanation is that *independent voters are driving the effect.* This hypothesis holds that lockstep party voting offends centrist, nonpartisan, independent voters who demand from their representatives the same independent-mindedness that keeps them happily unaffiliated. At the same time, party-aligned voters may punish lockstep voting in the opposite party's legislators but balance this by rewarding loyalty in legislators of their own party, leaving independents mainly responsible for the effect.

A second possible explanation is that *party-affiliated, aisle-crossing voters drive the effect.* While not contradicting the *independents* thesis, this explanation holds that a certain number of party-identified voters are willing to cross the aisle if an incumbent from the other party is perceived as effective and working for the good of her constituents. However, these party-identifiers may react to cues that the other-party incumbent is "too" partisan. Given the right campaign stimuli, these cross-aisle voters may view the incumbent as a warrior for the opposing team. Yet cross-aisle voters may accept or even admire an MC with strong ideological views. Additionally, they may lack the requisite understanding of ideological concepts or emotional ties to ideological camps—or both—necessary to punish an ideologically extreme incumbent.

Result 2: Partisans, Not Independents, Impose Electoral Sanctions

With some further analyses, we can start by dispensing with the idea that the effect is driven by the fact that voters in our sample are incapable of making use of ideological labels such as "liberal" and "conservative."[17] The tradition of Converse (1964) might suggest that a lack of sophistication led to a failure to punish roll call voting when it was characterized by ideology. But our sample did quite well in classifying issues along ideological lines. We asked all our participants a battery of issue-position questions,[18] gauging their opinions on several moral, fiscal, and other issues, which combined to form a highly reliable scale of issue-position-based left-right ideology.[19] Correlations this high indicate that our participants had no problem translating self-labels of any kind into the "correct" policy positions. They know very well what "liberal," "conservative," "Republican," and "Democrat" mean.

We can also reject the hypothesis that independent voters are driving the effect. That is, one might think that partisans do not react at all and that it is independents who want to see evidence that politicians think for themselves. Yet if we rerun our analyses with the independents removed, the key findings hold. Independents are not to blame—partisans are driving our results.[20]

This leaves two key questions. First, why do partisan identifiers punish extreme voting at all? We might at first expect partisans to like party-line voting if it's for their own party and perhaps punish it to an equal and offsetting degree for the opposite party.[21] Second, why is this punishment *not* observed for legislators whose extremity is characterized by ideological votes?

Result 3: Punishment Varies with Party
Loyalty of Opposite-Party Legislators

We begin by asking whether partisans punish all legislators equally for excessive party loyalty or punish only those who show loyalty to the opposing side. To answer this, we create a new dummy variable called *Legislator in Opposite Party* (LOP), coded 0 if the legislator votes (at least 60 percent of the time) with the participant's party (as indicated by the 7-point party identification variable) or coded 1 if the legislator votes with the opposition. We also specify an interaction between LOP and partisan lockstep voting to see if the effect of more extreme voting differs depending on whether the voter and the MC match each other in their party or ideology. These are then added to the model of table 3.1.

As shown in table 3.2, voters do punish the lockstep behavior of opposite-party legislators significantly. They also appear to punish lockstep behavior of same-party legislators too but not quite significantly (.05

TABLE 3.2. **Adding a variable for legislator of opposite party**

	Coefficient (se)	p-value (2-tailed)
Partisan lockstep roll call voting	−1.12 (0.32)	0.001
Partisan lockstep roll call voting × voter-legislator in same party	0.65 (0.44)	0.145
Voter and legislator in same party	1.26 (0.36)	0.001
Constant	−0.73 (0.27)	0.008
N	221	
R^2	0.28	
Wald test that (partisan lockstep voting + interaction term) = 0	$F = 2.40, p = 0.12$	

level).[22] In fact, the failure of the interaction by itself to achieve significance indicates that we cannot say with confidence that voters punish the opposite side any *more* harshly than they punish their "own" legislators. Thus the results do suggest that voters punish hyperpartisanship more strongly in politicians of the opposite party but do not reward hyperpartisanship for politicians of their own party.[23] Legislators may need to worry that excessive partisanship will turn off even partisans of their own party.

As in table 3.1, the strong effects of partisanship do not reappear when we replicate the analyses using ideology instead (not shown). Extremity is rewarded (though not statistically significantly so) whether the legislator is of the same or the opposite ideology as the voter.

*Result 4: Punishment Increases among Voters
Who Identify with the Opposite Party*

A possible explanation for the punishment of partisanship is that voters *socially* identify more strongly with parties than with ideologies and that the intensity of this social identity affects voting behavior. This account calls on social identity theory (Tajfel 1981; Tajfel and Turner 1979), which suggests that people should support a group strongly when they feel emotionally attached to that group or perhaps punish an out-group to boost the relative standing of their in-group. This is done in an attempt to boost a self-esteem that is intimately connected with feeling favorable toward their in-group.

We created an index that measured participants' level of "parti-

san social identity" and "ideological social identity" using three questions from the Mael and Tetrick (1992) "identification with a psychological group" scale, such as "When I talk about liberals, I usually say 'we'
rather than 'they.'" An additive scale was created to range from 0 to 1.[24]
The mean level of "socially identifying" with one's own preferred party
was 0.6825, while the mean level of socially identifying with one's preferred ideology was 0.6675. This small difference is nonetheless significant
in our sample of 252 ($t = 2.05, p < 0.05$) and is a first suggestion that perhaps partisan social identity might have different effects than ideological
social identity does.

More important than this small difference, we seek evidence that voters' stronger social identity with parties is associated with more punitive
voting behavior. Perhaps it is the voters who most emotionally identify
with a party who would be the ones most offended by legislators who vote
in lockstep with the opposite party. If these same voters do not reward
lockstep voting for their own party to the same degree, there would be a
net punishment.

Table 3.3 follows the model used for table 3.1 and adds the level of the
voter's in-party social identity and the interaction of that social identity
with legislator lockstep voting. We leave non-party-identifying independents out of the analysis.[25] In column A, we see the familiar finding that
lockstep voting brings a penalty—about 0.78 scale points of electoral support lost for lockstep voting at the mean level of partisan social identity.

TABLE 3.3. **Partisan social identity, partisan lockstep voting, and electoral support**

	A. Full sample		B. Voter, legislator in opposite parties		C. Voter, legislator in same party	
DV: change in support before/after seeing legislator's positions in partisan terms						
	Coefficient (se)	*p*-value 2-tailed	Coefficient (se)	*p*-value 2-tailed	Coefficient (se)	*p*-value 2-tailed
Legislator was very partisan	−0.78 (0.22)	0.000	−1.23 (0.29)	0.000	−0.43 (0.32)	0.18
Voter's party ID opposite of legislator	−2.45 (0.28)	0.000	−3.96 (1.09)	0.000	−0.64 (1.17)	0.581
In-party social identity	−0.02 (0.19)	0.921	0.10 (0.29)	0.712	0.03 (0.28)	0.924
Social Identity × legislator very partisan	−0.40 (0.24)	0.095	−0.53 (0.32)	0.108	−0.26 (0.33)	0.432
Constant	1.13 (0.22)	0.000	2.72 (0.98)	0.006	0.65 (0.33)	0.051
	$N = 221, R^2 = 0.33$		$N = 113, R^2 = 0.27$		$N = 108, R^2 = 0.03$	

Note that merely having strong partisan social identity, by itself, is little related to electoral reward or punishment—it is the interaction of lockstep voting and partisan social identity that appears to be meaningful. The coefficient ($-0.40, p < 0.1$) gives the additional penalty for lockstep voting imposed by opposite-party voters. It is half the size of the main effect, meaning that a *very* strong voter—for example, one standard deviation above the mean in partisan social identity—is predicted to punish a highly partisan MC about twice as much as an average-identifying voter. On the other hand, one would have to have very little identity with a party—roughly two standard deviations below the mean—to neither punish nor reward lockstep voting.

Strongly identifying voters simply do not reward lockstep partisanship by members of their own party. This is evident in columns B and C of table 3.3, where the same model is run separately for when the incumbent legislator and voter are in the same or opposite party, respectively. In an echo of table 3.2, these results show that even when the incumbent legislator is in the same party as the voter, stronger social identity predicts *more* punishment for lockstepping, not less. Thus while voters' punishing the opposition seems to drive much of the effect, there is no evidence that our participant voters—even strong party identifiers—*ever* reward excess partisanship, even in their own party's legislators.[26] By contrast, voters' ideological social identity does little to enhance or change the effect of legislative ideological extremity on electoral support (see the online appendix for table A.3.4).

To wrap up the discussion of social identity effects, it seems that people who socially identify strongly with parties set partisan concerns high in their political thinking. Hence it is these party-concerned voters who punish partisan loyalty the most severely; legislators need to be wary of them in their roll call decisions. These voters punish the lockstep behavior of the opposite side's legislators the most harshly but there is no evidence that they reward their own party's legislators for party loyalty either. They might even frown upon that too.

Result 5: Respondents Associate Party
Loyalty with a Loss of Independence

The answer to a final question tells us a lot of what is behind our results. The question: what do respondents think of legislators who engage in ideological and partisan lockstep voting? For example, does partisan lockstep voting (and not extreme ideological voting) cause voters to see legislators as insufficiently independent-minded? Are they seen as closed-minded or untrustworthy? We asked participants to rate the politicians as to how independent-minded, trustworthy, caring, intelligent, tough, open-minded, and predictable the legislator seemed after participants had seen his roll call votes.[27]

As it turns out, as shown in table 3.4, for party-characterized legislators, the change in vote is correlated significantly with six of the seven traits (toughness perceptions did not predict electoral support). Voters like politicians less in cases where those politicians were seen as less caring, less intelligent, less independent-minded, less open, less trustworthy, and more predictable. And it is the extreme partisans who are seen as less intelligent, less independent-minded, less open-minded, and more predictable. For ideology-characterized legislators, the change in their vote is correlated with four of the seven traits—with toughness, predictability, and intelligence failing to predict electoral support.

Looking only at the first two columns of table 3.4 (partisan-characterized incumbents), there is a suggestion of several pathways by which a legislator's party loyalty could affect a trait perception with eventual effects on electoral support. Four traits—independent-mindedness, open-mindedness, predictability, and intelligence—look to be important

TABLE 3.4. **Correlations: Lockstep voting, change in intent to vote for incumbent, and six incumbent trait perceptions**

Legislator seen as:	Partisan lockstep roll call voting (0,1)	Change in electoral support	Ideologically monotonous voting (0,1)	Change in electoral support
Independent-minded	−0.25	0.39	−0.14	0.32
	(0.0001)	(0.0000)	(0.03)	(0.0000)
Open-minded	−0.20	0.47	−0.18	0.35
	(0.002)	(0.0000)	(0.004)	(0.0000)
Predictable	0.35	−0.18	0.30	−0.04
	(0.0000)	(0.005)	(0.0000)	(0.54)
Trustworthy	−0.08	0.42	0.007	0.29
	(0.21)	(0.0000)	(0.90)	(0.0000)
Intelligent	−0.15	0.34	−0.11	0.09
	(0.02)	(0.0000)	(0.09)	(0.13)
Caring	−0.05	0.39	−0.08	0.32
	(0.45)	(0.0000)	(0.20)	(0.0000)
Tough	0.02	−0.05	0.10	−0.05
	(0.70)	(0.41)	(0.11)	(0.44)

Notes: $N = 250$; p-values in parentheses; correlations between dichotomous variables and trait variables are point-biserial correlations.

TABLE 3.5. **Preexposure/postexposure difference in intention to support incumbent: Incumbent roll call votes characterized by partisan description**

	Coefficient (se)	p-value 2-tailed
Lockstep voting (0,1)	−0.30 (0.19)	0.121
Coefficient for lockstep voting before trait mediator added to regression	**−0.67**, p = 0.002 before adding gen. likability	
Voter party ID opposite legislator	−1.83 (0.27)	0.000
General likability (6-item scale)	0.73 (0.10)	0.000
Constant	0.95 (0.21)	0.000
Sobel statistic	General likability as mediator: −0.36	
p-value	p = 0.0004	
Percentage of effect of lockstepping that is mediated	54%	
N	250	
R^2	0.40	

mediating factors. The pattern of partisan voting affects opinions on these traits, which then affect changes in electoral support.

However, voters might not be so much rating the politicians independently on each trait as using the different trait perception items as "indicators" of general likability.[28] We created an additive scale of these six trait perceptions (excluding toughness) and call it "general likability." These traits are closely related to each other, so ratings on one dimension are correlated with ratings on other dimensions.[29] Table 3.5 provides evidence that this general likability scale mediates much of the effect of lockstep voting on electoral support—adding likability reduces the effect of lockstep voting. Finally, when we switch to a two-dimensional structure we find that it is perceptions of open-mindedness, rather than likeability, that are punished.[30]

To summarize, then, it is clear that when a legislator votes a party line, voters withdraw a portion of electoral support because they interpret this roll call pattern as evidence of a lack of independent-mindedness. This mediates much of the direct effect of the legislator's lockstep voting for average party social-identifiers, but for voters who strongly socially identify with a party, there is an additional penalty associated with lockstep voting that has nothing to do with open-mindedness and probably relates more directly to highly emotional partisan politics.

Meanwhile, when a legislator's roll call behavior is *ideologically* monotonous, there is also a negative effect due to perceptions of a lack of independent-mindedness. However, this is more than offset by a direct electoral reward for ideological consistency.[31] We cannot fully explain this surprising direct effect, but there is evidence that part of it may relate to differential evaluations of legislative predictability, depending on whether that predictability is a result of partisanship or ideology. It would appear that a legislator who is strongly ideological gets low marks for open-mindedness, but this has little effect upon citizens' overall evaluation of politicians.

3.4 Conclusion

This chapter lays the foundation for our study of legislative parties. We found, in controlled experiments, that citizens seem to dislike partisan behavior by legislators. Of course, this does not apply to all voters. We found that subjects were more likely to disapprove of partisanship by (hypothetical) legislators (a) if the legislator was of the opposing party, (b) as the party loyalty of the legislator increases, and (c) the more the subject identified with the party opposed to the legislator. Meanwhile, excessive loyalty to the subject's own party is still not rewarded—and might be mildly punished. We also found that legislators who vote with their party frequently are perceived to be tools of their party: lacking independence, unintelligent, and uncaring. In contrast, legislators who are strongly ideological are perceived to be independent, unpredictable, and intelligent. In today's lingo, partisans are hacks while ideologues are mavericks.

The use of an experiment here to investigate voters' responses does leave room for questions. In particular, in what way does the "real world" provide voters with the same types of information about legislators' voting records? Investigating factors like the effects of the media, advertising, and social networks is beyond our scope, but it is telling that so many political advertisements provide summary information about roll call behavior. In addition, one study by Gronke, Koch, and Wilson (2003) shows not only that voters are quite good at perceiving their representative's level of presidential support in roll call votes, but also that voters use this information when deciding whether or not to support the incumbent for reelection.

The notion that voters punish partisan behavior by legislators is probably especially relevant to the American context. For decades, scholars have noted that European legislators are much more loyal to their parties than members of the US Congress. In part, this is a contrast of nominating and electoral rules; US politicians must win their own nominations and then compete in general elections in geographically defined single-member districts. However, this chapter also suggests that American voters expect their legislators to represent their districts first and foremost and may interpret excessive partisanship as evidence that a member of Congress has forsaken his or her district on behalf of party interests.

Of course, the experiments described in this chapter are limited to a particular point in time and space. How well do they explain patterns of congressional elections? The next two chapters build on our analysis by testing the claim that American voters punish party loyalty by incumbent politicians. As we do so, we focus on cumulative patterns based on millions of votes, but our intuition is based on the in-depth analysis of the sample we interviewed in this chapter: at the margin, many voters are uneasy with strongly partisan legislators.

The Electoral Costs of Party Loyalty in Congress

Coauthored with Jamie Carson and Ellen Key

The biggest legislative battle of President Obama's first two years in office was undoubtedly over health care reform. In mid-March of 2010, the House Democrats were still short the votes needed to pass the Senate's version of the bill. Among the final Democrats to agree to vote yes was four-term incumbent Tim Bishop of New York's First Congressional District, representing eastern Long Island. Bishop waited as long as he could to make his decision. He had hoped to avoid casting the vote that was unpopular in his district, but the party needed his help, and he ultimately acquiesced. His announcement of support finally came late Friday afternoon on March 19. When the bill was passed two days later, Bishop was one of 219 yes votes, giving his party an important legislative victory but putting him in a difficult position with his constituents.

In fact, Bishop had been comfortably elected in his previous elections to Congress. In his first three reelection campaigns, his percentage of the two-party vote had been 56 percent, 62 percent, and 58 percent. But 2010 was to be a tougher battle. Bishop's 2010 Republican opponent, Randy Altschuler, was a local businessman who would not have stood much of a chance in a typical year. But Altschuler was well funded and filled the airwaves with commercials tying Bishop to his party and its leader. "Bishop votes with Pelosi 97 percent of the time" was a consistent tag line in his advertisements. Bishop did all he could to fight back—even blitzing the district with former president Clinton in the waning days of the campaign. An extensive and seesaw recount followed the election, and the contest was the last in the country to be decided. Altschuler finally conceded on December 8, and Bishop was certified the winner by 593 votes.

Bishop's narrow victory illustrates how party loyalty can have severe consequences for an incumbent seeking reelection. While it is rare that a single legislative vote will have such detrimental electoral effects, legislators often worry that a *pattern* of controversial roll call votes may result in defeat during the subsequent election (Arnold 1990; Bovitz and Carson 2006). At the same time, legislators may accept some electoral risk to pass a bill for the sake of their party's overall goals. Realizing that their members often pay a price for their loyalty, party leaders strategically balance the party's collective interests against the electoral fortunes of individual members.

This chapter moves from laboratory tests to election results: collectively, do voters in congressional elections punish legislators for being too partisan?[1] We find that they do: controlling for other factors, legislators pay an electoral price for voting with their parties, especially those who represent competitive districts. As in the previous chapter, we are careful to distinguish between the effects of party loyalty and ideological extremism. In a series of tests, we find that ideological preferences are not directly related to election outcomes; they help us explain why legislators are loyal to their party (or not), but they do not directly explain why incumbent legislators gain or lose electoral votes. We also find evidence that—as one might expect, and even hope—legislators anticipate their electoral vulnerability when they are casting votes. Legislators and party leaders anticipate whether a particular member of Congress (MC) will face a difficult or easy reelection contest and factor this into their decisions about how loyal each MC should be to his or her party. Of course, party leaders trying to gain seats are unlikely to ask endangered legislators to take a lot of risks on behalf of their parties. Instead, we find that "safe" legislators vote with their party more often and pay little penalty for doing so, so that electoral costs are minimized by allocating risk to otherwise secure members.

These results offer a correction to a long tradition of testing whether MCs lose elections or vote share by being too ideological. Once we compare and contrast this explanation with the effect of party loyalty, we find that partisanship is a much stronger factor in elections. This is also a more satisfying account of the relationship between voting and elections because we can provide an answer to the question, why do legislators cast votes that could cost them the next election? It is not clear why a legislator would vote her ideology to the extent that she risked losing the next election.[2] Our party-based account, on the other hand, provides such an explanation: legislators cast votes that hurt their reelection prospects as a contribution to the collective reputation of their party.

This chapter highlights one of the most important features of American political culture. To an extent rarely seen elsewhere in the democratic world, voters do not simply focus on the party affiliations of candidates. Rather, the legislative records of incumbents are scrutinized and legislators are held individually accountable for their cooperation with their party organization. Consequently, both legislators and citizens have an uneasy relationship with political parties: however useful and essential parties may be, cooperating as a party will remain costly for legislators who deviate from their constituents' preferences to help their parties win.

4.1 Legislative Voting and Elections: Prior Research

A basic model of democratic representation is that citizens send representatives to act in their best interests for a fixed term. After each term, citizens (aided by challengers, interest groups, and the media) can evaluate the incumbent's record to determine if he or she has truly acted in their interests. In this system, an ambitious politician will strive to take positions that her constituents will reward and avoid positions they view as too extreme (Kingdon 1989; Mayhew 1974b). Legislators must be cautious about every vote because they cannot fully anticipate which votes will be critical to their campaign, so they must act as if any vote is a possible campaign issue (Fenno 1978, 142). We expect, then, that legislators who wish to continue their legislative careers will generally cast votes of which their constituents approve. Of course, constituents vary in their level of organization, information, and importance in the electoral process (Fenno 1978), so legislators may face complex choices as they weigh the preferences of different subgroups of constituents (Arnold 1990; Bishin 2000, 2009).[3]

Despite the electoral incentives to satisfy their constituencies, however, we often observe legislators casting votes that are disapproved of by (some of) their constituents. Our account, explained in chapter 2, focuses on the tension between collective party goals and the preferences of the constituents of party members. In order to achieve collective goals as a party, members must sometimes cast votes that are unpopular in their home districts with the expectation that the benefits of cooperating as a party will exceed these costs.

Another reason legislators may cast unpopular votes is that they are indulging in *agency slack*—acting on their own intense policy views rather than conforming to the views of their constituents (Bianco et al. 1996, 151). Several previous studies have tested this claim by studying the role of *ideological* extremity in affecting vote share for incumbents and suggested this relationship is constant across all districts (see, e.g., Canes-Wrone et al. 2002; Erikson 1971). Similarly, legislators may believe that they are acting in their constituents' best interests by defying their current *expressed preferences*, and they may hope that they can justify their decisions with the aid of time and persuasion.

In the context of research on legislative voting and elections, "ideological extremity" commonly refers to the relative proximity of an actor's policy views to other actors in the same game. Often the "game" is a spatial model of elections in which the selection and success of candidates are a function of how close their preferences match those of key actors (e.g., Downs 1957; Rogowski 2014; Stone and Simas 2010) or a spatial model of legislating in which the selection or success of bills depends on their proximity to key actors, given a distribution of legislators' preferences that is fixed and known. Conceptually, "ideology" implies an interrelated *pattern* of political views that is relatively stable over time. In practice, legislators' ideology is typically inferred from their behavior, not their views, using an applied item response model (Noel 2014, 69–71). As such, the term "ideology" is a misnomer: we do not really measure the coherent worldviews in legislators' heads. Instead, we have summary statistics of legislators' voting patterns (such as the DW-NOMINATE scores we use below) that are influenced by legislators' multilayered constituencies, including donors (Fenno 1978); the partisan socialization and primary selection process; the congressional party apparatus, which is a primary information source about policy proposals, a social group that promotes common bonds among partisans, and a source of rewards and punishment; and a legislator's own policy views.[4] These scores are constrained so that legislators' ideology can evolve over time, but in steady increments. This constraint is consistent with the meaning of ideology: while a legislator's coherent worldview may evolve with intellectual reexamination, we should look for a different explanation for rapid fluctuations in voting patterns.

There is some observational evidence that legislative voting affects elections. Using electoral and survey data from 1952 to 1968, Erikson

(1971) found that conservatism among Republican legislators had a pronounced, negative effect on their vote margins, while recent studies have found that ideologically extreme voting is linked to decreased vote share (Ansolabehere et al. 2001; Erikson and Wright 2001). In a key article, Canes-Wrone et al. (2002) examine the relationship between members' electoral margins and their overall ideological support as reflected by Americans for Democratic Action (ADA) scores. Using data from the 1956–96 elections, they find that incumbent legislators tend to receive smaller electoral margins as their ADA scores become more extreme— MCs are indeed held accountable for their roll calls. Canes-Wrone et al. also find that the electoral effect of being "out of step" is as important as campaign spending and facing an experienced challenger and that the penalty for ideological extremism affects both "marginal" and "safe" legislators.[5]

These prior studies have focused on the relationship between *ideological* patterns of roll call votes and electoral outcomes. Conceptually, this means the extent to which a legislator's guiding political ideas deviate from the mainstream of American politics, but in practice it means the extent to which a legislator votes for positions that are considered out of the political mainstream. But are voters really most likely to punish *ideological* voting and not other patterns of roll call voting? As demonstrated in the previous chapter, what we know about the individual psychology of voters tells us that voters see excessively partisan legislators as lacking independent-mindedness, while ideological consistency may actually be seen as a positive trait.

There are two ways that party unity can lead to electoral problems for an incumbent. The first is that challengers and other actors may criticize an overall pattern of party loyalty. This is often framed to link legislators to members of their party who are unpopular in the district or state, such as "Johnson votes with Speaker Pelosi 99 percent of the time" (or Newt Gingrich or Harry Reid). Carson (2005), for example, finds that experienced challengers are more likely to emerge and run against legislators who vote with their party on salient roll call votes. This would make sense if a high level of party loyalty enables challengers to portray incumbents as betraying their constituents' interests for the sake of party interests. A second mechanism is that party loyalty may be costly on specific votes: An incumbent who votes with his or her party to pass a critical piece of legislation (like the 1993 Democratic budget, the 2003 Medicare expansion, or the 2009–10 Affordable Care Act) may face criticism for a single act of loyalty. But this criticism is possible as part of a pattern that creates multiple opportunities for opponents to cherry-pick especially controversial votes. In both of these ways, challengers and the opposition party can use a pattern of partisan voting to portray an incumbent as too partisan for a district.

At the same time, it is not obvious that party unity will be a net cost. Some constituents—especially activists and donors affiliated with an incumbent's party—may prefer higher levels of party loyalty. This support may derive from general support of the MC-affiliated party agenda or a sophisticated expectation that each MC will cooperate with other party factions and intense policy demanders. This party base may function as a centrifugal force on congressional parties, encouraging MCs to be more loyal and to take greater risks to achieve their party's agenda or else suffer a decrease in voter turnout or campaign resources. Harbridge and Malhotra (2011) find, for example, that moderate and weakly partisan citizens approve of legislators with bipartisan voting records, while citizens with strong party affiliations *disapprove* of legislators who cross party lines. Bafumi and Herron (2010) find that these polarizing forces seem to influence candidate selection, as districts that flip party control swap partisan Republicans for partisan Democrats (and vice versa).

4.2 Party Unity in House and Senate Elections

We wish to build on the experimental results in the previous chapter by exploring the effects of *Party Unity* on the electoral success of members of the House running for reelection from 1978 to 2010 and for senators doing the same from 1974 to 2012. Our dependent variable is the incumbent i's percentage of the two-party vote share by year t. We exclude cases in which incumbents were unopposed or the major party challenger received fewer than 1,000 votes. This leaves 4,170 House races from 1978 to 2010 and 543 Senate races from 1974 to 2004. For House incumbents in our sample, the mean vote share was 65.7 percent with a standard deviation of 10.0 percent. For senators, the mean is 58.4 percent with a standard deviation of 10.8.

Our key variable is each incumbent's level of Party Unity in the two-year Congress preceding each election t. We collected *Party Unity* scores for individual representatives from Congressional Quarterly (CQ) Almanacs. CQ generates these scores by (a) identifying every roll call vote on which most Democrats voted against most Republicans and (b) calculating the proportion of these votes on which each legislator voted with his or her party.[6] Unity varies from a theoretical minimum of 0 to 1 with an actual minimum of 0.039 for Larry McDonald's (D-GA) House voting in the Ninety-Fifth Congress and 0.16 for Senator Clifford Case's (R-NJ) voting in the Ninety-Third Congress.[7]

This variable provides three forms of variation: individual legislators change their unity over time, the unity of legislators varies within a Congress, and there is variation as a district (or state) changes its representative/senator over time. There is a great deal of variation across legislators, of course, but legislators also vary over the course of their careers. Figure 4.1 illustrates the average range between House representatives' lowest and highest party unity scores during their House service, grouped by the number of two-year terms each member has served. The range tends to increase over time, with MCs serving eighteen or more years varying (on average) 20 percent or more. Even at the low end, however, MCs who serve two terms change (on average) 5 percent from one term to the next.

We view *Ideological Extremism* as one source of party unity in roll call voting. We use DW-NOMINATE scores (Poole and Rosenthal 2007) as measures of incumbents' ideological views on liberal-conservative economic issues. These scores are derived from roll call votes and place legislators relative to each other and, to some extent, relative to other legislators over time.[8] We use the first dimension scores, which explain much

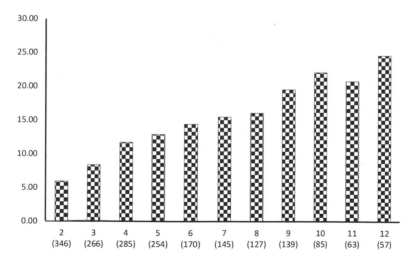

FIGURE 4.1. Average range in House members' party unity score by terms of service, 1978–2010

of the variance in legislative voting. Since the NOMINATE scale is centered at or near zero, we use the absolute value of these scores as a measure of Ideological Extremism; higher values on this variable suggest that the legislator has a noncentrist or "extreme" voting record. In conjunction with other factors, we expect that ideological extremism is correlated with higher levels of party unity.

The long history of scholarship on congressional elections has established several important factors that determine electoral fortunes, and we control for these factors. These include prior electoral success, the partisanship of the district, challenger quality, incumbent and challenger spending (when available), freshman status, presidential approval, the change in real disposable personal income, in-party versus out-party status in relation to the president, and majority status. We explain the operationalization of each below.

We control for legislators' electoral security with $IncumbentVote_{t-1}$, the incumbent's vote percentage in the previous election.[9] To conserve the many cases where new senators are appointed in the middle of another's term, we do not include this variable for the Senate analyses.

District Partisanship is the presidential two-party vote share of each incumbent's party candidate in his or her district (or state for senators) in the preceding presidential election. This vote share is a good measure of the partisan tendencies of a constituency (Levendusky 2009), and it helps us understand the extent to which legislators who vote with their parties on key votes are cross pressured (Jacobson 2009). *Challenger Quality* indicates whether the opposite-party challenger has previously held elected office (1 = yes, 0 = no). This is a classic proxy variable for challenger quality (Jacobson 1980). *Spending Gap* controls for the influence of challenger and incumbent spending. It is measured as the difference in the natural logarithm of dollars spent by the incumbent and the challenger (Jacobson 1980, 40).

Freshman is coded 1 for legislators running for reelection after their first term in office. These legislators are especially likely to be defeated, often because they were elected in electoral waves that quickly recede. *In Party* is coded 1 for legislators who are members of the president's party, 0 otherwise. *Midterm* controls for effects of midterm elections and is coded 1 for midterm elections with a president of the legislator's party, −1 with a president of the opposite party, and 0 in presidential election years. *Presidential Approval* and *Change in Personal Income* are also coded by in-party status, so a popular president and growth in income levels are likely to help members of the president's party and hurt those in the out-party.[10] *Senate Majority* is a dummy variable coded 1 if the senator is in that chamber's majority.

To account for the causal ordering of our hypotheses, we use a two-stage estimation technique.[11] The use of single-stage models is common in the congressional elections literature (see, e.g., Canes-Wrone et al. 2002; Jacobson 1993) but does not reflect the strategic decisions that members and leaders make as they decide how much each member should contribute toward party goals. Thus a two-stage modeling strategy has three distinct advantages over single-stage estimation techniques. First, *Party Unity* is an endogenous variable that is influenced by, and influences, a legislator's electoral margin. Party leaders look ahead to upcoming elections to decide which legislators' arms will be twisted to gain greater loyalty. Since we also expect voters to react to levels of *Party Unity*, this implies reciprocal causality and makes a two-stage model appropriate for estimation purposes.[12]

Furthermore, a two-stage approach corrects for the effects other independent variables in the model have on *Party Unity* such as *Freshman* status, *District Partisanship*, and *Presidential Approval*. By modeling these complex relationships we get a better estimate of how these variables affect election results.

A third advantage of a two-stage approach is that it allows us to test whether revealed preferences (measured by DW-NOMINATE) are an *antecedent* variable in the relationships between members' actions and their electoral fortunes. That is, we expect that, controlling for district partisanship and other influences, legislator ideology is a good predictor of unity but not a direct a predictor of vote share—as we have seen in chapter 3, voters are more likely to punish legislators for being too partisan rather than simply being too ideological. Our two-stage model tests both steps—preferences predicting unity and unity predicting election results.[13]

Our interest in correcting the endogenous relationship between party unity and electoral success does not imply that all other variables are strictly exogenous. Indeed, we anticipate that expectations about an incumbent's success in upcoming elections will affect the incumbent's decision whether to retire, a quality candidate's decision whether to challenge an incumbent, and donors' decisions to allocate donations across candidates. In the case of challenger emergence and campaign finance, failure to account for endogeneity may inflate the estimated effects of these control variables, because the <u>expectation of incumbent failure</u> leads to the emergence of experienced, well-funded challengers rather than (or in addition to) the existence of such challengers causing a decrease in incumbent vote share. In the case of incumbent retirement, legislators who retire because they believe that their voting records will lead to their defeat are dropped from our analysis. For this reason, their exclusion may lead to our results being *understated*; if these endangered incumbents had run for reelection, we would observe the effects of their roll call voting. While it would be ideal to treat each of these variables as endogenous, we are severely constrained by the lack of available instruments. For each endogenous variable, we would need a new instrumental variable that predicts incumbent retirement, challenger emergence, and campaign fundraising but *not* incumbent vote share. Given the scarcity of such variables, we have focused our attention on our key explanatory variable: party unity.

Figure 4.2 compares our strategic model (right) to the Canes-Wrone et al. model (left). For us, *Ideological Extremity* only has its effect <u>through</u> *Party Unity*. In addition, we consider two endogenous variables—the two arrows between *Party Unity* and *Incumbent Vote Share* indicate the reciprocal causality that demands a two-stage approach. Finally, we expect the level of *District Partisanship* to affect the relationship between *Party Unity* and *Incumbent Vote Share*.

These are controversial points, of course, and some readers may worry that by removing *Ideological Extremity* from our *Vote Share* equation we

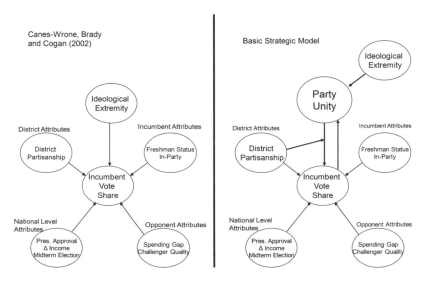

FIGURE 4.2. Model comparisons

fail to give *Extremity* a fair chance to demonstrate its relative value in a head-to-head matchup with *Party Unity*. Thus, to provide comparable single-stage estimates, we also present abbreviated results with voting extremity tested for its direct effects on *Incumbent Vote Share*. This allows us to evaluate its impact relative to unity.

Taken together, our model of general election vote margins at the second stage of the simultaneous equation model is

$$
\begin{aligned}
IncumbentVote_{it} = \tau_{2t} &+ \gamma_1 \widehat{Unity}_{it} + \beta_0 \\
&+ \beta_1 District_{it} + \beta_2 Challenger_{it} + \beta_3 SpendGap_{it} \\
&+ \beta_4 Freshman_{it} + \beta_5 InParty_{it} + \beta_6 Midterm_{it} \\
&+ \beta_7 Approval_{it} + \beta_8 \Delta Income_{it} + \beta_9 IncumbentVote_{it-1} + \upsilon_{it}
\end{aligned}
$$

where τ_{2t} is the election year effect, υ_{it} is the overall error component, β_0 is the estimated constant, β_1 to β_9 are regression coefficients, and γ_1 is the estimated effect of predicted values of the endogenous variable $\widehat{Unity}_{it}$, which is estimated in this first-stage equation:

$$
\begin{aligned}
\widehat{Unity}_{it} = \tau_{1t} &+ \delta_1 District_{it} + \delta_2 Challenger_{it} + \delta_3 SpendGap_{it} + \delta_4 Freshman_{it} \\
&+ \delta_5 InParty_{it} + \delta_6 Midterm_{it} + \delta_7 Approval_{it} + \delta_8 \Delta Income_{it} \\
&+ \delta_9 IncumbentVote_{it-1} + \theta_1 Extremism_{it} + \theta_2 Unity_{it-1}
\end{aligned}
$$

Here, θ_1 and θ_2 estimate the effects of the instrumental variables excluded from the second stage and $Unity_{it-1}$ is the lagged value of party unity for legislator i, which is a useful instrument.[14] We include this variable because we expect that it will help us generate better estimates of the true effect of party unity. To do so, we assume that incumbents' party unity from the previous Congress (three or four years ago) has little systematic effect on the upcoming election; typically, legislator i's party unity in Congress $t - 1$ was an issue (or not) in the previous election, after which voters are more likely to focus on the incumbent's recent behavior. Also, τ_{1t} estimates the effects of each election year for the first-stage model. To explore our data fully, we estimate several models that deviate slightly from these equations, but all preserve the same overall structure.[15]

4.3 Results

Our first results test the basic claims that incumbents suffer a loss of two-party vote share as their party unity increases and that party loyalty goes

down when incumbents feel electorally vulnerable. Next, we test variations on these claims: we determine whether vulnerable or secure legislators are more likely to lose vote share as a result of their partisanship,
we control for campaign spending, and we test for interactive effects. Last,
we present a model that uses change in vote share as the dependent variable, which controls for factors that are stable for each legislator, such as
ideology.

4.3.1 Vote Share Declines with Party Unity

Table 4.1 shows estimates of four variants of our basic House model.
Model 1 presents our base model, while model 2 incorporates the share of
the two-party vote an incumbent received in the previous election ($Vote$-
$share_{t-1}$) as a control variable. Whether we include it or not, our results
reliably confirm that legislators pay a price for party loyalty. Overall, the
models do quite well, with model 1 explaining 49 percent of the variance
and model 2 explaining 62 percent of the variance in incumbent vote
share.[16]

The results tell us many things about the process of incumbent reelection. To begin, the character of the district is very important in predicting
vote share. Not surprisingly, legislators tend to do better as their constituents' support for the incumbent's presidential candidate increases. Incumbents do worse when they are challenged by experienced politicians,
with quality challengers costing an average of 4.3 percent in model 1 and
2.8 percent in model 2. Finally, when we control for other electoral factors,
freshman legislators fare better than we would otherwise expect. This suggests that the real liability is the appearance of vulnerability. Legislators
who barely won the last election may continue to face difficult elections,
but once we control for this pattern, freshmen legislators actually gain
electoral share as they attain the electoral benefits of holding office.

The national political climate also has a strong influence on House
elections. As prior research has shown, members of the president's party
find that their electoral fates are partially tied to presidential approval
ratings and the state of the national economy. Controlling for these patterns, members of the president's party tend to lose vote share in midterm
elections (Jacobson 2009). MCs thus have an incentive to influence these
macrolevel conditions if they can, particularly presidential approval and
the state of the national economy.

The main finding of our four models is that incumbents' party unity

TABLE 4.1. **Explaining House incumbents' share of the two-party vote, 1978–2010**[†]

	1978–2010			
	Model 1 Coef. (se)	p-value <	Model 2 Coef. (se)	p-value <
Voteshare$_{t-1}$			0.48 (0.01)	.000
District Partisanship	46.89 (1.09)	.000	25.48 (1.17)	.000
Quality Challenger	−4.27 (0.29)	.000	−2.78 (0.27)	.000
Spendgap	−0.56 (0.03)	.000	−0.44 (0.03)	.000
Freshman	0.56 (0.27)	.019	0.41 (0.25)	.049
Presidential Approval (coded by in-party)	0.04 (0.01)	.000	0.10 (0.01)	.000
Midterm Election (coded by in-party)	−1.80 (0.24)	.000	−3.10 (0.22)	.000
Δ Personal Income (coded by in-party)	0.65 (0.14)	.000	−0.09 (0.14)	.249
In-Party	−1.80 (0.22)	.000	.11 (0.21)	.625
Party Unity[††]	−10.10 (1.01)	.000	−5.69 (0.94)	.000
R^2	0.49		0.62	
Observations	4170		3594	
Groups	17		17	
Obs/Group Min/Avg/Max	101 / 245.3 / 308		89 / 211.4 / 269	
Instruments excluded from second stage	Extremity, Party Unity$_{t-1}$		Extremity, Party Unity$_{t-1}$	
F-test of Excluded IVs (p)	3556 (.000)		3061 (.000)	
Sargan χ^2 statistic (p)	2.47 (0.12)		2.33 (0.13)	
Effect of Extremity on Unity in First Stage	$z = 15.82, p < .000$		$z = 14.74, p < .000$	
Extremity in Second Stage	Model 1b[†††]		Model 2b[†††]	
	Coef. (se)	p-value <	Coef. (se)	p-value <
Party Unity[††]	−5.91 (1.22)	.000	−3.57 (1.21)	.001
Extremity	0.92 (1.01)	.364	−0.50 (1.01)	.310

Notes: Group Min = minimum size of a group; Avg = average size of a group; Max= maximum size of a group
[†] Fixed effects panel-data models with instrumental variables and 2-stage least squares (2SLS). The results of both random effects models and multilevel random coefficient models are nearly identical.
[††] Instrumented variable.
[†††] Models are otherwise the same as above, but we show only the key results; p-values are based on one-tailed tests.

has a significant detrimental effect on their reelection vote share. Holding all other variables constant, voters clearly tend to punish legislators for voting too often with their party. This is the effect that forces party leaders to balance legislative goals (and the collective electoral benefits they can achieve) against the costs to individual members.

The results of model 1 suggest that a fifty-point increase in a House member's *Party Unity* score cost nearly 5 percent of the vote share in the next election—an effect similar to a quality challenger running against the incumbent. This effect is diminished in model 2 when we control for the effect of electoral security, but it is still statistically significant.

The tests of our modeling approach help clarify the relative roles of ideology and partisanship in congressional elections. First, *Ideological Ex-*

tremity <u>should not be used</u> in a model predicting incumbent *Vote Share*.[17] *Ideological Extremity* is an excellent predictor of party loyalty, but it is party loyalty that has the direct effect on vote share. When we compare the effect of the two variables head-to-head in the last two rows of table 4.1, it is *Party Unity*—not *Extremity*—that costs vote share.[18] Since *Ideological Extremity* fails to approach statistical significance in either of these revised models, we gain confidence that it is an *indirect* predictor of incumbent vote share—voters seem to penalize high levels of partisan loyalty by representatives, not the underlying ideology that may predict their voting record. *Party Unity*$_{t-1}$ also serves as a useful instrument—it predicts *Party Unity*$_t$ but not *Voteshare*$_t$. This is supported empirically by the Hansen-Sargan χ^2 tests that indicate our instruments are properly excluded from the second-stage equation.[19]

Similar patterns are evident in our analysis of Senate elections, shown in table 4.2. Senators are punished for party loyalty to roughly the same

TABLE 4.2. **Explaining Senate incumbents' share of the two-party vote, 1974–2004**[†]

	Coef. (se)	z
Constant	60.00 (3.52)	17.03***
State Partisanship	0.16 (0.06)	2.72**
Quality Challenger	−5.81 (0.97)	−5.97***
Spendgap	2.41 (0.20)	12.21***
Presidential Approval (by in-party)	2.80 (2.52)	1.11
Midterm Election (by in-party)	−2.89 (1.30)	−2.22*
Δ Personal Income (by in-party)	0.20 (0.26)	0.77
In-Party	−0.99 (1.31)	−0.76
Party Unity[††]	−11.22 (3.55)	−3.16***
R^2 within/between/all	0.44 / 0.23 / 0.43	
ρ	0.076	
Observations	418	
Groups	16	
Obs/Group Min/Avg/Max	18 / 26.1 / 29	
Instruments excluded from second stage	Extremity, Party Unity$_{t-1}$, Majority Party, Freshman	
F-test of Excluded IVs (p)	370.99 (0.00)	
Sargan χ^2 statistic (p)	0.83 (0.84)	
Effect of Extremity on Unity in first stage	21.17 (3.59) 5.90***	
Rerunning Above but with Extremity in second stage	Coef. (se)	z
Party Unity[††]	−13.53 (6.28)	2.16*
Extremity	−114.91 (552.54)	−0.21

Notes: Group Min = minimum size of a group; Avg = average size of a group; Max= maximum size of a group
[†] Fixed effects panel-data models with instrumental variables and 2SLS. The results of both random effects models and multilevel random coefficient models are nearly identical.
[††] Instrumented variable.
* $p < .05$, ** $p < .01$, *** $p < .001$, one-tailed tests.

extent as House members are in the fuller model 4 of table 4.1. *State Partisanship* is naturally a good positive predictor of *Vote Share*, as is the president's party at the *Midterm* dummy variable (negative), *Challenger Quality* (negative), and the *Spending Gap* (positive). Variables for *Presidential Approval*, *Personal Income*, and the president's *In-Party* fail to reach significance.

As in the House models, it is clear that *Ideological Extremity* is not directly related to electoral outcomes for senators. We find in the first stage of the model that extremity is a powerful predictor of the frequency with which a senator votes with her party, but all our tests indicate that extremity is not a direct cause of *Vote Share*.[20] When we ignore this and move *Extremity* to the second stage, it is not significant, while the effect of *Party Unity* grows in magnitude, becoming more strongly negative. Thus for both the House and the Senate, the story is clear: *Party Unity* leads directly to a loss of *Vote Share*, and *Ideological Extremity* does not.

4.3.2 Electoral Risk Predicts Party Unity

Our analysis also finds reciprocal causality between incumbent vote and *Party Unity*. A major claim of our strategic model is that parties attempt to win legislative contests while minimizing electoral costs. Thus party leaders will be less likely to ask vulnerable legislators to cast votes that will cost them electoral support and instead will tend to ask more secure legislators to cast unpopular votes. These judgments are grounded in the expected vulnerability of some party members. When legislators are perceived to be vulnerable, their party unity should decrease. In table 4.3, we test this expectation by reversing the causal sequence of our earlier models.

For the House, we predict changes in the level of *Party Unity* from one Congress to the next and find that vote share in the election to follow is a strong positive predictor ($p < .001$) of levels of *Party Unity*, so a 10 percent increase in future vote share correlates with a 1 percent increase in party unity.[21] In the Senate, this is again the case ($p < .05$), albeit with a weaker relationship. In addition, we can see some of the causal factors predicting changes in party unity. Legislators who are more ideologically extreme tend to increase their level of unity from one Congress to the next, controlling for electoral safety. That is, not only does *Ideological Extremity* predict levels of *Party Unity*, but it also forecasts the inclination to increase the level of *Party Unity* controlling for an MC's chances for reelection.

TABLE 4.3. **Explaining change in party unity using future incumbent share, House 1978–2010 and Senate 1974–2004**[†]

	House		Senate	
	Coef. (se)	Z	Coef. (se)	Z
Extremity	15.42 (2.87)	10.81***	33.41 (0.051)	6.53***
Party Unity$_{t-1}$			−0.68 (0.06)	−11.13***
Voteshare$_t$ [††]	0.105 (0.015)	6.97***	0.003 (0.001)	2.37*
District/State Partisanship	−8.17 (0.95)	−8.64***	−0.034 (0.057)	−0.60
Δ In-Party	−0.17 (0.08)	−2.17*		
Presidential Approval	0.046 (0.008)	6.04***		
R^2	0.03		0.29	
Observations	4009		270	
Instruments excluded from second stage	Spendgap, Challenger Quality, Voteshare$_{t-1}$		Spendgap, Voteshare$_{t-1}$	
F-test of Excluded IVs (p)	1552.96 (0.00)		70.49 (0.00)	
Sargan χ^2 statistic (p)	1.61 (0.45)		0.62 (0.43)	

[†] This a pooled-cross sectional time series model with instrumental variables and two-stage least squares. The dependent variable is the change in Party Unity from one Congress to the next, here calculated as a percentage, so the hypothetical range is −100 percent to 100 percent change, and the actual range is −47.4 to 77.0 percent.
[††] Instrumented variable. * $p < .05$, ** $p < .01$, *** $p < .001$, one-tailed tests.

4.3.3 Close versus Safe Districts

We expect that the penalty legislators pay for voting with their party depends on the partisan tendencies of their districts. A Democratic legislator with a record of high party loyalty, for example, should pay a much higher penalty in a heavily Republican district than in a highly Democratic district. Indeed, in very lopsided districts, legislators may find that party loyalists who *prefer* legislators who are loyal to their party (adding to the grievance parameter described in section 2.4.3) provide an electoral bonus for high levels of party unity. Figure 4.3 shows the effect of *Party Unity* in sixteen models—we show the key result in four subsets of our 1978–2010 House sample and do so for both the two-stage and one-stage models. The first eight models show the effect of party unity in the eight models of table 4.1. The next eight models parse our cases by presidential vote. They show the effect of party unity (in one-stage and two-stage models) for districts where the presidential candidate of the incumbent's party received (a) less than 40 percent of the two-party vote (n = 280), (b) less than 50 percent (n = 1106), (c) less than 65 percent (n = 3268), and (d) more than 65 percent (n = 908). The primary result is that party unity has a clear negative effect on incumbent vote share in districts that supported the presidential candidate of the opposite party. This effect

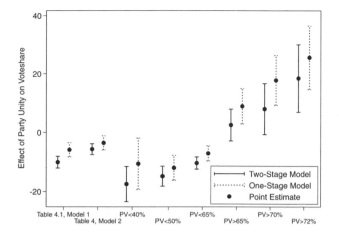

FIGURE 4.3. Effect of party unity on vote share in sixteen models: Coefficients and 95 percent confidence intervals

is diminished to near-zero in districts in which the incumbent's presidential candidate received 50 percent to 65 percent of the vote. This means that in more competitive districts, *Party Unity* has a clear negative relationship with voters' decisions.[22] In fact, in the 508 elections where the incumbent's party won above 70 percent, *Party Unity* actually tips from being punished to being rewarded.

As for the Senate, figure 4.4 shows that when the presidential candidate of the senator's party receives around 40 percent of the vote, senators pay a very steep price for partisan loyalty. As the state looks more aligned with the senator's party, the effect of unity is less harsh, but always a significant factor.

4.3.4 Explaining Change in Vote Share

Next, we use a dynamic-panel approach to test our expectations and present the results in table 4.4. A dynamic panel reconceives each observation as the change from one Congress to the next—that is, we seek to explain changes in incumbent vote share ($\Delta Voteshare = Voteshare_t - Voteshare_{t-1}$) based on shifts in key variables during the same time frame. For example, $\Delta Party\ Unity$ measures the increase or decrease in the incumbent's party unity score relative to the preceding Congress.[23]

This approach holds constant any factors that do not change from one election to the next, such as candidate valence and district characteristics.

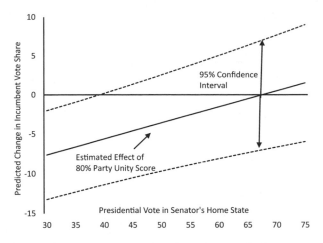

FIGURE 4.4. State partisanship and the negative effects of party unity, Senate

TABLE 4.4. **Dynamic model of house incumbent share, 2000–2010†**

	Coefficient (se)	p-value <
Δ District Partisanship	−34.99 (3.96)	.000
Δ Quality Challenger	1.60 (0.32)	.000
Δ Spending Gap	0.22 (0.02)	.000
Δ Presidential Approval (coded by in-party)	−0.27 (0.02)	.000
Δ Midterm Election (coded by in-party)	0.71 (0.32)	.013
Δ Δ Personal Income (coded by in-party)	−0.018 (.18)	.921
Δ Frosh	0.11 (0.26)	.678
Δ Party Unity ††	−0.48 (.21)	.010
R^2	0.45	
Observations	1073	
Groups	5	
Obs. per Group min/avg/max	117 / 214.6 / 258	
Instruments excluded from second stage	Δ Extremity, Δ In-Party, Party Unity$_{t-1}$	
Anderson LR test (p)	49.43 (.00)	
Sargan χ^2 statistic (p)	1.57 (.46)	

† Fixed effects panel-data model with instrumental variables and two-stage least squares. The results of both a random effects model and a multilevel random coefficient model are nearly identical.
†† Instrumented variable. One-tailed tests.

In particular, this strategy ensures that the incumbent's ideology is perfectly accounted for in the analysis. Since a legislator's underlying ideology is stable—and thus unchanging—between elections, its effect on vote share should be constant.[24] We focus on 2000 to 2010 because it is the period when the challenge of distinguishing between party and ideology is most acute.

The *Party Unity* coefficient tells us how much better (or worse) a House member will do compared to her last reelection if the incumbent's party unity score increases from the last Congress. The results indicate a considerable loss: a 1 percent increase in party unity correlates with a 0.48 percent decrease in vote share. Even for legislators who have already won at least two elections, voters can still dole out a hefty punishment for increased party loyalty regardless of how "safe" legislators perceive themselves to be. For the Senate (results not shown), too many cases are lost to make strong assertions, but the effect for $\Delta Unity$ is roughly the same size as for the House.

4.3.5 The 2010 Midterms

A final testing ground for our hypotheses at the legislator level is the critical 2010 midterm election, in which the Republicans regained majority status in the House by gaining sixty-three seats. To some extent, the Democrats' loss is attributable to structural factors: as the president's party in a midterm election with a struggling economy, some seat loss was expected. But the ambitious Democratic legislative agenda of 2009–10, passed over the nearly unanimous opposition of congressional Republicans, meant that high levels of partisanship defined the 111th Congress.

We see the 111th Congress as a high-stakes partisan contest between Democrats making a maximum effort to enact an ambitious agenda while Republicans risked their party brand on a strategy of maximum opposition. High-profile votes on health care, financial reform, and economic stimulus focused attention on members' positions. Our analysis of the 2010 House election shows that overall levels of partisanship were costly for legislators even beyond these high-profile votes: controlling for constituent partisanship and other factors, a 10 percent increase in *Party Unity* was correlated with a 3 percent decrease in incumbents' reelection *Vote Share*. This effect was stronger than during either of the 1956–2004 or 1978–2004 periods. Of course, as in the Tim Bishop story above, legislators were not naïve about the costs of being team players—they conditioned their party loyalty upon their constituents' preferences. In addition, members of both parties were rewarded with spending projects for supporting Democratic positions, which suggests that Democratic Party leaders were able to use their legislative influence to reward allies.

Before getting to those results, let's quickly review the history of the 111th Congress. The Democrats made large gains in the 2006 and 2008 elections and then won the White House with the promise of "change you can believe in." They thought they had received a mandate for an ambitious policy agenda and, additionally, a responsibility to fix a national economy devastated by a financial breakdown in 2008. The main Democratic agenda consisted of (1) a $787 billion economic stimulus bill to ameliorate the economic crisis and fund key Obama initiatives like "green jobs" and school reform; (2) an ambitious overhaul of the health care system; (3) a cap-and-trade system for carbon emissions to reduce the effects of climate change; (4) reform of the nation's financial regulation system; and (5) comprehensive immigration reform, including a provision for undocumented aliens to become citizens (Koger 2009).

The congressional Democrats moved swiftly and enacted the stimulus into law by February 2009. After that, House Democrats passed climate change (June 2009), health care (November 2009), and financial regulation (December 2009). In 2010, the House completed health care and financial regulation bills, some second-tier bills, and additional targeted economic stimulus measures. By the end of the Congress, the stimulus bill, health care reform, and financial reform became law. The House passed climate change legislation, but the Senate did not act on the issue, and neither chamber tackled immigration reform. These votes provided high-profile examples Democratic Party unity. Citizens who did not follow each roll call vote by their representatives could still use these votes to understand the links between their own legislators and the Democratic agenda.

Congressional Republicans responded with a strategy of solid opposition to the major measures of the Democratic agenda. This was a strategic choice; Democratic leaders sought their cooperation in writing these major bills, but Republicans believed their electoral interests would be harmed by public cooperation and supporting the Democrats' landmark legislation. Instead, Republicans denied their support and denounced the Democratic bills as reckless increases in the influence and expense of government. This strategy coincided with the emergence of a small-government "Tea Party" movement, which threatened incumbents and "establishment" candidates in Republican primary elections.

This Republican strategy forced Democrats to form majorities from their own membership to pass their bills and to take full public responsibility for their agenda. This meant that Democrats from swing districts ended up giving their challengers ample fodder for critical campaign ads. Indeed, as explained in chapter 2, passing major legislation posed a collective action dilemma for Democratic leaders—the party's reputation and base of support would improve if their agenda succeeded, but at the margins, individual legislators would suffer increased electoral risks to help provide this collective good.

4.3.6 Analyzing the 2010 Election Results

Looking at this single recent election provides us with data to test some additional hypotheses. Principally, we compare our results for over-all *Party Unity* to the effects of *Presidential Support, Party Unity on Key Votes*, and individual roll call votes. As before, we expect that the costs of maintaining party reputation will be borne by legislators whose districts share their partisan outlook, while legislators from districts that are marginal or lean to the opposing party will enjoy greater latitude to defect from the party position. Figure 4.5 shows the relationship between *Party Unity* (vertical axis) and the 2008 two-party presidential vote (coded by incumbent party) for each House member. The members of both parties have a high baseline of party unity (66 percent for Republicans, 69 percent for Democrats), and then their unity tends to increase steadily with the presidential vote.

There are also major subgroups within each party. Figure 4.6 illustrates the relationship between party unity and district partisanship for

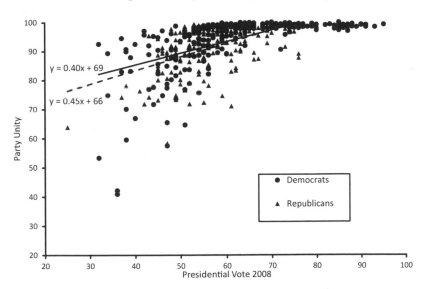

FIGURE 4.5. Constituency partisanship and party unity, 111th Congress
The data on party unity are from voteview.com; the data on presidential vote are from swing stateproject.com.

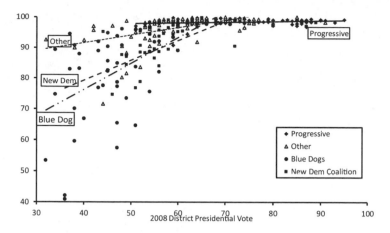

FIGURE 4.6. Partisanship and constituency for House Democratic subgroups
Trend lines are based on a bivariate regression.
Sources: Blue Dog membership is from voteview.com, Progressive caucus membership is from http://cpc.grijalva.house.gov, and NDC membership is from http://ndc.crowley.house.gov.

House Democrats with distinct markers for members of the moderate Blue Dog Caucus (circles), Progressive Caucus (black triangles), moderate New Democratic Coalition (NDC; squares), and nonaffiliated Democrats (empty triangles). These subgroups differed in their responsiveness. Progressive Caucus members voted consistently with their party regardless of their constituency partisanship, while Blue Dogs and NDC members exhibited a higher rate of responsiveness to district partisanship.

We can also subdivide the Republicans into members of the conservative Republican Study Committee (RSC) and the moderate Republican Main Street Partnership (RMSP), as shown in figure 4.7. Like the Progressive Democrats, RSC members (circles) exhibit a high level of partisanship that does not vary significantly, even for RSC members from marginal districts. On the other hand, RMSP members (triangles) and unaffiliated Republicans (empty diamonds) vary significantly from a baseline of 59 percent unity based on their district partisanship.

Next we turn to regression models to explain *Vote Share* in 2010. Using the additional data on caucuses and specific votes gives us some additional insights beyond the 1956–2004 analyses above. In addition to the high-profile votes that a House majority party must win for the sake of its reputation, there are dozens of votes on amendments and procedural agenda setting. We expect that higher rates of *Party Unity* on this broader

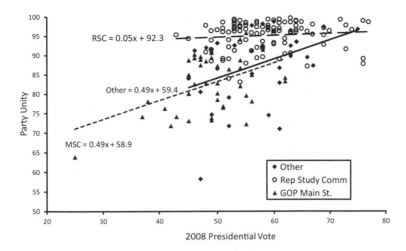

FIGURE 4.7. Partisanship and constituency for House Republican subgroups
Trend lines are based on a bivariate regression.
Sources: RSC, http://rsc.tomprice.house.gov; Republican Main Street Partnership, http://www
.republicanmainstreet.org/.

set of contested votes will be associated with a lower reelection vote share. In the 2010 elections, for example, the National Republican Congressional Committee ran attack ads against incumbent Democrats for "voting with Pelosi" (equivalent to *Party Unity* scores).

We compare the cost of *Party Unity* across all party votes against subsets of salient roll calls: *CQ Key Vote Unity* on all Congressional Quarterly "key votes" that were party votes and *Presidential support* scores calculated by Congressional Quarterly on a subset of roll calls on which President Obama took a public position.[25] We do so to determine whether voters are most likely to note and punish partisanship on these somewhat salient votes or whether they are more likely to learn about and evaluate partisanship across the entire roll call record. Like Brady et al. (2011) and Jacobson (2011), we also test the influence of highly salient votes on Democratic agenda items—health care, financial regulation, cap and trade, and the stimulus bill.

As before, we use an instrumental variable approach, but in order to avoid using a roll call–based measure as an instrument, we instead use membership in the Blue Dog, Progressive, and RSC caucuses to get predicted values of *Party Unity*. In doing so, we assume that caucus membership is correlated with party unity (it is) and not directly correlated with incumbent vote share. That is, few citizens vote for or against a legislator based on his or her affiliation with one of these congressional caucuses.[26] We estimate variations of this model substituting *Party Unity* on Congressional Quarterly *Key Votes* and *Presidential Support* (separately for each party).

Turning to the results, shown in table 4.5, our key finding is that there is a significant penalty for party loyalty: a 1 percent increase in *Party Unity* was correlated with a .3 percent decrease in vote share. For the dozens of Democrats who received 45 percent to 49.9 percent of their 2010 vote share, the penalty for party loyalty made a noticeable difference and was entirely within their own control.[27]

TABLE 4.5. **Analysis of 2010 House incumbent vote share, second stage of 2SLS**

	Party Unity (All) Coefficient (se)	CQ Key Vote Unity Coefficient (se)	Pres. Support (GOP) Coefficient (se)	Pres. Support (Dems) Coefficient (se)
Party Unity[†]	−0.301 (0.104)**			
CQ Key Vote Unity[†]		−0.199 (0.073)**		
Presidential Support[†]			0.556 (0.326)#	−0.243 (0.111)*
Democrat	−14.848 (1.342)***	−16.113 (1.636)***		
2008 Presidential vote	0.877 (0.052)***	0.899 (0.060)***	0.949 (0.144)***	0.849 (0.048)***
Pork Projects (FY 2010)	−0.028 (0.039)	0.012 (0.033)	−0.059 (0.068)	
Dem. Pork Projects	0.078 (0.055)	0.036 (0.047)		0.039 (0.027)
Spending Gap	−0.196 (0.031)***	−0.192 (0.031)***	−0.214 (0.050)***	−0.149 (0.043)***
Freshman	−3.747 (0.951)***	−3.727 (.936)***	−4.185 (1.907)*	−3.289 (0.982)***
New Democratic Coalition	−2.220 (0.972)*	−1.113 (.960)		−1.651 (0.785)*
GOP Main Street	−1.259 (1.344)	−0.522 (1.236)	−4.671 (3.514)	
Constant	47.037 (8.023)***	35.680 (4.496)***	1.084 (14.680)	27.569 (7.759)***
N	389	389	155	234
Centered R^2	0.777	0.528	0.521	0.404
R^2 of excluded instruments	0.207	0.173	0.078	0.181
Sargan test of excluded Instruments (p-value)	0.365	0.189	—	0.031

[†] Instrumented. Instruments used: membership in the Blue Dog Caucus, Republican Policy Committee, and Progressive Caucus.

#$p < .10$, * $p < .05$; ** $p < .01$; *** $p < .001$, one-tailed tests.

When we estimate the same model using *CQ Key Vote Loyalty*, the estimated electoral loss is lower and the R^2 is reduced, suggesting that the penalty for party loyalty is *not* the product of a few key votes. *Presidential Support* also cost Democrats, while Republicans may have *gained* vote share for moderating their opposition to President Obama.[28] The coefficients for *2008 Presidential Vote*, *Spending Gap*, and *Freshman* have the expected effects, while the sizeable coefficient for *Democrat* reflects the structural disadvantage the party faced in 2010. Interestingly, pork projects[29] were correlated with *Party Unity* (implying that they were a reward or enticement of some sort) but did not have a direct relationship with electoral vote share.

Next, we test the claim that, in addition to a general pattern of party loyalty, legislators paid an extra penalty for helping the Democrats pass major agenda items. The logic of this test is that high-profile roll call votes may have special significance in voters' evaluations of legislators. Incompletely informed voters may not follow each roll call vote or procedural choice, but they can understand and evaluate incumbents' choices on landmark legislation. Compared to similar work (Brady et al. 2011; Jacobson 2011; Nyhan et al. 2012), we estimate the effect of these votes while controlling for each legislator's overall pattern of party loyalty. We focused on five key votes: the conference report on the stimulus bill (February 13, 2009), final passage of the bill to "cap and trade" carbon emissions (June 26, 2009), final passage of health care reform (November 7, 2009), concurring with the Senate's health care reform proposal (March 21, 2010), and the conference report for revising the financial regulation system (June 30, 2010). We recalculated the 2SLS model with each vote as an additional second-stage variable.[30]

Figure 4.8 presents the estimated effect of each vote on reelection, controlling for overall *Party Unity* and other variables. The estimated effect of each vote is shown as a large dot with a 95 percent confidence interval (the dotted lines). With the exception of the vote to concur with the Senate health care bill, the effect of *Party Unity* was robust ($p < .05$ in each analysis) in each model. The stimulus and cap-and-trade bills did not have a clear *additional* cost above the general pattern of partisanship exhibited by each member. Also, the final passage vote on the health care bill has a substantively significant (-3.1 percent) effect but is only significant at the $p < .1$ level, which implies that the effect of this vote could vary significantly across members. However, the effect of the vote to concur with the Senate's health care bill in March 2010 was stronger (-4.8 percent) and

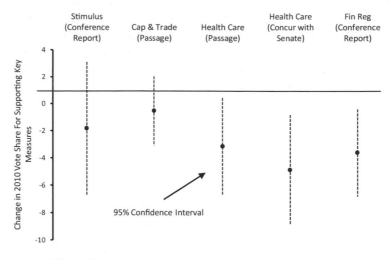

FIGURE 4.8. Effects of key votes on reelection vote share

statistically significant, suggesting that this particular vote was especially costly. Finally, the vote on financial reform appears to have cost around −3.6 percent in vote share on average, and this effect achieves conventional levels of statistical significance. While these are obviously different policy proposals with distinct political circumstances, it is noteworthy that the political costs seem to increase with proximity to Election Day.

Whether we measure partisan loyalty in terms of overall *Party Unity*, subsets of key votes, support for President Obama, or individual roll call votes, the central finding is that members of both parties paid a price for their partisanship. At the margins, this helps explain why some Democrats survived the 2010 elections while others lost their seats because they helped their party pass its ambitious agenda.

This leads to two possible interpretations. The first is that some individual Democratic incumbents may have been better off if they broke with their party more often, even if it meant the failure of Democratic priorities. While this may have helped individual Democrats avoid especially costly votes, it would have meant failure to pass major legislation despite a once-in-a-generation combination of unified government with large congressional majorities. The effect of this failure on the Democratic Party reputation and the support of core Democratic constituencies would probably also be very costly. Thus the Republicans' decision to present a united front against the Democratic agenda, in terms of both votes and public criticism, forced the majority party to face a stark trade-off between their collective party reputation and the loss of dozens of House seats. This implicitly validates the strategic calculus at the heart of the theory presented in this book.

A second view is that the Democratic majority successfully enacted a set of landmark laws without gaining enough political benefit to offset the risk to marginal Democratic legislators. Even after we consider the structural disadvantages the Democrats faced, the Democratic Party's losses in the 2010 elections were very high (Brady et al. 2011). We cannot know if a less ambitious policy agenda would have been a safer electoral strategy, since a middle-of-the-road agenda of incremental proposals would have left Democratic groups and liberal activists severely disappointed and unenthusiastic about helping the Democrats survive the 2010 cycle. But our results do suggest that the same agenda, pursued more quickly and at a greater distance from the 2010 Election Day, may have reduced the Democrats' electoral losses. In the long term, the Democrats can hope that the policy successes of the 111th Congress will yield political dividends, particularly if public support for the Affordable Care Act increases over time.

4.4 Conclusion

Chapters 3 and 4 began with a simple but important premise: citizens evaluate legislators based on their roll call voting records, including their loyalty to their political parties while in office. While past research on the effect of roll call votes on legislative elections has focused on the relationship between legislators' ideology and electoral outcomes, we posit that this approach overstates the influence of ideology on congressional elections. The literature on individual voting behavior shows that voters are more likely to use partisan cues than ideology when choosing between candidates (e.g., Kinder 1998; Mann and Wolfinger 1980). Voters may simply not understand political ideology as a distinct concept separate from political parties; they may know very little about candidate ideology per se; and if they do know about candidate ideology, they may be inclined to respect ideological "mavericks" as principled and conscience-driven.

On the other hand, both our experiments and our analysis of election results find that voters seem to view legislative partisanship as disloyalty to local interests. By directly testing the effects of party unity in Congress, we find that incumbent House members' and senators' vote share declines the more they vote with their own party on issues that divide the two major parties. While ideological extremity is correlated with party unity, we find that it has little *direct* effect on vote share. Moreover, party unity is almost twice as costly for members from moderate districts compared to lopsided districts, as defined by presidential vote share. Our findings suggest that many legislators face electoral costs for siding with their parties on divisive issues, even in this partisan era.

As we conclude our look at individual-level election results, we should note that further research in this area would help develop the strategic parties framework. For example, it is unclear whether legislators are more likely to be pilloried for a single "wrong" vote (on behalf of a party goal) or for a *pattern* of party unity. In practice, we observe both types of claims in campaign ads. It would be useful to know more about the mechanism by which legislative partisanship becomes a campaign issue or how partisanship is incorporated into campaign themes (e.g., tying a local MC to an unpopular party leader or as proof that the local MC is "out of touch" or has "gone Washington"). Finally, it would be useful to explore the role of legislative partisanship in fundraising and primary election campaigns to determine if these aspects of the campaign structure increase individual-level electoral incentives for MCs to be loyal to their parties.

In the next chapter, we go up one further level of aggregation and study the parties as whole entities. In that setting, we are able to see both the electoral consequences of increased party unity as well as their legislative results. Parties are careful to avoid the electoral costs we define here but must weigh these costs against the collective benefits of legislative victory. In trying to maximize both electoral and legislative victories, we will see the parties engaging in strategic interaction over the course of American history.

The Effects of Legislative Behavior
on Aggregate Election Outcomes

The previous two chapters have shown how voters punish legislators who exhibit high levels of party loyalty. In chapter 3, experimental data showed punishments being doled out by voters to strong partisans, and in chapter 4 we saw these patterns again in the reelection efforts of congressional incumbents. Here we focus on the big picture: how the partisan balance of the chambers of Congress varies according to party-level patterns of partisan cohesion. In this chapter, we also study the other side of partisanship—legislative success. Do victories in the legislative arena translate into collective victories in the electoral sphere?

As discussed in chapter 2, legislators are willing to take the risks that partisan unity entails for the sake of enhanced party reputation and public policy that they prefer. Here we can see the dual effects of partisan cooperation. First, there is the direct negative effect that unity has on election outcomes. Second, there is the indirect and positive effect of party unity leading to legislative victories that enhance party reputations and bolster reelection campaigns. This reputational benefit provides an answer to the skeptic's question: why would a legislator ever forsake constituency interests in favor of party cooperation (Krehbiel 1993, 1999)?

One additional focus of this chapter is on the role of the president in the legislative process and in the strategic and reputational goals of parties. Among the many key works on congressional parties, the role of the president is often marginalized or omitted entirely. But this is a costly oversight. The popularity and electoral successes of presidents are important factors in congressional elections (Jacobson 2009; Lewis-Beck and Rice 1984). Because presidential initiatives are a key component of party reputations, the president's copartisans in Congress have a strong incentive to advance the president's legislative agenda, while the opposing party has an incentive to prevent its passage. Legislators have good reason to believe presidential success or failure in the legislative process will affect future elections, both presidential and congressional (Lebo and O'Geen 2011). In this chapter, we demonstrate the effects of party and presidential success on the congressional elections that follow, and we also show how strategic partisan activity can work to pass or defeat presidential agendas. Overall, we find strong links between party behavior in Congress and electoral outcomes: an increase in partisan influence on legislative voting has adverse electoral costs, while winning contested votes has electoral benefits. Moreover, the passage of bills supported by the president has extra influence on party reputations and congressional election results.

5.1 Reputations and the Trade-Offs between Unity and Winning

As the drama over raising the federal debt ceiling played out in the summer of 2011, Senate Minority Leader Mitch McConnell (R-KY) made some frank admissions about his strategy. McConnell refused to accept the general terms of President Obama's offer that would cut social welfare spending by about three trillion dollars and find ways of increasing revenue by about one trillion dollars, saying, "I refuse to help Barack Obama get reelected by marching Republicans into a position where we have co-ownership of a bad economy. It didn't work in 1995. What will happen is the administration will send out notices to eighty million Social Security recipients and to military families and they will all start attacking members of Congress. That is not a useful place to take us. And the president will have the bully pulpit to blame Republicans for all this disruption." In fact, McConnell announced a plan that would essentially hand over responsibility for the decision to the president and was comfortable putting his declaration in the crassest political terms: "If we go into default he will say Republicans are making the economy worse and all of a sudden we have co-ownership of a bad economy. That is a very bad position going into an election. My first choice was to do something important for the country. But my second obligation is to my party and my conference to prevent them from being sucked into a horrible position politically that would allow the president, probably, to get reelected because we didn't handle this difficult situation correctly." A cataloguing of the items McConnell would rank as less important than party reputation would seem to include major policy victories (the president was offering major cuts and changes to Medicare and Social Security favored by many conservatives), lower deficits, and the credit of the United States—set to default on its loans within weeks of McConnell's statements. The minority leader basically said that he wanted no part in solving problems if he thought the Democrats and the democratic president were going to be blamed for the problems or get credit for the solutions. As he said after the 2010 elections, "Our top political priority over the next two years should be to deny President Obama a second term."

The connections between legislative behavior and electoral results are a key part of our understanding of party strategies in Congress. Cox and McCubbins (1993, 2005) place strong emphasis on the importance of reputation in the calculus of congressional party actions. Among several advances gained from this useful hypothesis, it serves as a strong argument against Krehbiel's (1999) theoretical challenge to explain *why* members of Congress would vote against their own preferences in order to support a party. Legislators can help themselves by helping their party achieve a collective goal that enhances their party's reputation.

Of course, this answer assumes that being on the winning side of legislative battles has positive electoral benefits. This is certainly a reasonable expectation; party reputations are likely an important part of voters' decisions. But we should know more about what reputations are made of and how they may be weighed in elections. In particular, since previous chapters show the punishments that voters dole out to those who support their own party too much, we should be able to answer whether or not the electoral gains from legislative success outweigh the costs of the unity it took to win those battles.

As discussed in chapter 2, party unity offers both benefits and costs, so each party selects a level of party influence that balances the *marginal costs* and *marginal benefits* of additional party unity. Party members attain a level of influence on voting by deciding how much vote-buying and agenda-setting power to delegate to their leaders and by selecting leaders who are more or less inclined to use their powers to advance the electoral interests of party members.[1] Congressional parties typically exert some influence but do not control every choice, suggesting that the equilibrium lies in between the extremes of zero and total influence. This chapter seeks to explain the electoral effects of these choices.

5.2 Party Reputations and Presidential Success

What are the elements of party reputation? Certainly, the two political parties and Congress as a whole are unpopular (Hibbing and Theiss-Morse 2001). Yet there is a great deal of variation in the parties' relative reputations over both time and issue area (Pope and Woon 2009). Both the parties' relative and absolute standings in the minds of voters vary based on an accumulation of their actions and the actions of their members. Successes and failures—both electoral and legislative—as well as positions, scandals, and personalities all play a role.

Cox and McCubbins (1993, 1994) make the theoretical connection between party reputation and incumbents' hope for reelection a central piece of what binds cartels closer together. More recent empirical work has sought to tie together some of the loose threads between roll call behavior, perceptions of members and parties due to that behavior, and voter reactions. Woon and Pope (2008; see also Egan 2013) find that the actions of Congress are a significant source of information for voters evaluating the parties and that these reputational effects translate into bigger effects for challengers than incumbents. Butler and Powell (2014) demonstrate that party leadership will pressure members when they believe it will positively affect the party label. In addition, Butler and Powell (2014) find that legislators will work to improve the party label through their roll call behavior, even in the absence of pressure from party leadership.

Mayhew's (1974b, 27) statement that "no theoretical treatment of the United States Congress that posits parties as analytic units will go very far" does not preclude the importance of party reputation to an individual member's success. As he states, "With voters behaving the way they do, it is in the electoral interest of a marginal congressman to help insure that a presidential administration of his own party is a popular success or that one of the opposite party is a failure" (29). Thus party reputations are developed within Congress and also across branches of government as well. A key point is that legislators *act* as if their actions matter. And in the long run, landmark legislation (or the failure to act) matters a great deal in shaping public perceptions of what the parties are about. For example, nearly fifty years after their passage, the 1964 Civil Rights Act and the 1965 Voting Rights Act continue to affect how voters and constituencies of voters judge the parties.

So what can affect party reputations? Of course, there are many possible answers—reputations may change based on scandals, leaders, or legislation. But for our purposes, being most concerned with the strategies employed toward legislation and the legislative agenda, we focus on two possibilities: the success of parties in Congress and the success of the president. In either case, parties will see legislative outcomes as vital to party reputations. But perhaps party leaders do more than simply concentrate on winning and losing. As shown by the Mitch McConnell quotes above, the victories and defeats that matter most to parties may be those of the president, the actor voters pay the most attention to. Relative to other roll call votes, the victories of the president should rally voters to his side, and his defeats should do the opposite.

In the remainder of this chapter, we investigate the pathways from patterns of party behavior to the elections that follow. We look at the effects of party unity but also party success—from the perspective of the party and the president. Throughout, the pattern seen in the previous chapters is evident: unity is punished. Yet here we see an additional and key piece of the puzzle: legislative victories make the risks of unity worth taking. We begin with a broad test of the relationship between legislative success and electoral success and then test three additional refinements. First, we test whether there are noticeable differences in the effects of success on policy rather than process roll call votes. Second, we test whether success is more important when defined in relation to the president. Third, we test whether the electoral costs of unity are higher for the majority party than for the minority party. Through each analysis, we hope to get closer to an understanding of exactly what type of legislative successes and failures have consequences for congressional elections.

5.3 Data

We claim that winning votes is electorally beneficial but that party unity costs seats. To test these claims, we use the Democratic Party's share of each chamber's seats as our dependent variable.[2] Of course, the "Democratic" and "Republican" labels were not used throughout the 1789–2010 time span. By "Democratic," we mean opponents of the Washington administration, the Jeffersonian Republican Party, supporters of Andrew Jackson, and members labeled "Democrat" or "Independent Democrat," all identified using Kenneth Martis's (1989) party affiliation coding. By "Republican," we mean supporters of the Washington administration, Federalists, pro-Adams and anti-Jackson factions, Whigs, and members labeled "Republicans" and "Independent Republicans."[3] We do not imply that these labels signify two constant coalitions. Rather, we merely posit that the coalitions we identify are similar to the group of legislators with the same label in adjacent years.

Figures 5.1 and 5.2 demonstrate these series from the 1st to 112th Congress in the House and Senate, respectively, with shaded areas indicating periods of Democratic majorities. In each chamber, we explain the change in the percentage of seats held by the Democrats using the change in the level of Democratic unity in the previous Congress as well as the change in the Democratic "win" rate—the percentage of votes on which the position preferred by a majority of Democrats prevails.[4] Figures 5.3 and 5.4 demonstrate the win rates for Democrats in the House and Senate, respectively.

Subsequent models also include the win rate of the president—the percentage of votes in which the president's stated position won, in each of the House and the Senate, in a given Congress.[5] We use control variables

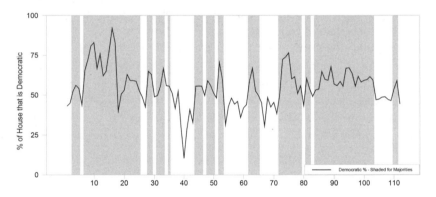

FIGURE 5.1. Democratic House chamber share, 1st–112th Congresses

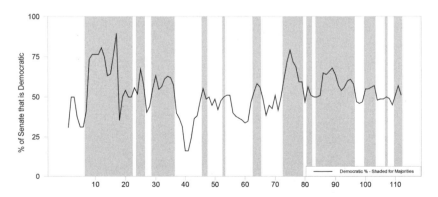

FIGURE 5.2. Democratic Senate chamber share, 1st–112th Congresses

when necessary for various election types—midterm elections with a Republican president, midterms with a Democratic president, presidential election years with Democratic wins, and a dummy variable for the unusual 1822 election.[6]

We also add in controls for presidential approval—measured as the average of monthly responses to Gallup's presidential approval question[7]—and the percentage of "quality" challengers (see chapter 4).

5.4 Results: Party Influence and Congressional Elections

What are the electoral consequences of party influence? Recall the two counterbalancing expectations here: as legislators vote more frequently with their party, they are being pulled away from the wishes of their con-

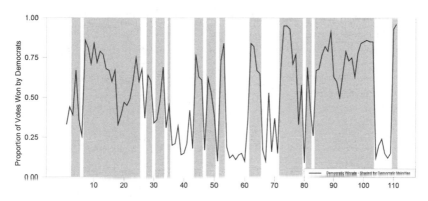

FIGURE 5.3. Democratic win rate in the House, 1st–111th Congresses

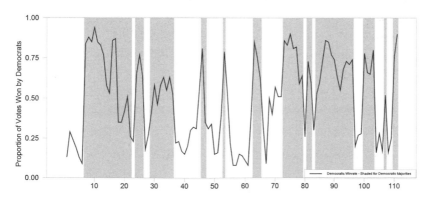

FIGURE 5.4. Democratic win rate in the Senate, 1st–111th Congresses

stituents and thereby risk defeat in their next election. Simultaneously, however, higher unity increases the probability of winning votes,[8] which, in turn, is rewarded by electoral gains for the party.

5.4.1 House of Representatives

Results for all party votes in the House are shown in the first model of table 5.1.

Each additional point of party unity costs the Democrats just over 0.22 percent in their share of the House (nearly 1 seat out of 435) in the next Congress. As party influence moves legislators away from the interests of constituents to those of party, the consequences are indeed felt at the ballot box. Looking at all party votes, we have some support ($p = 0.072$) for our expectation that legislative success leads to electoral success. For each additional 10 percent of the votes the Democrats win, they will win a 0.54 percent greater share (2.35 seats) in the next Congress.

Other results are predictable—the Democrats increase their share of the House in midterm elections with a Republican president and lose seats in midterms with a Democratic president. Coattail effects account for a rise in the Democratic House share when a Democrat is elected president, and the 1822 election, which marks the disintegration of the Jeffersonian coalition in our data, was a significant loss for the soon-to-be Democrats. Overall, the model explains 34 percent of the variance in Democratic House shares.

In the second and third models of table 5.1, we look at subsets of party votes, specifically those on policy and those on procedural matters. We expect that the public will reward victories on policy more than on procedure. We also expect that the punishments for unity on policy will be more severe. These are simply more visible to the public and of more obvious meaning to them. The effects fall in line with these expectations—victories on policy are significantly rewarded ($p = 0.04$), and the costs of unity are high. For procedural matters, on the other hand, the effects are comparatively small and do not achieve statistical significance.

5.4.2 Senate

Figure 5.5 shows the key results of multiple models for the Senate.[9] The changing nature of senators' selection makes for an interesting natural experiment here, and in fact, the story of partisan unity, legislative vic-

TABLE 5.1. **The electoral effects of party unity and party success on Democratic House share, 1st–111th Congress**[†]

Independent variable	All Party Votes			All Party Votes on Policy			All Party Votes on Procedure		
	Coefficient	(se)	p-value	Coefficient	(se)	p-value	Coefficient	(se)	p-value
Constant	-1.890	(1.643)	0.253	-1.761	(1.661)	0.292	-2.048	(1.701)	0.231
Democratic Party Unity in Previous Congress	-0.222	(0.106)	0.019	-0.173	(0.083)	0.019	0.031	(0.072)	0.659
Democratic Win Rate in Previous Congress	5.404	(3.677)	0.072	7.084	(4.009)	0.040	4.682	(3.206)	0.073
Midterm Election with GOP President	9.342	(2.339)	0.000	9.127	(2.349)	0.000	9.238	(2.379)	0.000
Midterm Election with Dem. President	-5.212	(2.204)	0.002	-6.581	(2.202)	0.002	6.621	(2.282)	0.002
Presidential Election with Democratic Win	4.726	(2.251)	0.019	4.553	(2.270)	0.024	5.145	(2.360)	0.016
1822 Election	-33.949	(8.587)	0.000	-34.550	(8.626)	0.000	34.647	(8.903)	0.000
Durbin Watson Statistic	1.94			1.92			1.79		
Centered R^2	0.34			0.34			0.31		
N	110			110			110		

[†] The dependent variable is the percentage of the House won by Democrats (differenced by 0.59); p-values are based on one-tailed tests.

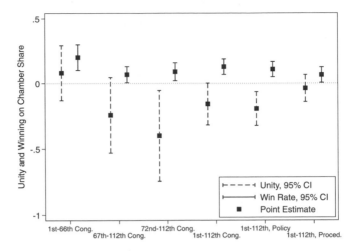

FIGURE 5.5. Effects of democratic wins and party unity on chamber share, Senate: Coefficients and 95 percent confidence intervals

tory, and congressional elections is even stronger in the modern Senate. We try our analysis on three separate periods, and the results confirm our expectations.[10] Before the Seventeenth Amendment and the adoption of direct elections in 1913, senators were selected by state legislatures and thus were only indirectly responsible to the voters of their states. During this period (which we extend to 1920), there is no consistent link between party unity and electoral fortune. This link becomes evident following the onset of direct elections, 1921 to the present, and solidifies for the 1931 to 2011 period. Indeed, party unity has an increasingly negative relationship with the Democrats' share of the chamber over these three periods. From 1931 to 2011, a 1 percent increase in party unity is associated with a 0.40 percent decrease in chamber seat share (i.e., .4 seats in a 100-seat Senate). Voting with one's party may be costly for senators who must be reelected by the voters of their states. State legislators, on the other hand, were either more understanding of party behavior or were beholden to their US senators prior to the Seventeenth Amendment (Rothman 1966).[11]

Winning contested votes, on the other hand, is associated with gaining Senate seat share in all three periods. For example, from 1931 to 2011, a 10 percent increase in the portion of party votes won by Democrats is followed by a 0.88 percent gain in seat share. This link is much stronger in the indirectly-elected Senate, with a 10 percent increase in win rate associated with a 1.99 percent increase in seat share. Overall, it is evident that by the modern age, the effects of party behavior on congressional elections that we identify are firmly in place.

Looking separately at votes on policy and procedure, the effects seen in the House models are repeated here. The direct punishment for unity and rewards for victories are much higher on the policy votes that are so much more visible to the public. Yet the effects of winning on procedural votes are still statistically significant ($p = 0.017$) in the Senate—an interesting pattern in a chamber where the procedural battles can be of as much interest as the policy outcomes. Thus in both the House and Senate, we see the same patterns of party unity leading to a smaller chamber share, but with the legislative victories bought by higher unity rewarded.

5.4.3 Presidential Success and Legislative Elections

Next, we can look more closely at the subset of key votes that are most important in explaining swings in chamber share in the modern era. Specifically, are votes on which the president takes a public position especially relevant to election outcomes? Answering this should give us a window into the idea of collective reputation.

The primacy of the president in the minds of voters seems reasonable. Thanks in large part to the different levels of media exposure (Cohen 2002), overall interest and knowledge about Congress is much lower than it is regarding the president. For example, fewer than half of Americans can identify the Speaker of the House, while more than two-thirds can name the vice president.[12] Recent work studying congressional approval has shown that the measure is mostly a general evaluation of the country as a whole and feelings toward the president rather than an accurate evaluation of the job Congress is doing (Lebo 2008). Voters are simply not nearly as attentive to the partisan struggles in Congress as they are to news on the president. Thus perhaps the wins and losses on the president's scorecard are of more central importance than those of the parties in Congress.

If so, it would be the level of presidential success that affects party reputations more so than that of the parties. This implies that parties will see costs and benefits of legislative victories in terms of the president's agenda and that it would be most strategic for parties to do what they can to either support a president of their party or to paint an opposing president as a legislative failure. As Mitch McConnell expects, legislators' reelection chances and even the balance of power in Congress may be swung through such strategies.

Certainly, the battles in which the president chooses to engage increase both media attention and the degree of partisanship in Congress (Lee 2009). As the most visible actor in American politics, the president's record is a vehicle for affecting the relative reputations of the parties and the elections that follow. Members of the president's party work to protect the president from the legislative defeats his opponents seek to hand him. These imperatives are a significant part of the cross pressuring between constituents and parties that legislators feel.

The bolstering or undermining of a president and his party's label is an important goal that is not separate from ambition and reelection but an important component of pursuing those goals. Indeed, in every other election, legislators share the ballot with presidential candidates. Beyond party reputations, the coattail effects of presidential elections can also have a large effect on the makeup of the Congress to follow. For example, the ability of the Democratically controlled 110th Congress to drive down the effectiveness of President George W. Bush led not only to the biggest victory for a Democratic candidate (Barack Obama) since 1964 but also to a large victory in the 2008 congressional elections—the 111th Congress was far more lopsided (256–178 in the House and 57–41 in the Senate) than one would expect from a roughly evenly divided electorate. Strategic maneuvers to affect the elections to come are integral to the behavior of partisans and stand quite apart from what we would expect legislators to do if they simply pursued their ideologically defined agenda. In the balance hang not just the seats that are needed for a majority status but also the benefits of holding additional seats beyond a bare majority. Electoral safety, rather than freeing up a legislator to vote her conscience, makes a legislator a prime target for furthering the goals of the party.

To explore this question, we use Congressional Quarterly's data on stated presidential positions, which is available from 1957 to 2006 (85th–109th Congresses). Figure 5.6 compares the win rate of the Democratic Party on the larger set of party vote bills to the win rate of presidents on issues where the president took a position. For both the House and Senate, the two series closely track each other, but they are distinct, in part because some presidential positions were supported by bipartisan majorities. While both parties will work to increase their "batting average" on roll call votes, when the president takes a position, the parties are more likely to gear up for a concerted effort. Legislators not of the president's

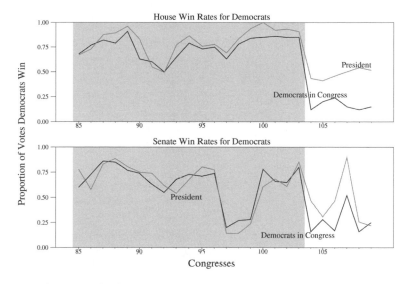

FIGURE 5.6. Democratic win rates, party and presidential

party will expend considerable effort to defeat the president's agenda in an attempt to paint him and, by extension, his party as ineffective. Policy preferences can certainly play a role as well in position taking. This is certainly a familiar scenario for witnesses to President Obama's first two years in office.

On the other hand, those in the president's party will work especially hard on passing his legislative agenda—not necessarily because they agree with those policies, although they often will; rather, they want to ride the wave of enhanced party reputation or stronger party coalitions brought about by a successful presidency (Erikson et al. 2002, ch. 7). There are several possible routes from presidential legislative success to party electoral success. Whether by riding coattails in an open election or in a re-election or by attempting to minimize the losses traditionally suffered in midterms, the president's copartisans will do what they can to burnish his reputation.

Table 5.2 tries to parse which level of success is most rewarded by voters. The analyses cover the last twenty-six congressional elections and explain the chamber share of the Democrats in the House. In the first model, we see that the effect of Democratic success is much larger over the more recent period than over the entire course of congressional history. In the more recent period, each additional 10 percent of the votes the Demo-

TABLE 5.2. **The electoral effects of party success and presidential success on Democratic chamber share in the House, 84th–109th Congress**

	Democratic Win Rate			Presidential Win Rate			Two Win Rates Compared		
	Coefficient	(se)	p-value	Coefficient	(se)	p-value	Coefficient	(se)	p-value
Democratic Win Rate in Previous Congress	17.39	(3.69)	0.006	—	—	—	7.74	(6.17)	0.113
President's Win Rate in Previous Congress	—	—	—	30.02	(7.19)	0.000	22.45	(9.30)	0.014
Democratic Party Cohesion	-0.39	(0.19)	0.026	-0.62	(0.20)	0.003	-0.64	(0.20)	0.002
Midterm Election with GOP President	4.65	(1.92)	0.013	4.62	(1.73)	0.008	4.38	(1.71)	0.010
Midterm Election with Dem. President	-10.26	(2.68)	0.001	-10.20	(2.36)	0.000	-10.98	(2.40)	0.000
Pres. Election with Democratic Win	6.52	(2.30)	0.005	6.46	(2.05)	0.003	6.89	(2.05)	0.002
Quality Republican Challengers	-0.10	(0.04)	0.016	-0.11	(0.04)	0.007	-0.12	(0.04)	0.004
Pres. Approval During Previous Congress	0.13	(0.06)	0.015	0.11	(0.05)	0.033	0.12	(0.05)	0.012
Constant	-0.97	(1.39)	0.491	-0.82	(1.25)	0.520	-0.71	(1.24)	0.574
Durbin-Watson	2.01			1.86			2.01		
R^2	0.67			0.73			0.76		
N	26			26			26		

Note: p-values are based on one-tailed tests.

crats win now lead to an increase of 1.74 percent (7.57 seats) greater share in the next Congress. Even more impressive are the gains the Democrats make when we instead look at the success rates of presidents in the second model of table 5.2. There the effect is dramatic—a 10 percent increase in the president's rate of success is followed by a 3 percent increase in chamber share, roughly thirteen seats or the entire congressional delegation of North Carolina.[13] The successes and failures of a president obviously do a great deal to alter reputations and perceptions of the party. Figure 5.6 shows the close relationship that we'd expect between the rate of Democratic wins and the rate of presidential wins (adjusted for party). The models in table 5.2 also control for the type of election, presidential approval, party cohesion, and the proportion of quality challengers with significant results in the expected directions. A final test of which of these is the best predictor of party size is to "horserace" the two variables against each other as we do in the final model of table 5.2. The result is pretty clear—despite the overlap, it is presidential success that matters most. This should tell us a lot about the working of the parties across branches of government—the president's partisans are right to team up on the president's agenda and priorities to work hard on passing them, and his opponents may benefit from derailing that agenda. Beyond the policies that emerge from a Congress, the reputational effects of legislative battles on presidential priorities are critical to the distribution of seats between the parties.

Table 5.3 tests the same questions in the Senate from the 85th to 109th Congress. For the Senate, the electoral effects of success are roughly equal for the party and the president. When each is included on its own, the effect is strong and statistically significant; increases of 1.01 percent and .93 percent of the party's share of the Senate follow increases of 10 percent in the win rates of Senate Democrats and the president (adjusted for party), respectively—that is, an increase of roughly one senator. Note that changes in the composition of the Senate are necessarily smaller than in the House, since only one-third of the Senate is elected in any election year. The last column of table 5.3 shows the rough parity in the contribution of party and president to electoral success in the Senate; the two variables are jointly significant. As Frances Lee (2009) has argued, presidential positions increase partisan calculations in the Senate—so much so that when the two variables are estimated simultaneously, they cancel each other out.

The effect of presidential success on party reputations and electoral returns implies that parties should be strategic in doing what they can to af-

TABLE 5.3. **The electoral effects of party success and presidential success on Democratic chamber share in the Senate, 85th–109th Congress**

Independent Variable	Democratic Win Rate			Presidential Win Rate					
	Coefficient	(se)	p-value	Coefficient	(se)	p-value	Coefficient	(se)	p-value
Democratic Win Rate in Previous Congress	10.13	(4.22)	0.01	—	—	—	6.36	(5.64)	0.14
President's Win Rate in Previous Congress	—	—	—	9.26	(3.98)	0.02	5.31	(5.28)	0.16
Democratic Party Cohesion	-0.49	(0.23)	0.03	-0.43	(0.23)	0.04	-0.50	(0.23)	0.03
Midterm Election with GOP President	3.37	(2.54)	0.10	3.67	(2.58)	0.09	3.69	(2.56)	0.08
Midterm Election with Dem. President	-4.36	(2.57)	0.06	-4.42	(2.60)	0.05	-4.55	(2.58)	0.05
Pres. Election with Democratic Win	4.30	(2.74)	0.07	4.63	(2.77)	0.06	4.54	(2.75)	0.06
Pres. Approval During Previous Congress	0.16	(0.07)	0.02	0.19	(0.08)	0.01	0.18	(0.08)	0.01
Constant	-0.69	(1.90)	0.72	-1.25	(1.91)	0.52	-0.94	(1.91)	0.63
Democratic Size$_{t-3}$	-0.49	(0.19)	0.02	-0.44	(0.19)	0.04	-0.45	(0.19)	0.03
Durbin-Watson	1.78			1.99			1.91		
R^2	0.62			0.61			0.64		
N	23			23			23		

Note: p-values are based on one-tailed tests.

fect the president's balance sheet of wins and losses. On issues where the president takes a stand, the stakes go up considerably. To be sure, an explanation of the success rate of the president is very much a partisan story. Lebo and O'Geen (2011) follow a long line of research on the causes of presidential success in the House (e.g., Bond and Fleisher 1990; Bond et al. 2003; Canes-Wrone 2001; Canes-Wrone and de Marchi 2002) and show the dominance of the partisan structure of the chamber over the popularity of the president. Figure 5.7 shows the effects of various measures on presidential success in both the House and the Senate.[14]

While the president's level of popularity (the last bar on each side) is a positive predictor of success, much more of the president's success is predicted by the partisan makeup and actions of the two legislative bodies. Members of the president's party can boost his level of success when they are more numerous and more unified. Majority status is not all that matters—the size of the president's party will matter, as will the ideological makeup of the chamber, both in the conditions of conditional party government (CPG) and in the distance between the president and the majority party leader. Party members will band together in an effort to affect the success of the president's agenda. In turn, these strategies affect the elections that follow. The reputation of the president as a legislative leader is more directly linked to congressional elections, and thus his reputation is a key focus of legislative behavior.

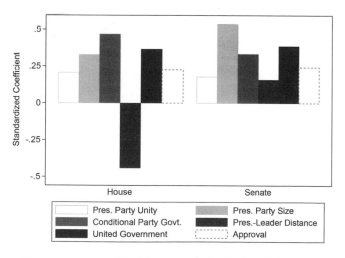

FIGURE 5.7. Determinants of presidential success, standardized coefficients: House and Senate, 1955–2005

5.4.4 Do Majority Parties Pay a Higher Price for Partisanship?

One additional question we can address with these data is the extent to which there are asymmetries between majority and minority parties in these effects. Are the positive effects of winning the same for the Democrats when they are in the majority as when they hold the minority? That is, are the rewards of passing the Democratic majority's agenda the same as those for squashing the Republican agenda when the Democrats are the minority party? Table 5.4 is based on a splitting of the data so that Democratic voting cohesion and Democratic win rate are separated by majority status for the 1st through 112th Congress in the House and for the 72nd through 112th Congress in the Senate.

Clearly there are differences based on majority status. When in the majority, Democrats reap great rewards in both the House ($\beta = 15.43, p = 0.007$) and the Senate ($\beta = 28.06, p < .001$) for winning legislative battles but pay costs for the voting cohesion those wins may require. The rewards of minority Democratic caucuses for winning do not approach statistical significance in either chamber—perhaps the public simply understands that the minority party does not often win. Yet if a party does not make large gains by winning votes as the minority, preventing the majority party from winning them denies the majority the chance to enhance its reputation and reap electoral rewards.

There is one final finding of note in these analyses: *the punishment*

TABLE 5.4. **The electoral effects of party success: Majority and minority status compared, House and Senate**

Independent Variable	House, 1st–112th Congress			Senate, 72nd–112th Congress		
	Coefficient	(se)	p-value	Coefficient	(se)	p-value
Democratic Win Rate – Majority$_{t-1}$	15.43	(6.12)	0.01	28.06	(7.77)	0.00
Democratic Win Rate – Minority$_{t-1}$	−4.97	(8.43)	0.56	5.55	(12.10)	0.33
Democratic Cohesion – Majority$_{t-1}$	−0.22	(0.10)	0.01	−0.42	(0.13)	0.00
Democratic Cohesion – Minority$_{t-1}$	−0.08	(0.09)	0.19	−0.17	(0.12)	0.08
Midterm Election with GOP President	8.55	(2.36)	0.00	6.64	(2.14)	0.00
Midterm Election with Dem. President	−6.58	(2.20)	0.00	−8.48	(2.04)	0.00
Pres. Election with Democratic Win	4.33	(2.36)	0.04	7.64	(2.11)	0.00
1822 Election (H) / DemSize$_{t-3}$ (S)	−38.16	(8.69)	−0.00	−0.38	(0.12)	0.00
Constant	−2.42	(2.38)	0.31	−1.94	(1.57)	0.23
Durbin-Watson		1.91			2.37	
R^2		0.36			0.60	
N		110			41	

Note: p-values are based on one-tailed tests.

for voting unity is also noticeably smaller for the minority party. This may again be due to a perception among the public that it is largely the job of the majority to govern. But it might also be the case that a minority party, by virtue of its size, will hold a core of "safe" seats with fewer evenly balanced or cross-pressured districts. On the other hand, as the size of the majority's caucus grows, a majority party will find itself defending an increasing number of districts that lean toward the other party in over-all partisan tendency. Especially in an era of polarization where so many swing districts, as well as the overall balance of power, are at stake in elec-tion after election, the minority party does well to force the majority to put its members in the position of having to cast electorally risky roll calls. A unified minority party forces members of the majority to unify in pur-suit of wins—and that action can be costly.

5.5 Conclusion

This chapter links the aggregate patterns of legislative battles to the elec-tions that follow them. Winning legislative battles has electoral conse-quences, and a party can boost its relative reputation by either helping a president of their party or frustrating an opposition president. Yet the costs of the party unity required to win those battles remain high, particu-larly for the majority party. The consistency of these findings—in earlier chapters at different levels of analysis and here in two chambers and for different time periods—establishes the robustness of the findings. For ex-ample, in the pre–Seventeenth Amendment Senate, there are no costs of party unity, which again points to the role of voters in enticing legislators to be as true to their constituents as their party interests allow.

Thus between this and the previous two chapters, the pattern of pun-ishment of excessive unity has worked its way up from the minds of indi-vidual voters to the aggregate swings of party fortunes over the course of American history. The pressure that legislators feel to follow their con-stituents is often ignored in the name of party interest, but the rewards to parties—and hence their members—are evident as well. In the chapters that remain, we will look at the role of party influence on roll call behav-ior at the aggregate (chapter 6) and vote by vote (chapter 7).

CHAPTER SIX

The Dynamics of Partisan Power

In previous chapters, we have shown how parties make strategic decisions and weigh the electoral consequences when assembling the votes necessary to achieve victories on roll call votes. On the one hand, we have seen the benefit of party unity: success in the legislative process *via* an enhanced reputation for their party (Cox and McCubbins 1993). Parties that cannot pass their agenda items due to internal dissent or that fail to contest controversial proposals by other parties risk disappointing their supporters and losing elections. On the other hand, parties and their members are certainly aware of the costs of excessive unity—they know that each time they ask for support, the member may lose votes in the election to come. Party leaders are thus careful to unify members of their party only as much as they can afford to.

Here we ask, what determines how unified a party needs to be? Our answer is the other party. Neither party exists in a vacuum. Beyond the ideological differences between them, each party must recognize and deal with the relative size and strength of its opposition. As parties strategize for the next legislative battle and the election beyond it, they look keenly at the opposition and attempt to muster the level of strength necessary to win in both arenas.

As discussed in chapter 2, these effects should lead to arms-race competition between the two parties, with strong pressure toward parity between the parties. When one party is noticeably more unified than a second party, the more unified party should have greater legislative success that should lead to greater party reputation and electoral benefits. However, the more unified party should pay direct electoral costs for having pulled its members from its constituents' preferences, leading to "fatigue" among party members. Thus the more unified party should feel some pressure to relax unity to the point that it still wins votes without asking its members to pay unnecessary electoral costs. And the less unified party should feel pressure to make a stronger response so as not to lose legislative battles and have its reputation suffer. Over time, we should observe that the two congressional parties' unity levels are tethered together—while other forces may push them apart, their natural tendency is for each to seek out the other.

This strategizing provides a clear explanation for the variation in party strength. In this chapter, we examine closely the strategic interaction of congressional parties over the history of the United States. We find overwhelming evidence that the strength of the opposition is the single best predictor of party strength. We elaborate on this finding by explaining how the tendency of parties to match the level of strength of their opponent explains the current period of partisanship in Congress. We also explore and dismiss alternate explanations for the two parties' unity levels to so closely match each other over time.

We begin with a theoretical discussion of the dynamics of party support over time and then demonstrate the empirical regularities we expect—the two major parties are continually moving toward a state of equilibrium. We then provide a descriptive account of the swings in party unity over the last several decades, demonstrating how our perspective helps explain the resurgence of congressional partisanship.

6.1 Explaining Variation in Party Unity

The two key hypotheses of this chapter, first presented in chapter 2, suggest that two patterns of strategic interaction should be evident in the data of party influence across time:

> *Hypothesis 6.1 (Response):* The level of party influence of one party will vary with the influence of the opposition party. Thus *Party Unity* for the Democrats will increase as *Party Unity* for the Republicans increases and vice versa.

> *Hypothesis 6.2 (Correction):* Parties will correct differences between themselves in party influence. Thus differences in *Party Unity* in one period will be quickly reduced in the next period.

According to hypothesis 6.1, the parties will make adjustments to each other within congresses—they will respond to the observed level of party unity within the opposition party. Gaps between the parties are still likely to occur due to incomplete information, to inflexibility in the structures of the parties, or to legislators' unwillingness to change their patterns of voting. When these gaps occur, hypothesis 6.2 states that the Democrats and Republicans will close them by adjusting their levels of influence in the direction of the other party's unity in the previous time period. This strategic interaction should dominate other explanations of variance in party influence across American history.

Hypothesis 6.1 is, of course, a key to our theory. If the Democrats get more unified, we expect an increase in Republican unity. Finding support for hypothesis 6.1 will establish a general tendency for the parties to *react* to each other over the course of American political history. But hypothesis 6.2 is also critical. It suggests that not only do the parties react to one another but they are in an equilibrium relationship—that is, each party is continually looking to match the level of unity of the other, and movements by one party that push the two parties apart prompt each to move back toward the other.

What is it that keeps levels of unity seemingly tethered to each other over time? Essentially, the costs of being too far out of sync in either direction ensure that the parties move toward an equilibrium of roughly equal levels of strength. Party leaders who unnecessarily enforce strict levels of discipline well above their opposition may win legislative battles in the short term, but they put their members at electoral risk. Ultimately, leaders will relax their pressure on members as much as they can get away with and still be competitive on the votes they deem important. From the other perspective, the party losing those legislative battles may gain benefits from having its members closely aligned with their respective districts, but repeated losses on roll calls can prove costly, and the party will seek to increase its influence over its members.

6.2 Analyzing Party Unity over Time

6.2.1 Measures of Party Unity

Untangling the effects of parties and preferences on legislators' roll call behavior is a difficult task and one that is aided by bringing as much data to the table as possible. We will examine data at the yearly level spanning the length of the republic, from 1789 to 2010. To see variation in party influence over time, we should first define what we mean by "party influ-

ence." As a concept, party influence refers to the ability of party apparatus, leaders, and fellow members to affect the decisions of a legislator. A
direct measure of these pressures on legislator behavior is somewhat elu-
sive, although some aspects, such as whip counts, are measureable. Upon
switching to legislator behavior that is directly observable, possibilities
for measuring influence emerge. For one, yearly scores of unity in voting
serve as a historically continuous measure of party influence. For each
"party" vote—those votes where a majority of one party votes against
a majority of the other party—legislators choose which side they are on
(or abstain). The proportion of times they vote with their party serves as
a measure of their allegiance to the party over some period of time. Congressional Quarterly has long published reports of these scores.

Aggregating among groups of legislators, yearly[1] party scores of unity
in voting serve as a historically continuous measure of party influence. For
each of the Democratic and Republican Parties, we define the yearly level
of unity as the average of party unity scores on all "party" votes. As Krehbiel (2000) argues, these party unity scores are the result of both legislators' preferences and party influences. Discerning whether a legislator's
choice on a single vote is due to constituent or party influence is not possible. But over a wider set of votes, if we can control for legislators' preferences or those of their constituents, we can then evaluate the party's
influence over those votes. Looking at the Democrats and Republicans
over longer periods, if we can control for the preferences of the parties,
we can see the influence of parties as institutions over time. We can then
ask, When have the Democrats and Republicans been strongest in their
abilities to bring together senators and representatives to fight the partisan cause? And what explains the variation over time?

Figure 6.1 shows us the variation in *Party Unity* for Democrats and
Republicans in the House of Representatives from 1789 to 2010, and figure 6.2 shows the same for the Senate.[2] *Party Unity* is defined for each
party as the average percentage of times its members vote with the majority of their party on votes where a majority of one party votes on one side
and a majority of the other party votes on the other side (so-called party
votes). Shading demarcates four distinct periods of party competition:
1789 to 1824, 1825 to 1860, 1861 to 1932, and 1933 to 2010. Several factors
are noteworthy. First, and most obviously, these party scores are changing
over time—for European legislatures, we might just see solidly horizontal lines at the 100 percent mark or perhaps some variation between 99
and 100 percent. Second, it is also obvious that the levels of unity in the

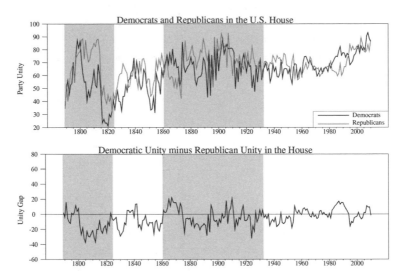

FIGURE 6.1. Variation in party unity in the House of Representatives, 1789–2010

two parties are closely related to each other. The series follow each other quite closely, and gaps that open up between their relative strengths are short-lived. The bottom panel of the figure shows the unity gap, the yearly difference between the unity levels of the two parties. While this gap fluctuates, it looks to have a natural tendency toward zero. A third noticeable pattern is the recent upward trend toward greater levels of unity.

In figure 6.2, we show the same variables over the same period for the parties in the Senate. The two series also follow each other closely, with three noticeable exceptions: the years prior to the 1824 election, when the parties underwent unique transformations; the Civil War to Reconstruction period; and to a lesser extent, the New Deal period of the 1930s. Again, it is evident that the parties have ratcheted up their levels of unity over the last few years—evidence of the increased polarization of the parties. For the Senate, the Unity Gap again looks to tend toward zero—a pattern we can call a *mean reverting* process. In both the House and Senate, the Unity Gap oscillates around zero as the two parties tend back toward equilibrium.

Such a relationship is an extremely close one and has been described in economics as *cointegrated* (Banerjee et al. 1993). In cointegrated relationships, the process of *error correction* can be explored—when two variables have moved away from equilibrium (the error), there is movement

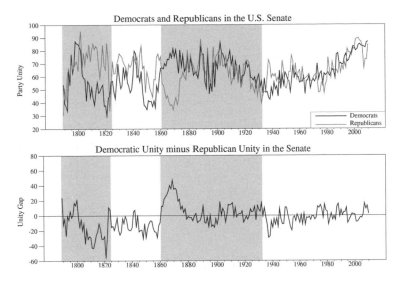

FIGURE 6.2. Variation in party unity in the Senate, 1789–2010

back (correction) toward each other in the period that follows.[3] Cointegration is an especially useful concept for studying action-reaction processes where one actor responds with similar behavior to either hostile or cooperative behavior from another actor (Lebo and Moore 2003).[4] Like a drunk walking a dog on a leash, the two may wander together, but they will never get too far apart from each other (Murray 1994). Finding such a close relationship in political-science data is rare. For example, the extent of the equilibrium relationship between Democratic and Republican *Party Unity* we find is considerably stronger than the one between presidential approval and public opinion about the state of the economy (Clarke and Stewart 1994). Thus not only do we expect the unity of each party to drive the other, but following hypothesis 6.2, we also expect to find error correction—the parties will strive to close any difference in unity from the previous period.

Among the additional factors to consider when explaining party strength is *Party Size* (Patty 2008). A larger caucus means that leaders may pass legislation without all their members, so its "response" parameter can be lower. In 2010, for example, on the final vote for health care reform, Speaker Pelosi needed the support of only 218 of the 253 Democrats voting. By winning the vote 219–212, the Democrats saved thirty-four members from casting votes that would have further hurt their prospects of reelection.[5] With smaller majorities, party leaders cannot let members off the hook so easily.

Party Size is also important when we think about the district of the marginal member. For example, all else equal, a Democratic Caucus of 260 instead of 250 would be adding 10 highly precarious districts, likely leaning Republican. We would expect Democrats elected from those districts to be poor party citizens who know that their reelections depend on their building reputations separate from the party. Since each additional seat moves a party into a district that is less safe, it should be associated with a drop in *Party Unity*. A majority party will not lean on the marginal member for key votes unless absolutely necessary—the party wants to protect the member and protect its majority. On the other side of the aisle, the minority party knows that for each one of its own members it can keep from voting with the majority, it puts a member of the majority at electoral risk. This gives us the following:

Hypothesis 6.3: Party Unity will be negatively associated with *Party Size*.

This is especially evident in a period such as the present, where the "natural vote" we might get from constituencies and states would lead to evenly split representation in the House and Senate. With majority status on the line every two years, this kind of party jockeying has become a hallmark of the twenty-first-century Congress. We next turn to other variables worth considering as explanations of party unity and then put our ideas and data to the test.

6.2.2 Measuring Preferences and Other Variables

We are also interested in testing the key hypotheses of the conditional party government (CPG) model alongside our hypotheses 6.1 and 6.2. Specifically, CPG expects that *Party Unity* will increase with the homogeneity of intraparty preferences (which lowers the *fatigue* component of a party's calculus) and with the degree of policy disagreement between the Democrats and Republicans (which increases the *response* component)—that is, parties will strengthen as each becomes more ideologically consistent and when the differences between the two parties grow.

To evaluate the effect of members' preferences on partisan voting patterns, we rely on DW-NOMINATE scores on two dimensions to operationalize preference cohesion within parties and disagreement between the parties (Aldrich et al. 2002; Aldrich et al. 2007). These scores are generated by treating every contested roll call as a choice between two alternatives and every vote as a choice between those alternatives; the more any two legislators vote together, the more we assume they have similar preferences. The first dimension is liberal-conservative and predicts most congressional voting. The second deals mostly with slavery in the nineteenth century but has "no consistent pattern" for most of the twentieth century (Poole and Rosenthal 1997). We use the standard deviation of each NOMINATE dimension for each party and the absolute difference between the scores of the median members of each major party as measures of intraparty unity and interparty differences, respectively. This leads to the creation of six time series for each chamber: *Democratic Cohesion—Nominate First, Democratic Cohesion—Nominate Second, Republican Cohesion—Nominate First, Republican Cohesion—Nominate Second, Ideological Distance—Nominate First,* and *Ideological Distance—Nominate Second.*[6]

The path of these variables over American history can be seen in figures 6.3, 6.4, and 6.5. As with *Party Unity*, the cohesion of preferences within each party also seems to be related to that of its opposition. In both of the DW-NOMINATE dimensions—figures 6.3 and 6.4—the measures for the two parties seem to track each other fairly closely. This may, in part, indicate the tendency of both parties to respond in a similar fashion to outside effects on the legislative agenda. As new and important issues become salient, members of both parties may respond by aligning their preferences. But it is also indicative of the variation in issue positions taken by party members. At times, the parties have been broad tents containing diversity in the opinions of their legislators. At other times, and certainly recently, the parties have sorted nearly completely on the issues of the day.

Figure 6.5 shows us a standard measure of party polarization in Congress over its history. The median-to-median distances between the two parties in the two chambers tell an interesting story, especially over the past fifty years or so. In the first dimension of DW-NOMINATE, the parties in both chambers have moved increasingly distant from each other. In the House, the level of polarization using this measure reached its all-time peak in 2007 as the Democrats took over the majority. In the Senate, one has to go back to the early 1880s to find a period of such high polarization. The CPG model would tell us that this polarization should be a key factor in explaining increased party influence over the last fifty years. We

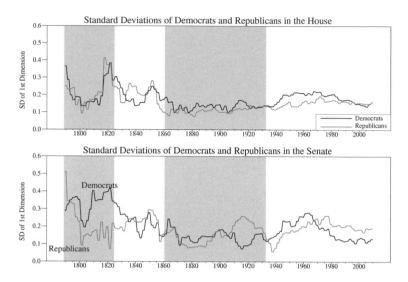

FIGURE 6.3. Ideological Cohesion: DW-NOMINATE first dimension, 1789–2010

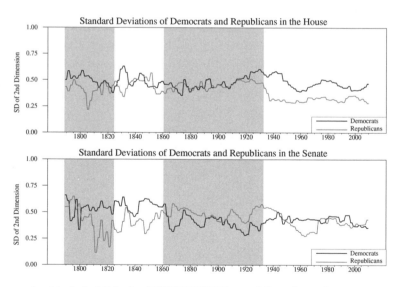

FIGURE 6.4. Ideological Cohesion: DW-NOMINATE second dimension, 1789–2010

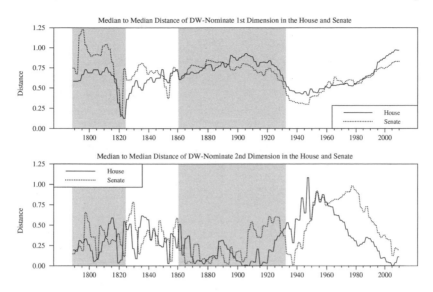

FIGURE 6.5. Ideological distance between the parties, 1789–2010

demonstrate below that this is a contributing factor, but that the strategic party government (SPG) model's factors dominate the movement of *Party Unity* over time.

The median-to-median distance in the second dimension of DW-NOMINATE (the bottom panel of figure 6.5) illustrates variation in cross party coalitions in American politics. During the mid-twentieth century, issues like civil rights led to persistent splits within and across parties, but since the 1960s, civil rights has increasingly become a partisan issue. The parties in both chambers have come ever closer together on matters of civil rights, with the House leading and the Senate lagging behind.

Measures of ideology are, of course, quite tricky. Having a pure measure of legislators' *personal* policy preferences would be a windfall to congressional scholars. Instead, what we have are measures of *induced* preferences, such as NOMINATE, that are calculated based on the *actions* of legislators. Those actions are naturally affected by the multiple pressures felt by members of Congress and senators, including pressures from their constituents, donors, and interest groups. One potential criticism of using NOMINATE scores as measures of induced preferences is that we are using variables derived from roll call votes to predict Party Unity, a measure also based on roll call votes. This is troublesome to the extent that parties directly influence members' votes and induce stable voting coalitions (Poole and Rosenthal 1997, 227). If so, our use of aggregated NOMINATE variables may *overstate* the role of constituency and personal preferences and *understate* the importance of strategic partisanship. Certainly these two measures—unity and NOMINATE—measure different aspects of party voting, a fact supported by Cooper and Young's (2002) thorough examination of measurement issues in examining party behavior. Thus using the best available measures of induced preferences, NOMINATE scores, does not create any methodological dilemmas for our analysis.[7] And here we are using not the scores but rather their distributions. So long as the scores are internally consistent, they serve us well in describing the cohesion of preferences within parties and the distance between them. Indeed, Poole and Rosenthal (1997) and Londregan (2000) argue that any bias in NOMINATE scores is minimized by pooling a large sample of legislators.[8]

Still, it would be useful to be able to measure the strategic actions of parties while holding constant the preferences of individual legislators. Since each Congress can be separated into two years with nearly identical membership, we can measure the year-to-year changes in Party Unity that occur between elections. Figure 6.6 shows that within congresses, changes in Party Unity by one party are to a large extent matched by the other party. With only minimal change in membership (and thus in ideological preferences), the correlation of 0.52 between the changes in the two parties' unity levels is a further indicator of parties tightening and relaxing their pressure on members in response to their opposition. This pattern will remain evident when we test our multivariate models.

In our more complete models of Party Unity over time, we will include the CPG measures of preferences as well as measures of opposition Unity. To account for hypothesis 6.3, we include *Democratic Size*, measured as a percentage of the chamber seats and based on opening-day tallies obtained from clerkweb.house.gov and www.senate.gov.

One interesting possible counterexplanation for the close relationship between the two parties' levels of unity is the legislative agenda. It is possible that the observed variation in party unity is actually the product of significant shifts in the legislative agenda—that is, items entering and exiting the legislative agenda might affect the levels of unity for both parties and make it appear as though the unity levels of the two parties are causing each other. This is an interesting challenge, and one worth testing. For one, we find that the relationships in the data are reasonably stable over time—that is, the two parties' unity levels move in tandem regard-

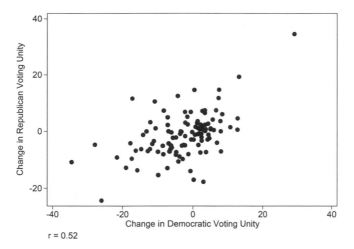

FIGURE 6.6. Within-Congress changes in voting unity: Second-year unity minus first-year unity

less of the agenda. In addition, we included a variable, *Democratic Majority*, for shifts in party control in each chamber. This variable is coded 1 for years in which the Democrats became the majority party, "−1" for the first year of Republican control, and zero otherwise. To be sure, this is an imprecise measure of issue variation, but it can account for the possibility that when new majorities enter with new agendas, each party may be temporarily cohesive with renewed purpose.

Turning back to the variance in unity over time, we should review our key assertions for the parties' movement. Put most simply, there are costs to be paid for being either too unified or not unified enough. To be too unified risks pulling legislators away from their constituents, risks having them seem "out of touch" with voters, and potentially risks their chances of reelection. To be not unified enough can be costly if it means losing important legislative battles to the opposition. These losses are costly to the extent that they result in less preferred policy outcomes, but they are also costly in the collective loss of reputation for the party.

Thus parties are forever moving toward the equilibrium of being just unified enough. Since "just enough" depends on the ever-shifting agenda and the votes of hundreds of legislators over many issues, levels of unity are always dynamic, and the two parties will adjust and readjust to each other's relative strengths. This should result in patterns of strategic interaction between the parties in Congress.

6.3 Models of Partisan Interaction and Party Unity in Congress

Studying the interactive behavior of parties requires the use of data over time, most importantly the levels of Party Unity by year from 1789 to 2010. Testing hypothesis 6.1 means regressing Democratic Party Unity on Republican Party Unity.[9] Hypothesis 6.2 states that parties will adjust to each other's level of unity over time by reducing differences between them. This type of equilibrium relationship over time can be tested using cointegration and error correction techniques (Banerjee et al. 1993; Clarke and Lebo 2003).[10] We test our two main hypotheses while controlling for legislators' preferences—the key aspects of CPG. We also test hypothesis 6.3 to see if Party Unity does vary with strategic need and the relative size of the parties. Since we believe that each of the two parties responds to the other, we have two dependent variables that simultaneously affect each other. Hence, for each chamber, we simultaneously estimate the determinants of both Democratic Unity and Republican Unity.[11]

To test whether our results were driven by our use of NOMINATE measures, we also estimated our equations for shorter time spans using Americans for Democratic Action vote scores and preference scores based only on lopsided votes (see Snyder and Groseclose 2000). These replications confirmed our findings that Party Unity is not simply a function of legislators' preferences—strategic interaction is a key factor. We also confirm this by testing our theory on those votes that require a simple majority to win, on those that pit most members of one party against most of the opposing party, and by reconfiguring our data to reflect majority-minority competition rather than Democrat-Republican competition.

Tables 6.1 and 6.2 show the results of our time series models explaining *Democratic* and *Republican Unity* in the House and Senate, respectively.[12] Our independent variables in each model are opposition-party unity, an error correction mechanism (ECM),[13] *Democratic Size*, a dummy variable for new Democratic majorities, measures of the ideological distance between the parties in each of the two NOMINATE dimensions, and measures for *Democratic Cohesion* (*Republican Cohesion* in the Republican equations) in the two dimensions.[14] In two of the equations, we add opposition-party cohesion as an explanatory variable.[15] We explain the models for the House and Senate together.

Our most important finding is the strong support for hypothesis 6.1—Republican behavior is a strong determinant of *Democratic Unity* and vice versa. Figures 6.7 and 6.8 demonstrate clearly that in both the

TABLE 6.1. **Strategic party voting in the House, 1789–2010: Model of yearly data**

Independent variable	Dependent variable: Democrats			Dependent variable: Republicans		
	Coef.	(se)	p-value	Coef.	(se)	p-value
Constant	0.39	(0.46)	0.40	0.17	(0.43)	0.40
Opposition Unity	0.82	(0.06)	0.00	0.70	(0.05)	0.00
ECM$_{t-1}$*	−0.31	(0.06)	0.00	−0.28	(0.06)	0.00
Democratic Size	−0.45	(0.08)	0.00	0.50	(0.08)	0.00
New Majority	1.83	(1.58)	0.12	−3.49	(1.47)	0.01
Ideological Distance N. 1st	−10.67	(11.11)	0.66	20.81	(10.44)	0.02
Ideological Distance N. 2nd	−8.84	(4.80)	0.94	9.27	(4.60)	0.02
Intraparty Cohesion NOMINATE 1	−4.80	(23.57)	0.42	−39.36	(18.97)	0.02
Intraparty Cohesion NOMINATE 2	−21.60	(16.58)	0.10	14.65	(15.32)	0.34
Intraparty Cohesion NOMINATE 2$_{t-1}$	−76.73	(16.80)	0.00	−5.08	(13.24)	0.35
Party Unity$_{t-2}$	0.09	(0.05)	0.07	—		—
Opposition Party Cohesion Nominate 2$_{t-1}$	—		—	61.03	(16.23)	0.00
Durbin Watson Statistic		1.99			2.05	
Centered R^2		0.45			0.35	
S.E.E.		7.08			6.69	
N = 220						

Note: p-values are based on one-tailed tests.
* ECM is the fractional error correction mechanism.

House and Senate and for both Democrats and Republicans, *opposition unity is the strongest determinant of Party Unity*. Indeed, it is of far greater importance than any measure of individual preferences. As these figures show, holding all else equal, when the opposition's unity level moves from its fifth percentile value to its median value, House Democrats' Unity jumps 20.5 percent, House Republicans' 23.5 percent, Senate Democrats' 11.6 percent, and Senate Republicans' 14.8 percent. Table 6.1 shows that in the House, when Republican (Democrat) Unity goes up by 1 percent, the Democrats (Republicans) counter with a 0.816 percent (0.701 percent) increase. These effects are clearly statistically significant ($p < .001$). In the Senate, the effects are a bit lower, 0.532 for Democrats and 0.598 for Republicans, but are still substantial ($p < .001$) and the largest among our set of independent variables. Hence legislators who are confronted with a more unified opposition party will more frequently forgo their induced preferences on roll call votes to help their party achieve legislative victories. Of course, this works in both directions. Seeing a less unified op-

TABLE 6.2. **Strategic party voting in the Senate, 1789–2010: Model of yearly data**

Independent variable	Democrats			Republicans		
	Coef.	(se)	p	Coef.	(se)	p
Constant	0.10	(0.45)	0.82	0.80	(0.50)	0.11
Opposition Unity	0.53	(0.05)	0.00	0.60	(0.06)	0.00
ECM_{t-1}*	−0.47	(0.09)	0.00	−0.20	(0.06)	0.00
Democratic Size	−0.42	(0.08)	0.00	0.34	(0.09)	0.00
New Majority	5.08	(1.43)	0.00	−3.79	(1.62)	0.01
Ideological Distance N. 1st	3.96	(6.93)	0.28	6.33	(7.78)	0.21
Ideological Distance N. 1st$_{t-2}$	13.47	(6.47)	0.02	—		—
Ideological Distance N. 2nd	1.86	(4.36)	0.34	−4.17	(4.69)	0.38
Intra-party Cohesion NOMINATE 1	−11.45	(18.08)	0.26	−100.30	(20.98)	0.00
Intra-party Cohesion NOMINATE 2	−40.45	(10.81)	0.00	−38.17	(12.67)	0.00
Opposition Party Cohesion NOMINATE 2	36.13	(10.88)	0.00	—		—
Party Unity$_{t-1}$	0.12	(0.08)	0.12	—		—
Party Unity$_{t-2}$	0.09	(0.05)	0.08	—		
Durbin-Watson Statistic		2.05			2.02	
Centered R^2		0.42			0.37	
S.E.E.		6.62			7.24	
$N = 220$						

Note: p-values are based on one-tailed tests.
*ECM is the fractional error correction mechanism.

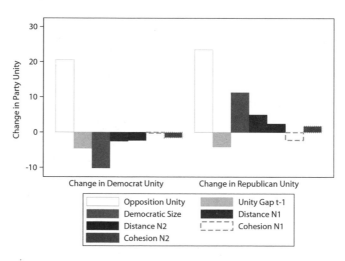

FIGURE 6.7. Effects of independent variables: Moving from fifth percentile to median, House

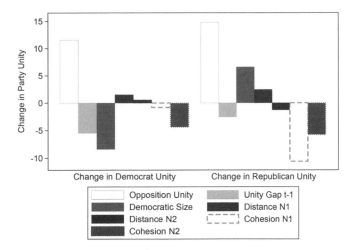

FIGURE 6.8. Effects of independent variables: Moving from fifth percentile to median, Senate

position, legislators are relatively freer to break from their party if it helps them get reelected.

As predicted by hypothesis 6.2, legislators look for cues for their strategic behavior not only from this year's opposition but also from the relative influence of the parties in the previous year. This action-reaction behavior ensures that the unity levels of the parties rise and fall to meet one another in a long-run equilibrium. This is apparent in two ways. First, tests for fractional cointegration suggest that the difference between the unity levels of the two parties naturally tends to some consistent level—the parties cannot remain apart indefinitely.[16] Thus any widening of the unity gap between the parties is quickly erased by strategic party behavior.

ECMs estimate the speed with which this gap is closed and thereby test hypothesis 6.2. To be sure, in both the House and Senate, the ECM coefficients are statistically significant. While error correction is strong for both parties in both chambers, it is noticeably stronger for Senate Democrats—evident since the ECM coefficient is more negative for Senate Democrats (-0.468) than it is for Senate Republicans (-0.203), House Democrats (-0.308), or House Republicans (-0.275).[17] This means that when the unity of the two parties strays from equilibrium, 46.8 percent of the gap is corrected in the first year by Senate Democrats, for example, and 46.8 percent of the remaining gap will subsequently be corrected by them in each following year. The Senate's smaller size and the leeway afforded by longer terms may explain why senators can adapt to the opposition more quickly than their House counterparts. But it is not clear why Democrats would be more active gap-closers than Republicans in both chambers.

Other results of these models are as expected. *Democratic Size* has a large negative impact on *Democratic Unity* and a large positive impact on *Republican Unity*. This supports the claim that party unity is costly and decreases when larger party size makes it easier to win without pressuring party members. As figures 6.7 and 6.8 demonstrate, with one exception, *Democratic Size* is the second-strongest independent variable in terms of effect size for both chambers. Only among Senate Republicans is this effect (marginally) below that of any of the NOMINATE variables.

We find some support for the classic claims of the CPG model with each of the four key CPG variables—distance in the first and second dimensions and cohesion in the first and second dimensions—passing statistical significance (.05 level) in at least one of tables 6.1 and 6.2's four equations. In the House, as the parties' preferences separate, Republicans increase their level of unity—$\beta = 20.812$ ($p = 0.023$) and $\beta = 9.266$ ($p = 0.022$) for the first and second dimensions of NOMINATE, respectively. Likewise, Senate Democrats increase their unity as the interparty distance of the first dimension grows (at $t - 2, \beta = 13.473, p = 0.018$).[18]

We also find a link between our measure of Cohesion—the standard deviation of members' scores in each year—and Party Unity; less variation in preferences leads to higher unity. We find this in the House where there are significant effects for Cohesion in the second dimension of NOMINATE (lagged) on Democratic Unity ($p < .001$) and for first-dimension Cohesion on Republican Unity ($p = 0.019$). As shown in the last two bars on each side of figures 6.7 and 6.8, the Cohesion variables are most relevant for Republicans in the Senate ($p < .001$). The voting Unity of Senate Democrats is likewise affected by Cohesion with effects in the second dimension ($p < .001$). This is consistent with Rohde's (1991) arguments regarding the increased homogeneity of the Democratic Party since 1970 due to the realignment of Southern districts.

Because we view the SPG model as an expansion of the CPG model, it is also useful to test for the added value of the SPG variables. Since the CPG model is nested within the SPG model, we can create the CPG model by setting the parameters for opposition Unity, Democratic Size, and the ECM to zero. Then, by testing the joint significance of those variables in the full model and finding strong evidence of their efficacy ($p <$

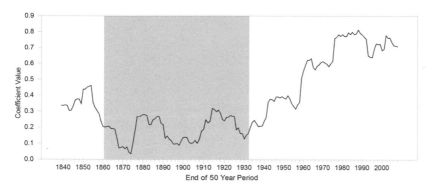

FIGURE 6.9. Effect of Republican unity on Democratic unity, US House: Fifty-year periods

.000001) in each of the four equations, we establish that the SPG model empirically *encompasses* the CPG model (Davidson and MacKinnon 1993).[19] That is, the SPG model explains everything the CPG model explains, plus additional variance in party unity over time. Overall, there is strong support for our strategic party hypotheses even when tested alongside measures of party preferences.[20]

One further issue is the consistency of our story over time. With more than two hundred years of data, do we see these relationships consistently present? Figure 6.9 shows the results of moving windows regressions— regressions of fifty years of data at a time ending in the year on the *x*-axis. Several factors are noteworthy in the figure. For one, the positive impact of opposition unity is *always* present, no matter which fifty years of data are used. Second, a low point in the action-reaction relationship between the parties occurs where we would expect, in the period that includes both the 1820s and the post–Civil War years. Third, the level of strategic interaction has entered a new era over the last few decades and presently sits near its historic high.[21]

Additional Models

Just to be sure that our results are not dependent on our particular choice of variables or models, we present some alternatives in this section. To begin, instead of looking at party unity on all party votes, we looked at unity across the smaller set of party votes that required a simple majority for passage. This excludes votes such as veto overrides, constitutional amendments, motions to suspend the rules, and cloture votes in the Senate and allows for the possibility that partisanship may be more intense on these votes (because it is cheap to do so when the outcome is not in doubt) or less intense (because cooperation is necessary to achieve a threshold that is typically larger than the majority party's chamber share). As with the wider set of votes, here we find strong and significant strategic interaction in both the House and Senate (see the online appendix figure A.6.1 for these results and others that follow).

Next, since the use of NOMINATE scores to account for legislator preferences is not uncontroversial, we try some alternatives. NOMINATE scores are calculated using roll call votes that are influenced by a combination of individual-, partisan-, and constituency-level factors and are thus not strictly a measure of a legislator's underlying ideology. One attempt to overcome this problem is Snyder and Groseclose's (2000) estimates of revealed preferences on lopsided votes in the House. Rather than looking at all roll calls, Snyder and Groseclose use this set of votes because they are the ones where outside influences, including those of the party, should be weakest. Thus an estimate of legislators' preferences based on these votes may be a more sincere measure of legislators' preferences. We substitute variables based on lopsided votes for our median-to-median distances and party cohesion for the House during the period they are available, 1868–1998. When this is done, the key relationship appears even stronger than with our standard data. And our strategic hypothesis holds when we forgo NOMINATE altogether and use Americans for Democratic Action (ADA) scores instead for the years 1947–2000 (ADA-H for the House and ADA-S for the Senate).

Lastly, to what extent, if any, are our findings the results of our choice to study the long-term trends of parties as Democrats versus Republicans as opposed to majorities versus minorities? Perhaps the strategic interaction of parties would appear different if we rethink our model in terms of majority-minority dynamics. To check this, we realign our data so that continuous strings of variables are created for the majority and minority parties. This means that each series contains within it data from each party. As the right-hand side of figure A.6.1 indicates, for both the House (Maj. vs. Min H) and Senate (Maj. vs. Min S), our key results are largely the same when we reorganize our data this way. In the complete models (see tables A.6.4 and A.6.5 of the online appendix), opposition unity proves again to be the most important predictor of both *Majority* and *Minority Unity* in both the House and Senate.

Two interesting findings in majority-minority models are worth further discussion. First, the coefficients on the ECMs are of roughly the same size in both chambers of Congress. This tells us that the majority party responds to disequilibrium in party unity to the same extent as the minority party—that is, gaps in the level of unity between the two parties will be closed by both sides. Of course, a united majority party forces the minority to become more unified to avoid losing every battle. But a minority party that is more unified than the majority also forces that majority to increase its unity to avoid legislative losses. In doing so, it forces members of the majority to take risks with their constituents for the sake of their party.

A second point is the impact of a new majority. In both chambers, the same pattern occurs—a new majority will have a lower level of unity than the outgoing majority, and a new minority will have a higher level of unity than the outgoing minority. This points to the fact that prior to losing their majority status, parties tend to have an excess of unity; this puts electoral pressure on the majority members and contributes to the loss of majority status. As well, minorities with relatively higher levels of unity can gain the majority by forcing the majority into this cross pressuring and by winning legislative battles in the minority.

How does our analysis of congressional partisanship help us understand the resurgence of congressional parties over the last five decades? The next section translates the insights of our statistical analysis into a synopsis of party development over this era. In particular, we focus on how competition—not voters, not legislators' preferences—has been a driving force behind the development of party organization and the gradually tightening bonds of party loyalty on the floors of the House and Senate.

6.4 The Rise of the Red and Blue Congress

Sixty years ago, scholars lamented the disorganized state of parties in Congress and proposed reforms to ensure that political parties were distinct and powerful (APSA Committee on Political Parties 1950). Today, the same association of political scientists laments the effect of partisan polarization on congressional decision making (Mansbridge and Martin 2013; see also Mann and Ornstein 2012). What factors explain the rise of a highly partisan Congress over the last five decades?

The classic answer of Rohde (1991, 46–47) is that the legislators' constituencies polarized first. The 1964 Civil Rights Act and 1965 Voting Rights Act triggered a realignment of the South to the Republican Party and the Northeast to the Democratic Party. As the voter bases of each party became more cohesive, they began to elect more conservative Republicans and liberal Democrats to Congress. These two trends—more extreme party bases and increasing disagreement between the two major parties—are the "conditions" in CPG. The voluminous literature on partisan polarization has suggested several other possible sources, including income polarization (McCarty et al. 2006), media coverage of politics (Levendusky 2013; Prior 2007; but see Arceneaux and Johnson 2013), and polarization of the politically engaged segment of the public (Abramowitz 2010; Hetherington 2001). Our contribution to this conversation is to highlight the role of partisan *competition* as an explanation for the increase in congressional partisanship: legislators deciding they want a stronger, more united party even when their own constituencies and operative policy views were diverse.

The rest of this chapter does two things. First, it details the sequence of *congressional* polarization relative to the American general public. This helps us parse our search for the root cause(s) of partisanship. We find that both chambers of Congress begin to polarize in the early 1970s, while partisanship in the general public lags behind by more than a decade. This helps us exclude several proposed causes of congressional partisanship. We conclude this section with a brief discussion of what we think are the root causes of polarization. Second, this chapter traces the expansion of congressional party influence over the last five decades and describes how each party uses these expanded powers to compete with the opposing party.

6.4.1 The Seeds of Polarization

Every story has a beginning. While our focus is on competition between parties as a major contributing factor to congressional partisanship, we do not think that legislators spontaneously decided to start acting like partisans. Indeed, our theory assumes that delegating power to parties is costly, so legislators would only do so to serve a purpose. And the increasing motivation for legislators to delegate to parties probably starts somewhere outside the legislative chamber.

A full analysis of the evolution of political parties in the mid-twentieth century is outside the scope of this book. We are persuaded, however, by

John Aldrich's (2011) account of the evolution of party "activists" as a major development in party history. For much of the first half of the twentieth century, many of the people who were active in party organizations and campaigns did so with the hope of material gain—jobs and contracts. As the federal workforce gradually became a professional civil service during the decades following the 1883 Pendleton Act (Skowronek 1982) and city machines faded away, politicians became unable to fulfill the expectations of these "party regulars." Instead, policy-seeking "amateurs" became the backbone of campaigns and party organization (Wilson 1962). These activists included donors who gave funds to candidates to advance their partisan and policy goals.

This shift had three consequences. First, as Aldrich notes, as the pool of activists became more issue-oriented, parties and candidates had to be more programmatic to appeal to them. The APSA report "Toward a More Responsible Two-Party System" channels the lament of frustrated amateurs of the late 1940s who observed that parties' campaign pledges were not worth the paper they were written on. Parties inside and outside of Congress began a *very* slow process of reforming their rules and behavior to articulate distinct policy promises and follow through on them. In response, activists began to exit, enter, and transfer between parties based on the clusters of policies each party advocated. Aldrich (2011, 164; figure 6.5) demonstrates that the ideological differences between Republican and Democratic Party activists—especially donors—became much more distinct between 1972 and 2008. This increased each party's incentive to respond to the opposing party's efforts, while increasing the "floor" of expected partisan loyalty.

Second, the polarization of party activists caused a growing political challenge for members of Congress. We show below that voter partisanship did not increase significantly until the 1990s, decades after activists began to sort themselves between parties. In the vocabulary of Fenno (1978), legislators' personal and primary constituencies (and we would add their *financial* constituencies) were increasingly different from their reelection constituencies. For members of both parties, this meant that there were a number of issues on which their different constituencies disagreed strongly, including well-known "wedge" issues like race-balancing busing, prayer in school, a constitutional amendment to ban abortions, or same-sex marriage.

Third, as Aldrich notes (2011, 188), issue-oriented activists may not expect nor reward policy compromise. Since their livelihoods are not at stake, they can afford to be farsighted and wait for the day when their most preferred policies are implemented. They may prefer that their allies in Congress shun compromises and incremental gains that would obscure the differences between parties on a key issue and thereby make transformational change *less* likely. The recent "Tea Party" faction is a particularly strong manifestation of this logic, but its traces are scattered throughout congressional elections and legislative research in the form of interest-group ratings based on roll call votes like the Americans for Democratic Action scores that date back to the 1940s. These organized groups evaluate legislators based on their positions, not their accomplishments, and legislators who seek the support of these groups have an incentive to take the "correct" positions whatever the consequences. This creates a second powerful reason for legislators to pay renewed attention to the legislative agenda to avoid votes that make them choose among party activists, interest groups, and centrist voters in their districts.

6.4.2 The Rise of Congressional Partisanship

Congressional partisanship began to increase in the early 1970s in both the US House and Senate. Figure 6.10 illustrates the party unity gap between the two parties in the US House and Senate. This is the absolute difference between average party unity among Republicans and the average defection rate (100 – party unity score) among Democrats and provides a view of legislative polarization in roll call behavior.

What is first noticeable is that both chambers seem to follow the same overall pattern and even share many of the same idiosyncratic shifts— the simple correlation between the two statistics is .95. Second, there is a similar historical pattern across both chambers: a period of medium partisanship (~55 percent gap) during the 1950s and early 1960s, followed by a period of low partisanship lasting from about 1967 to 1978, and then ever-increasing partisanship from 1979 to the present.

Third, partisanship in both chambers of Congress increased *before* their constituencies became more partisan. Figure 6.11 plots the partisan difference in the constituencies of Republican and Democratic members of the House and Senate. For each state and House district, we (1) measured the Republican share of the two-party presidential vote, (2) calculated the average Republican vote share for districts represented by (a) House Republicans and (b) House Democrats and states represented by (c) Senate Republicans and (d) Senate Democrats. Last, we (3) mea-

FIGURE 6.10. Party unity gap in the US House and Senate

sured the absolute difference between House Republicans and Democrats (figure 6.11A) and between Senate Republicans and Democrats
(figure 6.11B). For example, the average vote for 2012 Republican presidential candidate Mitt Romney was 59.32 percent in House districts won
by Republicans and 33.54 percent in Democratic districts. So for the 113th
Congress (2013–14), this interparty difference is 25.78 percent—the largest gap in this period.

In both chambers, electoral differences decrease from the 1940s (Senate) and 1950s (House) until the 1990s, then increase sharply after 1992.
This contrasts with the patterns of increasing legislative partisanship
shown in figure 6.10. Taken together, this pattern suggests that institutional reforms to strengthen congressional parties (discussed below) and
the increased partisanship in roll call voting *preceded* constituency polarization. The partisanship of congressional districts did not "catch up"
to the partisan behavior of House and Senate members until the early
1990s—more than a full decade after the resurgence of congressional partisanship began.

This is somewhat consistent with Bartels (2000), who finds that voters'
party identification and party voting in presidential elections reached its
nadir in 1972 and increased steadily afterward, while the correlation of

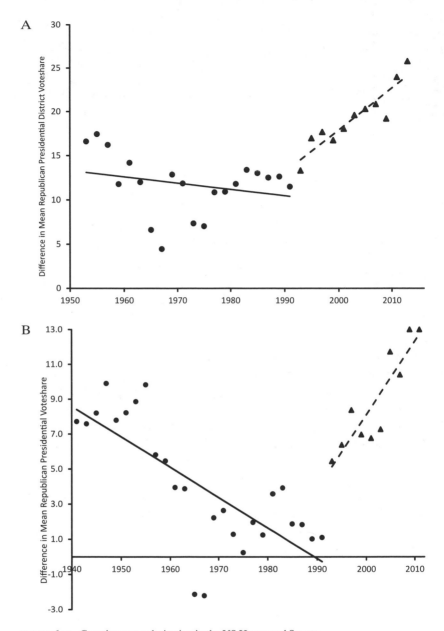

FIGURE 6.11. Constituency polarization in the US House and Senate
A, House; *B*, Senate

party affiliation and congressional voting reached its low point in 1978. Hetherington (2001) finds that partisan polarization of the electorate was a top-down process, with congressional partisanship increasing the partisanship of high-information constituents and, subsequently, the rest of the voting population. For this reason, Jacobson (2007) estimates that half of congressional polarization (measured in DW-NOMINATE scores) is *not* explained by electoral forces. The US Congress became partisan first, and then the general public followed.

6.4.3 Implications for Research on Congressional Partisanship

Given these patterns, we can safely downplay the role of individual legislators (such as Newt Gingrich), events (such as the 1985 dispute over the Eighth District of Indiana), or rules changes (such as the use of restricted special rules in the House) specific to a single chamber as *primary* causes of congressional partisanship. While these may have some minor influence on how legislators vote or might crystallize shifts in strategy in response to underlying changes in the political climate, it seems unlikely that they would have significant and nearly identical effects across both chambers.

Similarly, we can discount the decennial process of redrawing the boundaries of House districts as a primary source of partisanship. This is a common argument in the popular media, with some research supporting the notion that House districts are drawn to protect incumbents and, consequently, to make legislators more responsive to their primary electorate than their general electorate. Other scholars argue convincingly, however, that Americans are "sorting" into communities with similar political preferences, so the net effect of district boundary-drawing per se is minimal (Levendusky 2009; McCarty et al. 2006; but see Carson et al. 2007). For us, the comparison of House and Senate partisanship gives a further reason to discount the role of redistricting: Senate partisanship parallels House partisanship, but Senate constituencies (states) have constant boundaries.

Third, we can discount the popular notion that presidential persuasion can arrest or reverse the trend toward increasing congressional partisanship. American voters seem to hope—and perhaps expect—that their president will transform Congress and Washington, DC, into nonpartisan problem-solving zones. President Clinton promised to unite the two parties in a "third way" of governance, George W. Bush promised to be "a uniter, not a divider," and Barack Obama gained national attention in

2004 at the Democratic National Convention by saying: "There is not a liberal America and a conservative America—there is the United States of America. There is not a black America and a white America and Latino America and Asian America—there's the United States of America." During their presidencies, congressional partisanship soared to levels not seen in a century. Indeed, presidential involvement in an issue or vote only serves to make it *more* partisan (Lee 2009). By now, we can safely discount the "great president" theory of congressional bipartisanship.

6.5 The Evolution of Modern Congressional Parties

How and why did Congress become more partisan over the last five decades? This section provides an SPG perspective on this time period. We observe that party competition propelled the 1970s congresses to strengthen their institutional effectiveness and empower party leaders, laying the foundation for increasing contestation over the agenda as both parties sought to use the power *of* Congress to gain power *in* Congress.[22]

6.5.1 The Reemergence of Congressional Parties, 1969 to 1980

We begin our account at the nadir. Congressional parties reached their weakest point in the late 1960s. The 1968 election saw the candidacy of George Wallace as well as Nixon's "Southern strategy"—two events that, at the *presidential* level, signaled an end of the Democratic solid South. Subsequently, Southern white conservatives were increasingly likely to vote for the Republican Party and the Southern Democrats who represented them in Congress were increasingly likely to find their best chances of reelection to be in bucking their party. Thus the Democratic Party would remain the majority party in both chambers until 1980, but its caucuses included a significant number of legislators who considered party loyalty much more costly than beneficial.

The 1968 election also created an organizational challenge for the Democratic leadership. On May 25, 1969, the Senate Democratic Caucus convened to assess its situation. For the first time in eight years, they were without a Democratic president to set a policy agenda or lead the Democratic side of the political debate. The stakes of this discussion were high: "What was involved in what we did and how we did it in the Senate . . . was not only the future of the Democratic Majority in the Senate but also, in significant degree, that of the Democratic Party in the nation" ("Minutes of the Democratic Conference, May 20, 1969," 2). The Democrats agreed that the Caucus's Policy Committee should be empowered to identify a Democratic policy agenda so that the collective positions of the party would be known to all. This agenda was nonbinding: "Members will continue to vote on the issues on the basis of their conscience and wisdom," but by articulating a joint agenda, the caucus could "re-introduce among the Democratic members of the Senate some of the unifying party cement which was formerly supplied by a Democratic President in the White House (ibid., 3)." The meeting concluded with a report from Daniel Inouye (D-HI), the chair of the Democratic Senatorial Campaign Committee, who reviewed their electoral challenges in the 1970 cycle and an upcoming fundraising dinner, warning, "If you want to stay in the Majority Party . . . you had better get with it. If we don't gross $1 million with this dinner, we don't deserve to be members of the majority party (ibid., 10)."

Congressional Democrats also worked to reestablish the autonomy and effectiveness of the legislative branch. The Legislative Reorganization Act of 1970—passed with Republican support—increased the transparency of committee and floor proceedings, including a provision for recorded votes when the House was deliberating bills as the Committee of the Whole. In practical terms, that meant that it would be possible for members to get roll call votes on their amendments even if the amendment was defeated (Zelizer 2004, 126–28). The War Powers Act of 1973 followed, passed over President Nixon's veto with the aid of Republican votes, and was intended to guarantee Congress more influence on military deployments. Finally, the Budget and Impoundment Control Act of 1974 institutionalized Congress's role in the budget process and curtailed the practice of presidential "impoundment" of funds. Taken together, these measures were intended to improve institutional capacity, but this coincided with the interests of the party that held a majority in both chambers.

In addition, Democratic leaders began addressing the lost opportunities of their healthy majorities—for example, with a comfortable majority of 56 percent of House seats, Democrats' unity level was 58 percent in 1972. In particular, a faction of the House Democratic Party known as the Democratic Study Group worked during the 1970s to overhaul the rules of its party, with one of their primary aims being to empower party leaders and increase committee chairs' accountability to the party caucus (Rohde 1991). One key reform was the decision that the Democratic Caucus should elect all committee chairs using a secret ballot. On the day of that reform's passage, Speaker Carl Albert said, "The Seniority system—for sixty-two years the path to legislative domination—died that day." In its place was left a party leadership and caucus that both had expanded powers over individual members.[23] Notably, however, these party-strengthening reforms were not enacted by parties meeting the "conditions" of CPG theory. They were enacted out of Democratic frustration with their high levels of disunity and not as the result of internal party homogeneity or division between the parties. And while Rohde (1991) argues that the primary motive of Democratic Study Group reformers was to facilitate the passage of liberal legislation, John Wright (2000) notes that some of the 1970s committee reforms made it easier for junior legislators to raise funds, suggesting that these reforms may have been motivated by legislators' electoral goals.

Meanwhile, in 1975, the Senate revised its cloture rule so that three-fifths of all senators could bring major legislation to a vote. Senators continued to refine their cloture rule and further restrict obstruction so that by 1980 the cloture process was fairly effective. This was a double-edged reform: on the one hand, the reforms helped institutionalize the Senate filibuster so that senators and observers increasingly considered supermajority rule to be the norm of the Senate (Koger 2010). On the other hand, the fixed sixty-vote threshold set an attainable goal for Senate majority parties: as long as they could unite their members and attract the support of minority-party moderates, the Senate could be a productive legislature.

The election of Jimmy Carter brought back a united Democratic government and, in the wake of Watergate, gave the Democrats a chance to use the newly reformed Congress to consolidate a long-term majority among the American electorate. This opportunity was squandered as congressional Democrats failed to cooperate with President Carter to unite on a popular agenda. Rather than giving the electorate legislative progress with which to evaluate them, the Democrats left themselves to be judged on their partisanship and the infighting between Congress and the Carter administration. In addition, House Republicans became adept at using their new prerogative to obtain recorded votes on amendments. This forced Democrats to choose sides between key subconstituencies on hot-button "wedge" issues such as school prayer or race-conscious busing plans and to do so on the record. In response, House Democrats urged the Rules Committee to propose more restrictive "special rules" so that the amending process was less chaotic and less politically hazardous (Smith 1989, 40–42).

6.5.2 Divided Government, 1981–92

Ronald Reagan's 1980 victory brought with it a new Republican majority in the Senate and a thirty-three-seat Republican gain in the House. All that stood between Reagan and the implementation of his conservative agenda was the House Democratic majority. President Reagan famously shepherded his 1981 tax-cut package through the House by "going public" to arouse public interest in the bill and convince conservative Democrats that voting against Reagan's plan could cost them their jobs (Kernell 2006). Otherwise, however, the postreform House gave tremendous power to Speaker Tip O'Neill, and Speaker O'Neill tempered the House Democrats' legislative agenda to protect the conservative wing of his caucus—a set of members that the Democrats needed to retain the majority. As described in John Farrell's biography of him (2002, 404): "O'Neill defended the 40-odd conservative-democrats from charges that they should be disciplined for failing to toe the party line. 'Let's forget about punishment or anything of that nature. I have seen Congresses when we needed those 40 . . . They are in our party, and there is room for everybody in our party, and always remember that. . . . They have to think, too, of the next election.'" Even with this approach, O'Neill still corralled votes to push issues like a national holiday in honor of Martin Luther King Jr. The House Democrats fought the battles of the 1980s by increasing their level of voting unity steadily over the course of Reagan's two terms. In 1981, Democratic voting unity stood at 65 percent, but by 1988 it had risen to 82 percent, its highest since the first year of the Sixtieth Congress back in 1907.

House Speaker Jim Wright (D-TX) followed O'Neill with a more aggressive agenda. Working with the House Democratic Caucus, Wright pushed legislation on clean water, deficit reduction, highway spending, trade, welfare reform, and a farm bill (Sinclair 1995, 271–72). Wright was targeted by ethics charges filed by Newt Gingrich (R-GA) in 1988. Gingrich would soon win a critical election for House Republican whip over Tom Madigan (R-IL) in 1989, setting the tone for a more confrontational minority party. When Wright resigned in June 1989 and Tom Foley (D-WA) took over the Speakership, he inherited a similarly ambitious agenda for the 101st Congress but nonetheless faced criticism that Democratic leaders were not being aggressive enough (Sinclair 1995, 274), suggesting a high "grievance" component to the Democrats' calculations. From 1989 to 1992, the congressional Democrats highlighted contrasts between the two parties by sending popular legislation to President George H. W. Bush to force him to publicly veto the bills. This included legislation to raise the minimum wage, allow government workers to be more involved in politics, guarantee family and medical leave (twice), and allow citizens to register to vote when they receive a driver's license or other government benefits. This veto baiting (Gilmour 1995) provided the party with a set of election issues for the 1992 presidential election.

With Bill Clinton in office, Republicans in the 103rd Congress set out to finally end the decades they had spent as the House minority. Their chief weapon in doing so was to limit their members' voting with the opposition and thereby reduce the Democrats' ability to form winning coalitions (Fenno 1997). In 1994, Republican unity on party votes reached 75 percent—the highest of their forty years in the minority (see figure 6.1 to see the uptick). This was not a unilateral shift, however, but a response to the partisanship of the Democratic majority of the previous three congresses—the most unified House Democrats since the Speakership of Joseph Cannon in 1911. As Republican unity surged, many House Democrats faced difficult choices between the failure of major Democratic agenda items and the preferences of their own constituencies on issues like taxes, trade, and guns. In the 1994 elections, Republicans targeted Democrats who provided the margin of victory on these close House votes, and aided by a slow economy and low presidential approval, the Republicans gained seventy-three seats and a majority of the House.

6.5.3 The Republican Congress, 1995–2006

After the 1994 election, Republican unity increased even more, peaking at 84 percent in 1995 as they sought to enact their ambitious election promises. Over the next four years, the two parties' voting scores converged as Republicans moderated slightly while Democrats sought to match the Republicans by increasing their unity from 68 percent in 1995 to 80 percent by 2000. In the Senate, the new Republican majority ratcheted up party unity in the 104th Congress to its highest level (81 percent) in one hundred years. The Senate Democrats countered in the 105th Congress with their highest level of unity in nearly ninety years and by the 106th Congress were the most unified (83 percent) they had been in their history as a party. This unity was accelerated by party reforms that gave House Republican leaders more influence on committee assignments and—after

Mark Hatfield's (R-OR) vote helped defeat a balanced-budget amendment in the Senate—that committed the Senate Republicans to formulating a party agenda all party leaders were expected to support.

Early on, the Republicans attempted to enact a set of conservative bills proposed in the House Republicans' campaign agenda, the Contract with America. The Republicans sought to bundle a number of these proposals into an omnibus budget reconciliation bill with a debt limit increase and the fiscal year 1996 appropriations bills, forcing President Clinton to choose between accepting the Republicans' "take it or leave it" offer or taking the blame for a government shutdown and debt default. Clinton's veto of this bill set off a high-stakes public-relations battle that resulted in a Democratic victory. The Republicans relented, reopened the government, raised the debt limit, and spent the rest of 1996 working with Clinton to enact major legislation on telecommunications, terrorism, and immigration. Their election-year agenda included two "veto bait" bills on welfare reform and same-sex marriage. Clinton did not take the bait, allowing both bills to become law. Once Clinton and the congressional Republicans were reelected in 1996, they cut a budget deal and avoided further scuffles over appropriations.

Despite President George W. Bush's promise to bring the congressional parties together, they continued to ratchet up their levels of voting unity during his presidency. For the Republicans, unity was essential to push through an early agenda of a $1.35 trillion tax cut in 2001 (with another $550 billion in 2003), a major change in federal education policy, and an expansion of Medicare prescription drug coverage in 2003. Mann and Ornstein (2006, 1–6) detail the extraordinary passage of the Medicare bill, which required party leaders to use all their power—including holding a roll call vote open for three hours in the middle of the night—to obtain the votes for passage.

Congressional Republicans worked hardest on education and health care initiatives that are hard to describe as strictly conservative. Further, the Bush tax cuts of 2001 and 2003 were not offset by reductions in social welfare or other government spending. At the same time, the Republican-dominated Congress routinely enacted appropriations bills that increased discretionary spending faster than the rate of inflation while budget deficits increased. Thus the Republican agenda traded ideological consistency for an electoral strategy of rewarding base supporters and middle-class voters with tax cuts, buying the support of senior citizens with Medicare expansion, and reaching out to swing voters with support for education and other domestic programs.

Just as a president committed to uniting the two parties did not staunch partisanship in Congress, the shock of massive terrorist attacks on September 11, 2001, also did not have long-term effects on congressional partisanship. In the short term, there was a massive surge in public support for both President Bush and Congress. Congress swiftly enacted several measures to respond to the crisis: the antiterror PATRIOT Act, the creation of the Homeland Security Department, and the authorization for military action in Afghanistan and Iraq. By the 2002 election, however, disputes over the Homeland Security Department and the looming conflict with Iraq, combined with President Bush's active campaigning for Republican candidates, brought the post-9/11 era of good feelings to a close. Congressional parties returned to normal.

Normal, for the Democrats, meant unity levels around 81 percent in the House and 77 percent in the Senate. The House Democrats' selection of Nancy Pelosi over Steny Hoyer for minority whip in 2001 was broadly considered to be a recommitment to a policy of opposition, and this interpretation is borne out by the Democrats' continued level of opposition. In particular, the Democrats' staunch opposition to the 2003 Medicare expansion was a clear demonstration of the Democrats' party cohesion; after all, it was the biggest expansion of Medicare since its creation in 1965, but the Democrats opposed it because it was not *their* proposal.

After the narrow reelection of President Bush in 2005, Republican unity saw a last hurrah with the passage of a bankruptcy reform bill and the Central American Free Trade Agreement (CAFTA). CAFTA was a particularly interesting case of partisan effort because a primary reason for taking up the agreement was to demonstrate that the congressional Republicans were still effective, because the House Republicans had to convert votes from a large segment of their party in order to win, and because the House Democrats employed a strategy of pain maximization to ensure that Republicans paid full price for their victory (O'Connor 2005a, 2005b, 2005c). However, congressional Republicans also refused to act on President Bush's proposal to create private Social Security accounts, confronted Bush on prisoner torture and funding for stem-cell research, and divided internally on Bush's proposed immigration reforms.

6.5.4 Democratic Resurgence and the Rise of the Tea Party, 2007–14

Congressional Republicans' differences with Bush did not spare them during the 2006 elections, when Democrats gained majority control of both chambers. Congressional Democrats spent the next two years using the legislative process to clarify the distinctions between Bush and the Democratic Party on the Iraq war, stem-cell research, and health care for poor children in preparation for the 2008 election.

As the 110th Congress drew to a close, however, the US economy was jeopardized by the disintegration of the financial sector. This led to the Bush administration's proposed Troubled Asset Relief Program (TARP), which authorized the secretary of the Treasury to buy up to $700 billion in bad loans and other financial assets. This bill was a difficult political choice for every legislator: in order to stave off complete economic collapse, they were being asked to dedicate public funds to compensate for the mistakes and misdeeds of homeowners, banks, and investors. The proposal was contrary to the proclivities of free-market conservatives who were inclined to allow private actors to suffer the consequences of their own economic decisions. And liberals were equally offended by a bailout of corporations and wealthy investors while individual homeowners were left to fend for themselves. Consequently, the Democrats were a "split majority" as defined in chapter 2, but the Republican minority was also split.

Despite lobbying for TARP by President Bush, congressional leaders, and the Chamber of Commerce, public outrage at a taxpayer bailout of reckless financial institutions led to an initial House vote of 205–228. The Democrats split 140 to 95 in favor and Republicans opposed the bill 65 to 133. Afterward, Speaker Pelosi blamed the Republican leadership for the bill's failure because they had agreed that at least half the Republican members would support the bill (Hulse and Herszenhorn 2008). The fallout was immediate and dire: the Dow Jones stock market indicator dropped about 5 percent (778 points) the afternoon of September 29, highlighting the extraordinary economic importance of passing the bill. A bipartisan team of senators salvaged the legislation by adding some modifications and sweeteners, and TARP soon became law.

TARP is a case study in enacting legislation with positive policy payoffs—in this case, avoiding a complete breakdown in the global financial system—and negative political costs. The political costs should not be downplayed. In the 2010 cycle, Sen. Bob Bennett (R-UT), a conservative running for his fourth term, was denied the Republican nomination at a party convention by activists who heckled him with chants of "TARP! TARP! TARP!"[24] On the Democratic side, former Speaker Nancy Pelosi (D-CA) blamed the TARP vote for the Democratic losses in 2010 because it led to the rise of the Tea Party movement (Blake 2013).

President Obama's First Term, 2009–12

The 2008 elections reinforced Democratic majorities in the House and Senate and ushered in President Barack Obama, a Democrat who intended to "turn the page on the ugly partisanship in Washington." Obama was elected by 52.9 to 45.6 percent, the largest margin of victory since 1996 and the highest vote share by a Democrat since 1964. The Democratic share of congressional seats grew to 59 percent of the House and 59 percent the Senate, rising to sixty Senate seats in April—the highest it had been for either party in either chamber for decades.[25] In true "responsible party" fashion, the Democrats attempted to implement an ambitious campaign agenda that included economic stimulus, health care reform, and climate change legislation, with banking reform thrown in.

After such a decisive victory on top of Democratic gains in the 2006 midterm elections, one might expect the Republicans to accept their status as the minority party and cooperate in the passage of the Democratic agenda. To the contrary, Republican leaders in Congress reiterated their 1993–94 strategy of maximum opposition. Draper (2012) reports that conservative Republicans met the night of Obama's inauguration and agreed that they would "show united and unyielding opposition to the President's economic policies," even opposing economic stimulus bills in the midst of a recession and banking reform in the wake of a financial crisis. For House Republicans, united opposition reinforced their message that the Democratic agenda was a radical shift toward big-spending government control. For Senate Republicans, unity was also the key to legislative power: by voting together on cloture votes, they could prevent the Senate Democrats from passing major bills and nominations.[26] Sixty votes are required to limit debate on most legislation and (at the time) nominations. In addition, Senate Republicans slowed down the Senate and the Democratic agenda by insisting on debate time and roll call votes (Hulse and Nagourney 2010). This strategy helped keep climate change and immigration-reform bills from making it to the Senate floor.

The Republicans' strategy of maximum opposition contributed to Republican gains in the 2010 election, including a return to majority status in the US House. While it is common for the president's party to lose seats in a midterm election, the combination of a still-weak economy and voter disapproval of Democrats who voted for the Affordable Care Act (Jacobson 2011; Koger and Lebo 2012; Nyhan et al. 2012) contributed to Republican gains of sixty-three House seats and six Senate seats.

These electoral gains came at the expense of intraparty harmony. Soon after the inauguration of President Obama, disaffected Republicans and conservatives billing themselves as the "Tea Party movement" began to protest and organize opposition to President Obama and the Democrats (Bailey et al. 2012; Parker and Barreto 2013; Williamson et al. 2013). However, Tea Party supporters were also disappointed with the Republican Party for failing to adhere to the "limited government" elements of the conservative creed during the Bush administration, so they distrusted Republican officeholders as well (Hirsh 2013). Dozens of Tea Party–aligned candidates ran for office in 2010 against both Democratic and Republican incumbents (Zernike 2010). Senator Lisa Murkowski (R-AK) was defeated in the Republican primary and had to win reelection as an Independent, and in 2012, Richard Lugar (R-IN) lost in the Republican primary to a Tea Party candidate. Figure 6.12 illustrates the result: ideological differences between the parties grew while partisanship leveled off.

In the House, the membership of a newly founded Tea Party Caucus swelled from four members in July 2010 to forty-eight in early 2013, while the membership of the long-standing conservative group, the Republican Study Committee, surged to more than 170 members—about three-fourths of all House Republicans. This influx of antiestablishment conservatives presented a major challenge for Republican leaders. In order to make a deal on the budget or any policy issue with the president, they would have to acknowledge the legitimacy of President Obama and to convince Tea Party activists that no better bargain could be struck.

In terms of our theory, the post-2010 House Republicans delegated less power to their leaders than their recent predecessors. The Tea Party activists' "grievance" was with the Republican leadership, so while they approved of Republican confrontation with President Obama, they also applauded backbenchers who dissented from party leadership. John Boehner (R-OH) enjoyed the substantial formal powers over the chamber agenda and committee assignments granted to Speakers by the rules of the House and Republican conference, and he also enjoyed the fundraising ability and media access that attends the office. But the members of the conference afforded him comparatively less informal influence over their voting and public relations than Speaker Pelosi enjoyed. During the debate over raising the public debt limit in the summer of 2011, for example, several House Republicans refused to vote to raise the limit under any circumstances, no matter what policy concessions were paired with the legislation.

Given these constraints, the Republican strategy was, first, to pass a series of "message" bills through the House, especially legislation to repeal Obamacare entirely (Hawkings 2013; O'Keefe 2014). Second, they sought to force Democrats to accept their policy goals by making the enactment of critical measures (debt limit increases, tax policy revisions) conditional upon the acceptance of Tea Party priorities like repealing Obamacare, making significant reductions in social welfare spending, or adopting a constitutional amendment requiring a balanced budget. This amounted to a repeated game of "chicken" in which both parties waited until—sometimes literally—the final hour before passing legislation to avert a national catastrophe. By doing so, Republicans sought to maintain the purity of their conservative brand and either win their showdowns because the Democrats "blinked" first or convince the Republican base that they tried very hard to win before accepting a compromise.

There are, however, two downsides to this strategy. First, the gulf between the parties ensured that Republicans' preferred positions are not nearly moderate enough for Democrats to accept as fair nor popular enough that Democrats lose popularity for rejecting them. Thus Democrats rejected the Republicans' take-it-or-leave-it proposals, and budget disagreements dragged on. In December 2012, for example, Congress was considering how to extend the Bush-era tax cuts. Speaker Boehner was undercut by his conference when Republicans refused to vote for his "Plan B" proposal that was moderate enough that some Democrats might actually accept it. To Boehner's Republican conference, however, it meant an affirmative vote to raise taxes and thus a tremendous blemish on their voting records. For this reason, "Plan B" never made it to the House floor, and the House ended up passing the Democratic Senate proposal ("Last-Minute Deal Averts Fiscal Cliff, Punts Big Issues to New Congress"; Montgomery and Helderman 2012).

A second downside to the Republicans' legislative strategy is that public opinion may assign them most of the blame for policy gridlock. After several inconclusive rounds of crisis bargaining, the Republicans lost a decisive showdown in October 2013. Two fiscal deadlines arrived in October: the beginning of a new fiscal year on October 1 and a projected deadline of October 17 for raising the federal limit on debt. A first-year senator, Ted Cruz (R-TX), convinced Republicans to attempt to block funding for Obamacare in the House appropriations bill to continue federal spending past October 1. Senate Democrats refused to budge on this demand, and a government shutdown began on October 1. Republicans insisted that repeal, delay, or significant changes in Obamacare be included in any legislation to fund the government and raise the federal debt limit (Carney 2013). This was a very controversial strategy within

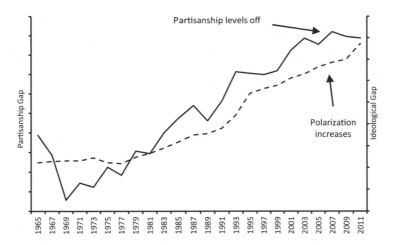

FIGURE 6.12. Ideological polarization and partisanship in the US House of Representatives
Partisan gap is the absolute difference between the percentage of votes taking the Republican side on party votes cast by Democrats and Republicans. *Ideological gap* is the absolute difference of the difference between the median House Republican and Democratic first-dimension NOMINATE scores. The data are by Congress, so the *x*-axis shows the first year of each two-year Congress.

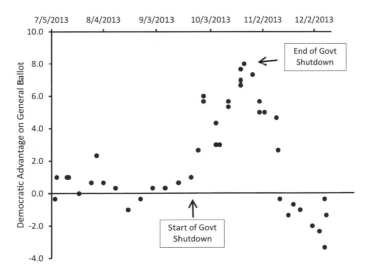

FIGURE 6.13. Generic ballot polls and the 2013 shutdown
Source: http://www.realclearpolitics.com, which aggregates polls from multiple sources. Accessed December 20, 2013.

the Republican Party, with many legislators concerned that it would be both completely ineffective and disastrous for their reputation. Republican leaders were nonetheless unable to unite their members behind a more realistic strategy.

Ultimately, the Republicans' strategy was costly to their public image. A *New York Times*/CBS poll before the shutdown found that respondents would blame the Republicans more than the Democrats by a 44 to 35 percent margin, while a Quinnipiac University poll found that voters opposed shutting down the government in an attempt to block the implementation of Obamacare by a 72 to 22 percent margin (Carney 2013; CQ staff 2013). Not surprisingly, then, when the shutdown occurred, the Democrats surged from dead even to 8 percent ahead in "generic ballot" polls asking voters which party they were more likely to vote for in the 2014 election, as shown in figure 6.13.[27]

While the media focused on the Republican Party during the October 2013 shutdown, the Democratic strategy is particularly interesting for our narrative. Senate Majority Leader Harry Reid (D-UT) united his caucus—and the White House—behind a strategy of *not* negotiating with Republicans over policy riders to the debt limit or budget legislation. In particular, the Democrats would not make any amendments or delays to Obamacare, which was still not a popular policy (Catalini 2013). Republicans were reportedly surprised that Democrats flatly refused to bargain. Instead, Senate Democrats decried the Republican strategy of holding the country's fiscal policy hostage and cast votes to reject all House-passed bills with health care restrictions attached. This was a risky move for many, including incumbents up for reelection in 2014 in Republican-leaning states like Arkansas, Louisiana, and Virginia. This is a classic case of *strategic* partisanship: instead of heeding their constituents' likely preferences, these legislators took risks to achieve the collective good of united opposition to the Republican strategy. By doing so, they focused attention on the nature of the Republicans' *tactics* rather than the policy content of their demands.

6.6 Conclusion

The underlying story of our account is that congressional partisanship is not driven primarily by personalities or events, nor does constituency cohesion precede legislative partisanship and cause legislators to grant party organizations and their leaders more power. Presidential candidates routinely promise to enact bipartisan solutions only to find that the minority party is not interested in cooperation—at least not on the president's terms. Major events like 9/11 or the outbreak of a war may induce a short-term truce in partisan competition, but in due time, legislators return to the long game. Other events, such as conflicts between Newt Gingrich and Democratic Speakers in the 1980s, may serve as crystallizing moments that linger in politicians' memories, but if these events had never occurred, it is likely we would observe nearly identical behavior in the long term.

Instead, the waxing and waning of party strength over the course of American history are the product of strategic interaction. Each party does its best to beat the competition on the floors of Congress and in the voting booth. The actions of one party determine just how much pressure the opposing party must bring to bear on its members.

Between this and preceding chapters, much of this story has been covered. Senators and Representatives know that voters will punish them for excessive partisanship. But they also have party goals to enhance their collective reputation among voters. Thus legislators will vote as they see fit to win reelection but may cave to party pressure when necessary for party goals. With the two parties watching each other, their overall levels of unity move together over time. Seemingly tethered together, they may move apart for a time, but both will feel heavy costs for doing so, and they will quickly return to their equilibrium level.

While this story is one that we can find in even the earliest years of Congress, the level at which this interaction occurs now is indicative of the high level of party polarization that typifies the modern Congress. The fact that majority control of each chamber seems contested every two years is certainly a principal reason for party strategizing to be at its highest. A few key votes won or lost can mean a tremendous amount for the reputations of the parties. And since roll calls are subject to greater media attention than ever before, legislators weigh these decisions very carefully. In the next chapter, we will investigate these partisan battles at the roll call level. Looking at the individual battles on the floors of Congress will help demonstrate the underlying patterns we have found here.

CHAPTER SEVEN

Party Competition in Legislative Voting

The last stage of our analysis is the study of individual contests. Do parties match each other's investments in roll call votes? We begin with a case study of the passage of the Central American Free Trade Agreement (CAFTA) through the House in 2005.[1] This case was a motivating example of strategic party interaction for us and helped us formulate our theory, so we use it to illustrate how modern party contests unfold.

The chapter then presents an analysis of how roll call partisanship in the House and Senate varies across votes and how these relationships have evolved over time. We find that procedural partisanship has increased in both chambers since 1950, and this has partially shielded majority parties from the need to respond to minority party unity. Nonetheless, strategic interaction between parties continues to influence legislative behavior.

7.1 The Central American Free Trade Agreement (2005)

Compared to other trade agreements in American history, CAFTA has had a relatively minor impact. It faded from the national political conversation soon after its passage. However, the struggle to push this agreement through the US House left behind a compelling behind-the-scenes account by *The Hill*. We think it provides a clear example of (a) the willingness of party leaders to override their members' individual interests on behalf of a collective victory, (b) a minority-party strategy of maximum opposition, (c) the primacy of politics over policy, and (d) the close ties between institutional actors and allied interest groups.

Following the restoration of fast-track trade-negotiating powers in

2002, the Bush administration negotiated a free-trade agreement with Costa Rica, El Salvador, Guatemala, Honduras, Nicaragua, and later, the Dominican Republic. This was CAFTA. The Bush administration submitted the pact to Congress in June 2005.

Compared to major trade agreements like the North American Free Trade Agreement (NAFTA), CAFTA was a minor issue. As Congressional Quarterly noted, "The six Central American and Caribbean economies together generate a little more than $200 billion a year in trade, roughly equivalent to the economy of Missouri. Even the pact's most ardent proponents emphasized CAFTA's effect on national security, immigration and regional stability more than its economic benefits" (Norton 2005a). In the wake of NAFTA and the creation of the World Trade Organization, however, CAFTA had enormous *political* importance. The Republicans sought its passage as a signal of their commitment to free trade and their competence as a party, while Democrats and allied interests sought to derail the Republican agenda and protest the broader effects of trade on labor and environmental regulations (Norton 2005c). Partisanship was not the only consideration, however. Domestic textile and sugar producers were concerned about the effects of the treaty, causing many Republicans to express private and public concerns about CAFTA (Norton 2005b).

At first glance, there seems to be almost no role for partisan agenda setting in this case. Once a trade deal is submitted to Congress under fast-track rules, each chamber must vote on the deal by simple majority vote with no amendments. This sets in motion an up-or-down vote within ninety days on the agreement in each chamber. However, Republican leaders did influence the timing of the submission of the trade deal to Congress by encouraging the Bush administration to hold onto the treaty until after the 2004 elections (O'Connor 2005a). House leaders also waited until the Senate voted on the pact, thereby building momentum for the deal.[2] Next, the House Ways and Means Committee delayed its report until the House leadership was ready for a vote; otherwise, the statutory time limits on fast-track bills might have forced a premature vote (Norton 2005c).

The focus of party leaders' involvement, however, was on whipping the vote. House Majority Whip Roy Blunt began counting votes six weeks before the House vote—the longest whipping effort of his tenure (O'Connor 2005a). Blunt and the Republican leaders augmented their formal team with a vast team of business lobbyists and administration officials, including direct involvement by President Bush and Vice President Cheney (O'Connor 2005b, 2005c). Business lobbyists were especially useful for lobbying House Democrats (Ota 2005). The focus of this effort was a group of fifty undecided or wavering Republicans and a handful of probusiness House Democrats (O'Connor 2005c).

The Republican leaders' efforts converted dozens of Republican members' votes and ensured the passage of a treaty that otherwise lacked enough support to succeed. Some of these votes—as many as ten—were won over when House leaders held a separate vote on a China trade bill (Norton 2005a, 2005b). Several other members switched to supporting CAFTA after they were assured that the effects on the domestic textile industry would be limited (Norton 2005c; O'Connor 2005b).

On the other side of the aisle, House Democratic leaders sought united opposition to CAFTA to defeat the agreement or, failing that, to maximize the costs to the Republican majority: "Many of the Democratic opponents are motivated by partisan politics: They want to see Bush lose a major legislative initiative or, at the very least, make Republicans from districts hit hard by international trade take a dangerous vote in favor of a deal their constituents oppose. Dozens of Republicans in districts dependent on the textile industry, the sugar growers or small manufacturers have already said they will vote against the bill. House Minority Leader Nancy Pelosi (CA) privately warned Democrats last month that a vote for CAFTA is a vote to stay in the minority" (Weisman 2005). This strategy exemplifies the *strategic party government* explanation for minority-party opposition: they seek to defeat high-profile initiatives and, failing that, to inflict maximum political pain on majority-party members. Specifically, the arguments in chapter 2 suggest that, based on minority-party behavior, party-loyal majority-party members would have to pay higher costs for voting *for* CAFTA than conflicted minority-party members paid for voting *against* CAFTA. In this case, the minority Democrats successfully inflicted these costs: "A core group of as many as 50 pro-trade Democrats [voted] against CAFTA" (Weisman 2005), citing CAFTA's weak labor provisions. Each of those party-loyal Democratic votes forced another Republican to cast a vote that he or she considered to be politically costly.

On the day of the vote on passage, Republican leaders were uncertain if or how they would win (O'Connor 2005c). President Bush came to give a speech to the Republican conference while several top administration officials lobbied swing voters (O'Connor 2005b). As the vote actually unfolded in the evening of July 28, 2005, the vote total was close and stalemated at 214–211, with eight or nine Republicans and one Democrat waiting to vote. After a half hour of negotiations, the Republicans settled on a path to victory: Robin Hayes (R-NC) switched his vote from a "nay" to an "aye," two other contingent Republicans voted "aye," and the rest were freed to vote against the measure or not vote at all. CAFTA passed the House 217–215 and was swiftly passed by the Senate and became law (Norton 2005b; O'Connor 2005b). Afterward, Pelosi made it clear that she was furious with some of the Democrats who voted for CAFTA—specifically, those from safe seats and those sitting on good committees (Billings 2005).

This case illustrates the importance of *party reputation* as an incentive in agenda setting. In this case, House Republican leaders were not pushing a trade agreement because their members supported it. Rather, for the sake of the Republican Party's reputation with the business community and the general public, Republican leaders pushed a measure despite high levels of opposition within their own party. Second, the Democrats pursued a strategy of pain maximization. The Democratic leadership regretted every Democratic vote for the agreement that allowed a Republican to vote "nay." Interestingly, this case also illustrates that the party budget can include the efforts of external actors like the president, the executive branch, and interest groups. Third, there is a role for party leaders influencing members to cast votes against their individual interests, but only to help the party achieve collective goals. Party leaders do not expect party orthodoxy for its own sake, even Pelosi's condemnation was only targeted at defectors who would have paid a minimal cost for supporting their party.

7.2 Partisanship across Roll Call Votes

The CAFTA case illustrates that positive action on major legislation requires leaders to bring together coalitions on key votes, often over the opposition of rival leaders or the objections of disappointed constituents. To better understand when parties will unite, this section turns to a broader analysis of interparty competition in roll call votes.

Our interest in partisanship is motivated by the expectation that party unity is linked to legislative success. As figure 7.1 illustrates, parties that mobilize votes are more likely to win. It plots the relationship between

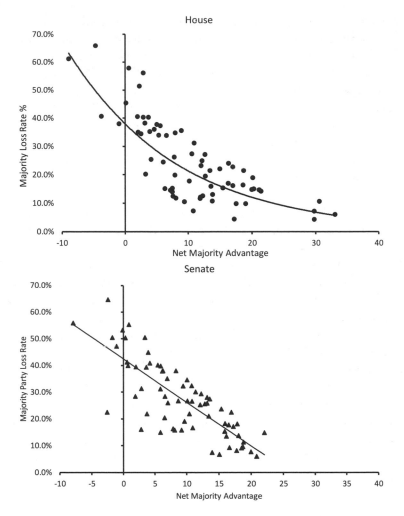

FIGURE 7.1. Net majority advantage and majority loss rate in the House and Senate, 1877–2013

net majority-party influence and the majority party's "loss rate" as a percentage of all simple-majority party votes in a Congress from 1877 to
2013. Influence, in this context, is the interaction of the majority party's
chamber share and its party unity, and *net* influence is the majority's influence minus the minority's influence:

Net Majority Influence = (Majority Chamber Share * Majority Party Unity)
                        – (Minority Chamber Share * Minority Party Unity)[3]

The "loss rate" on the *y*-axis is the percentage of all party votes in a Congress lost by the majority party. In Cox and McCubbins's terminology, it combines the roll rate and disappointment rate across all simple majority votes.

The central pattern of figure 7.1 is that party influence *matters*. The more votes a party can muster from its members, the less likely they are to get "rolled." Conversely, if a minority party is united and taking on a disunited majority party with a narrow advantage in chamber share, the minority party can win a large proportion of party votes—even more than half the votes! While it is not groundbreaking news to find that the legislative party with more votes usually wins,[4] it is worth underscoring that our interest in party unity and party size is not an abstract concern; party unity and party size directly relate to patterns of legislative outcomes and, as we showed in chapter 5, electoral outcomes as well.[5] Next, we continue with a discussion of our theoretical expectations, then test our hypotheses on roll call votes using the entire scope of congressional history.

7.2.1 Theoretical Expectations

Symmetric Party Effort

We expect that the pattern of strategic matching, which we observe at the macro level, also exists at the micro level of individual votes. That is, when one party decides to invest effort into winning a vote, the opposing party will also invest effort, *ceteris paribus*. Our reasoning follows (among others) Snyder and Groseclose (2000) and King and Zeckhauser (2003). Parties that care about winning legislative contests and that have limited resources to invest will allocate their effort across votes to have maximum effect on the party's legislative record. Let us assume that on any important question, party leaders have a general expectation about what the victory margin will be in the absence of party influence. On many questions, this expected margin is lopsided, so party leaders either anticipate an easy win or anticipate a defeat that cannot be avoided without investing more effort than the bill is worth. When the expected margin on important legislation is close, however, the majority party has a collective interest in converting enough doubtful members to solidify a chamber majority. By doing so, the majority party bolsters its reputation by winning on a salient issue or bill, or at least avoids the damage to its reputation that could result from a defeat. The minority party, on the other side, hopes to inflict a political and policy defeat on the majority, or at least to compel the winning coalition to convert all its reluctant members into public supporters.

In our framework, both parties should have similar notions of which votes are "important" even if they have different policy priorities. Even if, say, Republican members of Congress (MCs) are more interested in tax issues than are Democrats, and Democrats are more interested in social welfare issues than are Republicans, the competition for party reputation induces interest in legislation and votes that are relevant to party reputation, regardless of issue content. And, as discussed earlier, any battle will take on only greater salience when the reputation of the president is also at stake.

This is the rationale behind our first claim:

> *Hypothesis 7.1 (symmetric party effort)*: As majority-party influence increases, minority-party influence should increase as well.

By "influence," we mean the collective efforts of party leaders and party organizations to sway the votes of party members, including side payments, vote trading, peer pressure, threats of retribution, and so on.

Variation by Vote Type

Of course, the fact that a vote is expected to be close does not guarantee that parties will fight to win it. The rewards for winning the battle must exceed the costs. The costs for party unity may vary across the type of vote— for example, whether it is a "procedural" vote with indirect linkage to policy outcomes or a direct vote on policy (Froman and Ripley 1965). Froman and Ripley (1965) suggest that the costs of voting with one's party are lower on procedural votes than on substantive votes. This logic yields a second hypothesis:

> *Hypothesis 7.2 (vote salience)*: Party unity will increase as the public salience of a vote decreases—for example, on procedural votes.

Below, we operationalize the vote-salience hypothesis as testing whether party unity increases on procedural votes.

7.2.2 Data and Methods

In this section, our units of analysis are *party votes* from the 1st to the 111th Congress, House, and Senate (ICPSR 0004), and our variable of

TABLE 7.1. **Summary statistics: Party Unity and Rice difference scores**

	House		Senate	
	Mean	Standard deviation	Mean	Standard deviation
Majority Party Unity	67.2	29.9	62.9	30.6
Minority Party Unity	69.8	29.1	67.4	30.5
Democratic Party Unity	67.0	29.7	65.4	30.6
Republican Party Unity	70.0	29.3	64.9	30.6
Rice Difference Score	68.5	23.2	65.1	23.3
Cases		27,527		25,076

interest is the *party unity* of the majority party. While chapter 6 focused on patterns of aggregate partisanship over time, these analyses focus on partisanship across roll call votes. Like Cox and Poole (2002), we assume a baseline of party influence and preference homogeneity across all votes but seek to identify which votes within a Congress or era are especially likely to be partisan. We again exclude all votes that require a supermajority threshold—for example, Senate cloture votes, treaties, veto overrides, and constitutional amendments. This yields a total of 27,527 observations in the House and 25,076 in the Senate. Table 7.1 summarizes the cohesion of the majority, minority, Democratic, and Republican Parties and the Rice difference index (absolute percentage difference between majority party voting "aye" and minority party voting "aye") for all votes.

As in chapter 6, the "Democratic" label is shorthand for, respectively, opponents of the Washington administration, the (Jeffersonian) Republican Party, supporters of Andrew Jackson, and members labeled "Democrat" or "Independent Democrat," all identified using Kenneth Martis's (1989) party affiliation coding. And by "Republican," we mean supporters of the Washington administration, Federalists, pro-Adams and anti-Jackson factions, Whigs, and members labeled "Republicans" and "Independent Republicans."[6] We do not imply that these labels signify two constant coalitions.

Our main explanatory variable is the party unity of the minority party on each vote, *Minority-Party Unity*. We expect that the unity of the two parties will be highly correlated; in the pooled data set, the Pearson's *r* correlation is 0.202. A second key variable is *Procedural Vote*: we seek to test the classic Froman and Ripley (1965) claim that partisanship is higher on procedural votes. This claim also underlies the notion of a "procedural cartel" in the US House of Representatives (Cox and McCubbins 1993, 1994, 2005): party members stick together on votes to allocate parliamentary powers to their leaders and to set the chamber agenda. This allows them to then have more discretion in their votes on policy issues.

We also test whether voting becomes less partisan as elections approach[7]—that is, does *Majority-Party Unity* decline as elections draw closer? *Date of Vote* measures the effect of the proximity of elections. We calculate this variable by (1) identifying the date on which each roll call vote occurred and (2) assigning a percentile ranking the dates of these votes, so all votes on the first day of a Congress will have the same low ranking, while votes on the last day of a Congress have a high rank. We expect this variable will be negative if legislators expect that voters (a) punish partisanship and (b) are especially likely to punish partisanship as elections draw close.[8] If legislators expect voters to behave this way, they will structure their agenda and choose their votes to appear less partisan as elections draw near.

Our final vote-specific variable is *Disappearing Quorum*, which measures *Majority-Party Unity* on votes with a significant deficit of minority-party participation.[9] This is a historic form of obstruction—similar to the quorum-breaking we observe at the state level in modern times, when legislators flee across state lines to deprive their chambers of a working majority, except in the nineteenth-century House and Senate, legislators could remain in the chamber and refuse to vote (Koger 2010). We anticipate that this tactic, whether it breaks a quorum or not, forces the majority party to support its own measures to ensure passage without any support from the opposing party.

In addition to these predictors that are specific to each vote, we employ a set of year-by-year variables that are familiar from chapter 6. There are year-level variables for *Democratic Majority*, *Majority President* (coded 1 if the president shares the party affiliation of the majority), *Short Session*, and *Long Session*. In addition, there are year-level variables for the vote-specific variables described above: *Minority Party Unity (Year)*, *Procedural Votes (Year)*, *Date of Vote (Year)*, and *Disappearing Quorum (Year)*. Collectively, these year-level variables emulate the macrolevel results presented in chapter 6. Our goal is to understand the effects of our four key variables on roll call votes while simultaneously estimating the expected effects at the yearly level.

Methods. Our data are *repeated cross sections*: each of the 222 years of data contains a unique sample of votes.[10] Votes nested within the same year will share commonalities with each other that set them apart from other votes in other years—for example, the set of legislators and the political circumstances are particular to that year. Such nesting issues can cause statistical problems, which we control for using the time-series multilevel model shown in Lebo and Weber (2015).[11] Essentially, we filter out the temporal relationships between sets of roll call votes, then estimate the relationships at both the yearly level (as in chapter 6) and the vote level. That is, our multilevel approach allows us to study how the parties interact with each other at both the vote level and the yearly level. A critical benefit of this approach is that we can estimate the time-varying effects of key variables.

7.2.3 Results

We first present the key results for the pooled data set and then illustrate how the dynamic estimates for *Minority-Party Unity* and *Procedural Vote* in both chambers vary over the course of congressional history. We find that the pooled results generally conform to our expectations, but the effects of the key variables vary significantly by chamber and over time.

The results of our pooled model are displayed in figures 7.2A and 7.2B for our four key variables, grouped by whether they are continuous (2A) or dichotomous (2B).[12] The pooled results generally confirm our expectations, with some notable differences between the chambers. First, and most importantly, we observe a pattern of strategic balancing on roll call votes: controlling for other factors, the unity of the two parties is correlated. Consistent with hypothesis 7.1, a 1 percent increase in *Minority-Party Unity* is correlated with about a 0.095 percent increase in *Majority-Party Unity* in the Senate and 0.14 percent in the House. Second, when the minority party abstains from voting en masse (a "disappearing quorum"), *Majority-Party Unity* spikes by about 16 percent in both chambers. Third, *Majority-Party Unity* does decrease in both chambers as elections draw closer: there is about a 7 percent decrease (Senate) and a 5 percent decrease (House) from the beginning to the end of a Congress. Again, it is likely this is the result of both changes in how legislators vote and, since leaders expect this voting behavior, a shift in the legislative agenda toward issues that do not require legislators to cast costly votes in support of their party.

Finally, consistent with hypothesis 7.2, we find the expected pattern of partisanship on procedural votes in the House. This is consistent with a century of scholarship noting that parties in the House often clash over the organization and agenda, while legislators vote more freely on policy

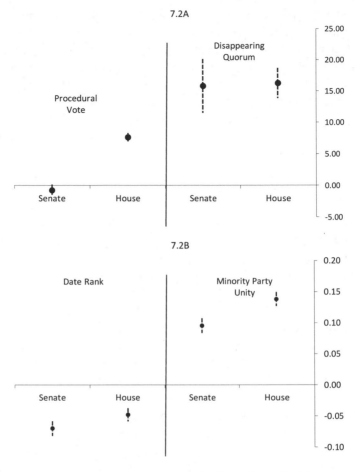

FIGURE 7.2. Patterns of partisanship: Pooled analysis of the US House and Senate

issues. However, we do not observe the same pattern in the US Senate: in the pooled data set, these votes are not noticeably different from other policy and housekeeping votes.

This null result in the pooled data obscures tremendous variation over time. Using a multilevel time series approach, we estimated the coefficient for procedural partisanship in each chamber on a year-by-year basis while controlling for other factors. These dynamic estimates are displayed in figure 7.3, with the jagged line indicating the coefficient for procedural partisanship's effect on *Majority-Party Unity* in each year—a Loess smoother shows the general trend in the relationship (surrounded by an error esti-

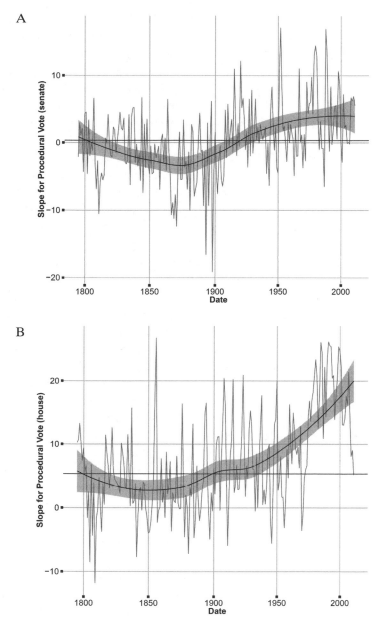

FIGURE 7.3. Procedural partisanship in the US Senate and House: Dynamic estimates
A, Senate; *B*, House of Representatives

mate for each year), and a horizontal line shows the average effect over all the data. Figure 7.3A displays procedural partisanship in the Senate from 1789 to 2012 and suggests that for much of the nineteenth century, procedural votes were *less* partisan than other votes. During that period, these votes allowed senators an opportunity to defect from their parties. Instead of voting against their party's position on the final passage of a bill, for example, a senator might vote for a motion to switch from debating the party's proposed bill to another issue. A well-known example was the Senate debate over the 1891 "Force" Bill accompanied by a majority-cloture proposal: rather than vote against these measures directly, a subset of Republican senators voted to switch to alternative agenda items: first legislation to purchase silver as a basis for US currency and later a reapportionment bill (Koger 2010, 74; Welch 1965, 519–22; Wawro and Schickler 2006, 76–87). Around the 1940s, Senate majority parties began to adopt a pattern of procedural partisanship, but this has not yet emulated the high levels of procedural partisanship in the US House.

The House exhibits a similar pattern of slightly below-average procedural partisanship during the nineteenth century, and then procedural votes become more partisan beginning around 1940. The members of the US House are especially partisan in the modern era, with procedural votes around 20 percent more partisan than nonprocedural votes.

The modern increase in procedural partisanship seems to compensate for a decrease in competitive partisanship. Figure 7.4 illustrates the year-by-year effect of *Minority-Party Unity* on *Majority-Party Unity* in the Senate and House. In both chambers, the historical trajectory of this variable is like a mirror image of procedural partisanship. This suggests that, on an everyday basis, congressional parties have substituted battles over the agenda for battles to win individual votes. There are still battles over key legislation, such as CAFTA, the Troubled Asset Relief Program (TARP), the Affordable Care Act (Obamacare), and budget resolutions. And, as chapter 6 demonstrates, there is still a pattern of strategic partisanship from Congress to Congress (see also Fenno 1997).

Overall, these results suggest that *Majority-Party Unity* varies systematically across votes. To some extent, this is a reaction to minority party strategies, including *Minority-Party Unity* or collective abstention from voting. Or the majority party can structure the chamber agenda and its expectations to allow its members more discretion as elections draw closer and shift the focus of party efforts toward procedural control of the chamber floor.

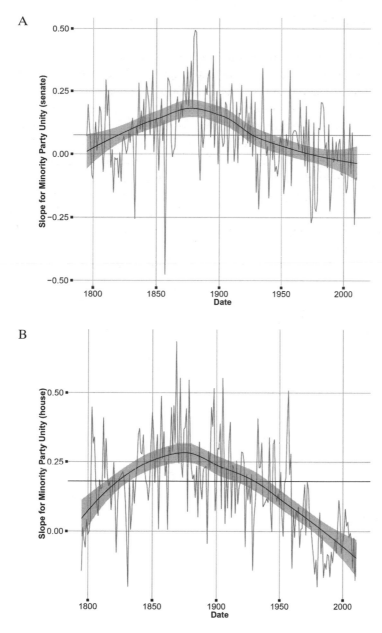

FIGURE 7.4. Strategic partisanship in the US Senate and House: Dynamic estimates
A, Senate; B, House of Representatives

7.3 Conclusion

This chapter explains how parties allocate their influence across roll call votes. First, the CAFTA case study illustrates how leaders whip votes and can gradually build coalitions out of ambivalent or conflicted legislators. It also highlights the role of strategic interaction, as the minority party sought to maximize the political costs of this legislation by minimizing the number of Democratic votes for the agreement. Our statistical analysis finds that this is a broader pattern in congressional voting. One of the clear predictors of majority-party unity in both the House and Senate is the unity of the minority party. In recent years, there has been elevated party unity on procedural votes, which has allowed a diminished level of strategic partisanship in the US House. Overall, these findings confirm that partisanship is not simply a function of legislators representing their districts or acting on their own ideology; it is the result of competition for political advantage.

CHAPTER EIGHT

Conclusion

This book offers a fresh perspective on the strategies and behavior of legislative parties. We build upon a robust body of research with a retooled explanation of why legislators cooperate with fellow party members. We started with an assumption as old as the Constitution: legislators want to get reelected. To do so, they must represent their constituents and work together to pass legislation. These two strategies, however, are often in conflict. The teamwork required to build coalitions and unite behind a single proposal may be electorally costly for legislators who pay conformity costs when they settle for less than exactly what their constituents want.

8.1 Overview

The model of *strategic party government* that we propose in this book posits that legislators join coalitions to manage the benefits of collective action and the costs of conformity. At any point in time, each party will strike a balance between individualism and cooperation that reflects the costs and benefits of each *and the strategy of the opposing party*. This framework builds on the traditional model of *conditional party government* by claiming that similarity of political interests within a party and differing interests between the members of opposing parties can influence legislative partisanship. We add a second claim: over time and across votes, each party's effort will respond to the behavior of the opposing party. Like firms in a duopoly or teams on a football field, we should expect parties to choose strategies that are a best response to their opponent's expected behavior.

A second distinguishing feature of this work, however, it its effort to test the model's predictions in *both* the electoral and legislative realms. We began with individual-level experiments to determine whether voters disapproved of legislative partisanship and why. We found that voters disapprove of legislators who vote with their party at a high rate. Why? Because voters perceive that a high rate of party unity implies that legislators are probably failing to represent the views of their districts on some issues. An underlying distrust of partisanship in Congress is evident as well—voters hate a party hack. How does this result compare with the long research tradition evaluating the effect of ideological extremity on elections (e.g., Canes-Wrone et al. 2002; Downs 1957)? We also asked our respondents about how they viewed ideologically extreme legislators and found that voters were not inclined to punish ideologues; they viewed ideological extremism as a sign of intellectual sincerity.

Our second clue that voters punish partisanship and not ideology came when we studied individual House and Senate elections in chapter 4. Using multiple statistical approaches, we found no direct relationship between ideology and election results but a robust negative relationship between partisanship and the vote share of incumbents running for reelection.

Viewed in isolation, these results have a clear implication: legislators—especially those in competitive districts—should minimize partisanship, since party unity jeopardizes reelection. Our analysis of party-level election results in chapter 5 adds nuance to this claim. On one hand, we find that parties tend to do worse as their party unity increases. On the other hand, *winning* legislative votes is correlated with improved election results. Our results for the Senate suggest that the mechanism is voter sanctions against partisanship. During the 125 years that senators were selected by state legislatures, party unity had no consistent effect on subsequent elections, but winning contested roll call votes did have a positive effect. Once the Senate was directly elected, however, Senate parties paid a penalty for partisanship that exceeded those of the "people's House."

How do legislative parties balance the rewards of winning with the costs of voting together? Chapters 6 and 7 tested the claim that parties engage in strategic mirroring—reacting to the partisanship of the opposing party. Chapter 6 finds this pattern at the macro level: the party unity of one party increases with the unity of the opposing party. Furthermore, to the extent that the unity of the two parties in a chamber differs in one Congress, that gap tends to shrink in the succeeding Congress. This suggests that elections serve as informative signals to "correct" parties that are excessively partisan (and hence punished by voters) or insufficiently partisan (and thus punished by disappointed party activists). Chapter 7 goes on to find that a similar pattern holds true for individual votes; partisanship in voting is highly interactive. These results support our treatment of legislative partisanship as an arms race: each party's unity is a response to the actions of the opposing party.

Taken together, the strategic party government model and the extensive empirical testing we have done make a contribution to the study of legislative politics. The next two sections explain the implications for future research on legislative parties and for the US Congress.

8.2 Implications for the Study of Congress

How should this book affect the way that reporters cover Congress? First, observers should abandon the assumption that the majority party schedules legislation for the sole purpose of changing public policy or that legislators cast their votes in order to make good public policy. Instead, we see agenda setting as an exercise in party brand management. Since 2010, the House of Representatives has voted dozens of times to repeal all or part of the Affordable Care Act (ACA, or "Obamacare"), but these efforts have resulted in very little policy change. Was this effort wasted? Not if we think the House Republicans' primary goal was to make public their opposition to the law. Nor should we interpret Republicans' votes to repeal the law as a genuine expression of their preferences for the future of health care policy. More broadly, as Arnold (1990) argues, when legislators vote, they are thinking primarily of the position they are taking rather than the policy they might be making.

Second, journalists, citizens, and scholars seeking to understand the trend toward increasing partisanship—or, perhaps, a later turn away from partisanship—should avoid the temptation to explain these trends in terms of personalities or single events. In our account, legislators are influenced by a complex electoral environment and work with their parties to compete in an intense competition. No one individual makes legislators more partisan, no one event made parties happen, and no single leader— not even a president—can fundamentally alter legislators' incentive structure for the long term.

Third, we should take legislative partisanship with a grain of salt. The simple fact that the majority and minority party in a legislature are voting against each other does not mean that either party is acting in bad faith or the bill or nomination they are voting on is somehow tarnished by the disagreement. In practice, such votes often reflect the decision by most members of one party—or both parties—that public disagreement suits their political interests.

What might cause the current era of high partisanship to end? While it is possible that parties will simply agree to some form of mutual disarmament, it is more likely that it will take an exogenous shock to congressional parties to fundamentally change their calculations. Strangely enough, the Tea Party movement might provide such an outside shock. By sowing dissension within the Republican Party—including the ouster of Speaker John Boehner in the fall of 2015—the Tea Party movement might lead to the decentralization of party leadership and increased cooperation between Democrats and non–Tea Party Republicans.

Future Research

The strategic party government model has implications that extend beyond this book and raises new questions that are worthy of study. First, there are several opportunities for further research on the electoral connection between partisanship and elections. How exactly does partisanship become costly to incumbents? One opportunity is to study campaign advertisements to measure how often roll call partisanship is used against an incumbent and the extent to which it comes in the form of criticizing individual votes ("Congressman Y voted for Obamacare") versus a pattern of behavior ("Congresswoman X voted with Newt Gingrich 99 percent of the time"). Second, it would be interesting to know more about which voters are responsive to such a message and which messages induce them to switch from supporting an incumbent to supporting a challenger.

A second general topic of study would be to better understand the electoral rewards for partisanship, particularly at the nomination phase. Are members of Congress with relatively low party unity more likely to face quality challengers in a party primary and more likely to lose? To what extent do party-aligned interest groups and donors reward party loyalty? Theriault (2013, 73–88), for example, notes that "Gingrich senators" seem to be able to compensate for the electoral costs of staunchly conservative and Republican voting records by raising additional campaign funds.

Third, this book has not analyzed legislative agenda setting in much depth. There remains an opportunity for scholars to study the role of party leaders in selecting which proposals come to the House and Senate floors in which order, also known as *positive* agenda setting. Scholars have studied this topic at the level of individual members (e.g., Anderson et al. 2003), the level of individual bills (e.g., Krutz 2005), and institutional (e.g., Adler and Wilkerson 2013) levels, and Barbara Sinclair (1995) provides an inside account of party agenda setting, while Cox and McCubbins (1993) and Patty and Penn (2008) offer formal models of agenda setting. What we lack, however, is a study that systematically explains which proposals are selected as the majority party's "message" agenda and how legislators select the remainder of the chamber agenda.

Above all, we hope that this work redirects legislative scholars away from trying to explain Congressional parties using unidimensional spatial models and ideology scores. Legislators have multiple constituencies that they seek to satisfy simultaneously, and they work with their parties to minimize the conflict within their own constituencies while highlighting and exploiting the divisions within the opposing party. Among both voters and legislators, a great deal of what we label "ideology" is really partisanship, and it is simpler and more useful to treat it as such.

8.3 The Future of Parties and Congress

As we discussed in chapter 6, Congressional parties have returned to historically high levels after a period of low salience during the mid-twentieth century. This resurgence has led to apprehension about the ability of Congress to pass laws during periods of divided government (but see Mayhew 2002) and criticism of the Senate filibuster as a brake upon the majority party's agenda. From 2007 to the present day, only the 111th Congress (2009–10) can be deemed productive, and that required large Democratic majorities in both chambers of Congress and a Democratic President elected in the middle of an economic crisis by the largest margin of any Democratic candidate since 1964. Even then, the yield was three landmark laws (a stimulus bill, health care reform, and financial reform) and several major laws such as the Lily Ledbetter act and student loan reform. It is hard for Congress to govern a nation when it can only function during once-in-a-generation conditions.

One interpretation of this gridlock is that the policy views typical of each political party are so different that they are irreconcilable. Yet this was not really the case for the contests over the landmark bills of the 111th Congress. The stimulus bill spent money in the middle of a financial crisis to avoid the next Great Depression—a practice embraced by the Bush administration. The health care law was based on a blueprint proposed by the Heritage Foundation and adopted in Massachusetts by a Republican governor who would become the Republican nominee for President in 2012. And the Dodd-Frank financial reform law was relatively mild given the global recession sparked by the failures of Wall Street firms.

An alternative explanation is that there are ample opportunities for major policy reforms if legislators can agree to compromises on the issues that do divide them. However, legislative parties are increasingly loath to act on these potential compromises because obtaining *political credit* for enacting these proposals is a zero-sum game, with the President's party often accruing the majority of the credit. From the perspective of the party that does not hold the White House, major legislation with bipartisan support strengthens the reputation of the President's party, legitimizes the President and leaders of the President's party, and probably disappoints party activists who have to accept less than their ideal outcome. In a highly partisan political environment, uncompromising opposition helps the opposition to minimize its losses and perhaps inflict embarrassing setbacks to the President's party.

In this stagnant environment, there is also a risk that legislators' skills will atrophy. Legislating requires a base of policy knowledge and skill at building coalitions, identifying areas of compromise, and managing legislation on the chamber floor (Fenno 1997). If legislators do not hone these skills during periods of divided government, they will be ill-prepared if the political stars align and their party enjoys a turn as the dominant party for a while.

Results, Not Positions

To some readers, our account of Congressional parties may appear bleak. Legislators who care mostly about keeping their jobs form gangs and lock into a struggle that stretches from the chamber floors to the streets of America. As citizens, we might hope that our representatives will work across the aisle out of sheer commitment to the public good. As James Madison says, however, "But what is government itself, but the greatest of all reflections on human nature? If men were angels, no government would be necessary." Neither the US Constitution nor our model is based on unrealistic assumptions about human nature.

But career ambition and party competition are not all bad. In the marketplace there are duopolistic firms that compete with each other for the primary purpose of making money, but in the process they develop new products at low prices. In the political marketplace, teams of office-seeking politicians *could* be induced to improve the lives of their constituents—not out of patriotism or altruism, but for fear of getting fired. The challenge for citizens is to harness their legislators' career ambition to serve public ends.

One positive step would be to shift the emphasis of campaigns from *positions* to *results*. Citizens, reporters, interest groups, and challengers focus a great deal of attention on incumbents' past votes and the future votes of challengers and incumbents. The result is that legislators enter (or return to) office with a set of constraints on how they vote, but few commitments on which legislative proposals they will advocate, nor what policy change they will accomplish. As individuals and parties, their incentive is to accumulate a set of favorable issue positions, not a set of positive accomplishments. Unless the White House and both chambers of Congress are staffed by politicians who have an identical set of issue positions, this is a recipe for inflexible bargaining positions and status quo policy.

Whatever direction political parties take, scholars and citizens benefit from a model that explains the challenges that politicians face and the role of competing parties in addressing those challenges. We hope that *strategic party government* is useful for this purpose.

Notes

Chapter One

1. Laws per Congress data are from Ornstein et al. (2013). For "worst Congress" columns, see Bolton (2014), Marcos and Cox (2014), Milbank (2014), and Topaz (2014). David Boaz (2014) and Charles Cooke (2015) respond that a Congress that "governs least" is commendable for not making any errors of commission, but clearly conservatives had disappointed aspirations as well.

2. Examples include Republican efforts to pass a tariff bill in 1883 (McCown 1927) and Democratic leaders' efforts to pass the Interstate Commerce Act in 1887 (James 2000).

3. For our purposes, it is necessary that a model do more than merely predict outcomes. A useful model of politics also provides the conceptual framework for explaining why we observe the behavior and outcomes that we do and provides the foundation for evaluation. Is this the way politics *should* be organized? What sort of reforms would change the political system to better achieve social goals?

4. The "party effects" literature is voluminous; as an introduction, we refer the reader to exemplary works on voting (Ansolabehere et al. 2001; Cox and Poole 2002; King and Zeckhauser 2003; Sinclair 2002), agenda setting (Covington and Bargen 2004; Cox and McCubbins 1993, 2005; Gailmard and Jenkins 2007; Marshall 2002; Sinclair 1994, 2002; Talbert and Potoski 2002) and outcomes (Cox and McCubbins 2005; den Hartog and Monroe 2008; Lawrence et al. 2006; Snyder and Groseclose 2000).

5. As discussed in chapter 2, Patty (2008) develops a CPG-like model of delegation to party leaders, which predicts that party voting will vary with party size. Our model shares some of the logic of Patty's equilibrium party government model approach, although we differ on whether legislators seek policy outcomes per se.

6. Specifically, in the cartel model the majority party seeks to protect status quo policies that lie between the majority party median and the chamber median.

7. In November 2003, for example, the Republican majority in the US House

narrowly passed a bill to expand the Medicare program to provide prescription drug coverage to senior citizens. At the time, Medicare offered no drug coverage, and the bill did not offset the cost of the program, so it was expected to add at least $400 billion to the federal deficit. As such, we would expect "conservative" members to vote against the bill and "liberal" members to vote for it, with the overall margin reflecting the extent to which the bill changed the status quo relative to the median member of the chamber. Instead, "liberals" voted *against* expanding Medicare while just twenty-five members of the "conservative" party voted against the bill. Using the NOMINATE process, these twenty-five votes are classified as "errors" because they are actual expressions of personal and constituency views instead of party strategy.

8. Here Cox and McCubbins's (1993) analogy of parties to firms is helpful: in theory, firms seek to maximize profits for shareholders, who in turn use the money to pursue a limitless number of ends.

9. See Bawn (1998) for a discussion of how party leaders may be responsive to intense subgroups within their legislative caucuses.

10. An interesting pair of articles finds that this diversity is reflected in the initial stages of congressional representation—funding requests and bill cosponsorship—and is subsequently "organized" by legislative parties (Potoski and Talbert 2000; Talbert and Potoski 2002). Harbridge (2015) also finds that party leaders are more likely to select bills with partisan supporting coalitions for the chamber agenda and less likely to prioritize bills with bipartisan support coalitions.

Chapter Two

1. Cox and McCubbins use the analogy of legislators "posting a bond" so that leaders can punish them (revoke the bond) if they are insufficiently loyal—for example, by stripping them of committee assignments or committee seniority. Below we use a similar notion, in which legislators provide leaders with a "budget" of delegated power; unlike a "bond," this budget can be used to reward as well as punish.

2. Cox and McCubbins document the existence of partisan electoral tides (1993, 112–22) but do not further explore the connections among legislative actions, party reputations, and election outcomes.

3. To be clear, this is only a portion of Aldrich's formal account of parties. He goes on to discuss the incentives for ambitious politicians to develop political parties to institutionalize cooperation while running for office (1995, 45–57) and the incentives for legislators to strengthen or weaken their parties (1995, 208–40).

4. The "bond" notion adds clarity to Patty's model of voting decisions, while our "budget" approach better reflects the range of rewards and punishments meted out by party leaders. But both conceptualizations involve legislators making a col-

lective decision to give power to party leaders to resolve the tensions between individual and collective interests.

5. Some valence traits are ascriptive: race, gender, age, attractiveness. Other valence traits are based on a "life profile": hometown, school affiliations, prior career. For our purposes, *electoral skill* (personal aptitude at speaking, fund-raising, and other campaign activities) and *legislative skill* (including past policy and pork delivered for the district) are considered valence, ignoring any interactions with ideology or generic incumbency advantage. On the complex relationship between valence and candidate positioning, see Carter and Patty (2015) and Stone and Simas (2010).

6. For our purpose, it is not important to resolve here whether voters evaluate candidates in terms of distinct policy issues or based on overall ideology. In chapters 3 and 4, we focus on overall ideology measures derived from roll call votes.

7. Strong views on policy do not necessarily mean a strong preference for legislators with high levels of partisanship. Since 2009, the Republican Party has been coping with a "Tea Party" faction of voters and activists that combines strongly conservative policy views with high levels of skepticism toward party leaders and legislators who cooperate with their parties.

8. While we are interested in how public opinion of political parties responds to the actions of election leaders, it is also clear that individual voters exhibit a great deal of loyalty to their preferred political parties (Campbell et al 1960; Green et al. 2002) and that these loyalties can affect how citizens interpret events and public debates (Gaines et al. 2007). The key point here is that party evaluations are at least partially endogenous (Fiorina 2002).

9. It is worth noting some of what we do not know about party reputations. In particular, we know very little about how voters process political information into party reputations. Far more research has studied the mechanisms working in the other direction—for example, how ideology and opinions about parties affect the processing and updating of political information.

10. This is a loose translation. More precisely, Madison is concerned with self-interested "factions" that seek their own interests above the national interest or at the expense of another group. Madison expects that cohesive factions are unlikely to form a majority in an extended republic. In our interpretation, this further implies that any cooperation (i.e., a party) between the representatives of different factions would falter because it would be difficult for legislators to defend their vote-trading roll calls in their home districts.

11. This could occur if a vote poses a choice between two core constituencies, such as a Democrat facing a choice that pits labor unions against environmentalists so that either way an MC must provide fodder for a potential primary election challenger and, if nominated, risk diminished general election support from the disappointed group. Or a vote may force a choice between the preferences of a core group of supporters and general public opinion so that an MC must choose

between an increased risk of losing a primary election and an increased risk of losing a general election. Some votes on gun restrictions present Republicans with this kind of difficult choice.

12. The dividing line illustrates the case of a legislator who assigns roughly equal weight to political and policy payoffs. We could assume that legislators care primarily about policy outcomes (in which case, the line would be more vertical) or electoral implications (making the line more horizontal). Our logic applies as long as legislators attach value to both reelection and policy making.

13. A recent example is the 2008 Troubled Asset Relief Program (TARP), which authorized the federal government to purchase up to $700 billion in low-grade investments. While many policy makers were convinced that this was necessary to stabilize the financial system, it was also a very unpopular policy.

14. For this discussion, we assume that party leaders care primarily about the electoral implications of votes for individual legislators and the effect of collective *outcomes* on party reputation. It is possible that leaders may care about the political implications of vote margins per se—for example, wanting to see their own proposals pass by large margins, striving to ensure that the proposals of the opposing party pass by narrow margins, or being concerned about the message sent by a single vote. Jeanette Rankin's (R-MT) 1941 vote against declaring war on Japan is an example of how a single legislator's vote can impact collective party reputations.

15. Obviously, it is an oversimplification to state that the majority party enjoys agenda-setting power in the US Senate, in which the minority party is able to filibuster majority proposals (Binder and Smith 1997; Koger 2010), which allows both a minority veto over legislation and bargaining over the terms of floor debate. A full discussion of obstruction and agenda setting is outside the scope of this chapter, but we concur with den Hartog and Monroe (2011) that the majority party in the Senate retains a significant degree of agenda-setting power.

16. Readers who prefer to think in terms of ideology can think of this as a liberal versus conservative dimension.

17. It may even be possible to "buy" the votes of party members to the left of A in figure 2.2 if leaders offer sufficient incentive. We expect, though, that explicit quid pro quo agreements are relatively rare, since they are difficult to negotiate and enforce and because there are usually "cheaper" votes available.

18. To simplify presentation, this section leaves out a couple nuances: (a) minority party opposition may influence the PR benefits of winning (i.e., whether the bill was a "bipartisan triumph" or a "partisan steamroller") and, similarly, (b) individual legislators' payoffs for voting may be affected by the voting of the other party; a majority party member may be willing to vote for a measure if there is some support from the other party.

19. Since 2011, there have been multiple violations of the "Hastert Rule" in the US House—the expectation that a majority party will not allow bills on the floor

that a majority of the majority party opposes. In each high-profile case, however, there is a compelling explanation for why the majority party's reputation is better off allowing a policy defeat to avoid a political disaster. See "House Votes Violating the 'Hastert Rule,'" *New York Times*, 2014.

20. Formally, committee assignments are now approved by the US House and Senate, but in action, each party arranges its own committee slates without challenge. On change in party rules, see Rohde 1991; on the revision of chamber rules to empower party leaders, see Binder 1997; Koger 2006; Schickler 2001.

21. Sinclair (1995, ch. 2) makes this point. When House conservatives calling themselves the "Freedom Caucus" revolted against Speaker John Boehner during the fall of 2015, a major underlying complaint was the extent to which policy making was centralized in the Speaker's office, leaving lay members with little influence (Sherman 2015).

22. See also Patty 2008; Smith 2007.

23. Obviously, here we invoke the median voter theorem (Black 1948). Patty (2008) makes a similar claim. The coevolution of party rules, chamber rules, and leadership is, however, a potential topic for further research.

24. We ignore here the possibility that there are multiple levels of party influence that yield the same optimal level of net benefit.

25. This section also draws heavily on Intriligator and Brito (1976, 78–79) and Simaan and Cruz (1975, 96–98).

26. Rohde (1991, 120–61) anticipates this claim in his account of the Republicans' response to the strengthening Democratic Party. Also, Volden and Bergman (2006) predict symmetric party pressure in a modified pivot model.

27. It is also possible that international conflict will increase "fatigue" by increasing the political cost of domestic conflict (Bafumi and Parent 2012).

28. Legislators will differ about how much party influence maximizes this balance, and so each party will end up choosing the level preferred by its average member—that is, given perfect information, the median member of the party will choose a level of party influence so that there is enough party influence to "buy" all bills for which the potential benefits of party influence outweigh or equal the associated cost.

29. In figure 2.3, the costs and benefits of PU_D correspond to specific areas, so we can think of the Democrats' goal as maximizing the benefits region minus the cost region. The gain from PU_D is a quadrilateral demarcated by the x-axis, the y-axis, the marginal electoral gains line, and a horizontal line extending from PU_D on the y-axis to the benefits line. The cost region is everything above the marginal electoral costs line and below a horizontal line extending from PU_D to the costs line. PU_D^* maximizes the net difference between the costs and benefits of opposition.

30. After the 2008 election, for example, the Republicans might have decided that their losses were attributable to being (a) too conservative in the past, (b) too

moderate in the past, or (c) unlucky to hold the White House when the economy suffered a sudden downturn. In the end, they opted for "b," but there was a case to be made for each explanation of the results.

31. For example, the decision of legislators to vote with their party is an ongoing one.

Chapter Three

1. The spatial model is applied more plausibly to party activists since these actors by definition possess the high interest levels necessary to develop their own political thinking and collect information about available candidates (e.g., Aldrich 1983; Miller and Schofield 2003).

2. Indeed, in papers that discuss voting by mental shortcut, it is more or less obligatory to open not only with a reference to the lack of knowledge and competence of voters as uncovered by Converse and others in the late 1950s and early 1960s (Campbell et al. 1960; Converse 1964) but with a reference to the very ubiquity, since Converse, of references in the literature to this lack of knowledge.

3. Like Rahn (1993), Lau and Redlawsk (2001) consider both ideology and partisanship as schemata—rich stereotypes—that contain a lot of information. Partisanship appears to be more the stereotype and ideology the more deeply informative. Lau and Redlawsk find that all the heuristics are used and that most participants used both ideology and party, but that increasing political sophistication generally increased the use of ideology and decreased the use of party. This is some evidence that, perhaps, ideology is functioning less in the classic role of a heuristic.

4. Both adult samples were recruited mainly by visiting professional offices or coffeehouses and asking for volunteers. The adult sample was recruited because, after attaining the expected results from the student sample, we wished to ensure that the effect was not sample specific. In particular we worried that the word "liberal," seen as a pejorative in wide swaths of American politics, was not sufficiently toxic to the students.

5. Examples of low-diagnostic information given are age, marital status, number and age of children, hobbies, and charitable interests.

6. Using the change from the initial electoral support to the level of support after the roll call information allows us to control for a great many unmeasured factors, including a participant's tendency to support any new politician at all.

7. Additional details on the experimental design and samples of these pages are shown in the online appendix, available at http://press.uchicago.edu/sites/koger, tables A.3.1a and A.3.1b.

8. Randomization was carried out with the caveat that the probability of a participant seeing a "full lockstep voter"—that is, a politician who was a 90 percent

or 100 percent ideologue or partisan, was exactly 0.5. This ensured a deep enough pool of subjects who encountered each of the two legislator types. Care was taken so that the following aspects of the presentation were randomized for each subject: whether the partisan-described legislator was predominantly a Democrat or a Republican; whether the ideology-described legislator was predominantly liberal or conservative; on which issues the legislator was shown to "deviate" from his party or ideological camp; on how many issues the legislator deviated; whether the partisan-described or the ideology-described legislator was shown first; the order in which the ten issues were presented; and the particular issues on which the legislator deviated. The randomization helps us obtain, as purely as possible, a measure of the effect of lockstep voting on our participants' change in electoral support. It avoids some possible confounding effects, such as the possibility that participants might base their support only on politicians' votes on the first and/or last issue presented, or on representatives' deviations from ideological or partisan orthodoxy on particular issues of systematically greater import to the subjects in the sample.

9. Note that nowhere on the politician page does it say, explicitly, that the politician took a side any certain percentage of the time. Subjects were left to gather this perception simply by looking at the issue positions one by one.

10. See the online appendix for additional information on randomization, the use of distracter questions, and more on trait evaluations.

11. We believe this dichotomous coding reflects the likelihood that the differences between, say, a 9-out-of-10 and a 10-out-of-10 politician may not seem so large to a voter. Instead, voters more generally may see politicians as being predictably one-sided or less so.

12. For example, if the incumbent votes more often with the Republicans and the participant is a strong Republican (7 on the 7-point scale), the participant is scored 0 on this variable, indicating that the voter and the legislator match. If the incumbent votes more often with the Democrats, this same voter would be scored a 1, indicating a strong mismatch. All pure independents—people who did not identify with, say, either the Republican or the Democratic Party, were recoded to 0.5, indicating neither a voter-incumbent match nor a mismatch.

13. The estimation is from a seemingly unrelated regressions design, which allows the creation of a single covariance matrix of coefficients for the purposes of comparing coefficient sizes between the partisan-incumbent and the ideological-incumbent equations.

14. A Wald test shows that the coefficients for partisan and ideological extremity are significantly different from each other ($p < 0.001$). These results hold when we adjust our coding of the key independent variables. See the online appendix for details.

15. One exception here: the coefficient for partisan lockstep voting is absolutely larger at -1.22 for the higher incomes in the adult sample ($p = 0.04$), the only sample for which income was asked.

16. It is worth noting the extent to which subjects were paying attention to legislative behavior at all. While a laboratory experiment cannot speak directly to what real-world voters attend to, it would not have surprised some if our subjects had reacted barely at all to a bland list of roll call votes characterized merely by ideological or partisan labels when the stakes for "voters" could not have been lower. Many of the issue positions likely had no personal relevance to participants, and yet they were clearly aware of the extent of the legislator's devotion to one side or the other.

17. Unless otherwise stated, the two subsamples are combined for the analyses that follow.

18. The issue questions dealt specifically with: abortion; gay marriage; the acceptability of "alternative lifestyles"; posting the Ten Commandments on government property; constitutional literalism versus contextualism; support for income redistribution; support for regulating business to protect the environment; support for government assistance to the poor; support for a public versus a private, profit-driven health care system; the death penalty; English-only laws; and foreign-policy unilateralism versus multilateralism.

19. Crohnbach's $\alpha = 0.83$. And ideological self-identification is slightly more highly correlated with issue-position-based ideology ($r = 0.72$) than party ID is ($r = 0.66$).

20. There are precious few nonpartisans or nonideologues (those choosing 4 on the 1-to-7 self-placement scales) in our sample so running the model on them alone is not a reliable exercise.

21. Recall that due to randomization, a participant in our sample, regardless of her own party identification, was exactly as likely to see a legislator from her own party as from the other.

22. The Wald test is not quite significantly different from zero.

23. This finding is somewhat in contrast to Harbridge and Malhotra's (2011) finding that strong partisans dislike partisanship in the aggregate but approve of it with respect to individual members of Congress.

24. A fourth question was included for the student sample.

25. Here, social identity is standardized so that the "main" effect of the legislator's partisan lockstep voting is estimated at the mean level of partisan social identity.

26. We ran additional models to ensure that our findings here were not due to partisanship serving as a proxy for political sophistication. See note in the online appendix, *Social Identity or Sophistication?*

27. Notably, the predictability question characterized "predictability" not pejoratively but instead asked whether the participant gets "the impression that this candidate relies on ideological principles, so that you know what to expect" of him. This wording intended to test for our suspicion that ideological extremity in a legislator might cause voters to see the legislator as principled, whereas partisan

lockstepping might produce an impression not of principle but of a failure to be independent-minded. The trait questions were randomized with respect to each other so that no particular trait question would systematically prejudice answers to the others. The final measure of electoral support was also asked as part of this series of questions so that participants would not always indicate electoral support after having committed themselves to a certain personality profile as describing the incumbent.

28. Indeed, an exploratory factor analysis of the 7 trait perception items yields a first eigenvalue of 2.4 and a second eigenvalue of 0.47—consistent with the presence of only a single factor. "Toughness" does not significantly load on this factor, however.

29. Crohnbach's $\alpha = 0.79$.

30. See the online appendix and tables A.3.3, A.3.4, and A.3.5.

31. See the online appendix and table A.3.4 for more detail on this comparison.

Chapter Four

1. Parts of this chapter appear in Carson, Koger, Lebo, and Young (2010) and Koger and Lebo (2012).

2. Of course, there are possible reasons why legislators might do this: they may be indifferent to their electoral fortunes or completely uncertain about the relationship between roll call votes and elections. They may feel "locked" into the ideological positions they adopted early in their careers, or their campaign fundraising may be tied to their ideological position such that they would suffer a net electoral loss by shifting to better reflect their constituents' views.

3. One form of "unpopular" vote not listed below arises when interest subgroups within a district have conflicting preferences—for example, doctors contesting with lawyers over medical malpractice laws. These votes force MCs to choose which group they prefer, and in doing so, they create subsets of disappointed constituents.

4. Lee (2009, 25) points out that for much of congressional history, congressional observers did not use ideological terminology to explain legislative behavior, instead focusing on whether legislators adhered to "party principles"—that is, ideology had little meaning outside of a partisan context, and legislators were either loyal or disloyal to party positions. Noel (2014, 78–92) contends that distinct ideological coalitions developed in the mid-twentieth century among elite thinkers permeated to political activists and gradually led to a "takeover" of the two major parties by conservatives and liberals. Lee and Noel may disagree about the extent to which the modern divide between Republicans and Democrats can be characterized as ideological. We think they are both correct: modern political parties consist of coalitions of actors and organizations with shared policy views

(see Koger et al. 2009), and legislators of each party strive to act in a manner that pleases these coalitions. Like Lee, however, we do not suggest that legislators' actions conform to the assumptions of the spatial models used to infer their ideology nor that their revealed behavior accurately reflects the true extent of policy (dis) agreement between the two parties.

5. Bovitz and Carson (2006) provide evidence of electoral accountability in conjunction with legislative voting on individual roll calls in the US House. Bonney, Canes-Wrone, and Minozzi (2011) find similar evidence with respect to crime policy in Congress.

6. For members of the House, we use the average score for each two-year term. For senators, we use the average score for each six-year term. For some years, CQ counted absences against one's unity score, while for other years they did not. We recode the data so that absences do not count for or against one's score. We recognize there are limitations of using party unity scores in analyses of legislative behavior, especially in terms of measuring how much influence parties exert over member actions independent of preferences (see, e.g., Krehbiel 1993). Since we are interested in understanding the electoral consequences of party unity on a subset of divisive roll call votes and *not* trying to measure party influence on these roll calls, however, we do not view this limitation as adversely affecting the scope of our analysis.

7. McDonald's record of voting with his party less than 4 percent of the time fits with his conservative credentials. As a Democrat from Georgia's Seventh District from 1975 to 1983, McDonald became the president of the John Birch Society while serving in the House. He once said, "We have four boxes with which to defend our freedom: the soap box, the ballot box, the jury box, and the cartridge box" (Avlon 2010). McDonald was aboard Korean Air Flight KAL-007, which was shot down by the Soviets in 1983, thus becoming the only US member of Congress killed by the Soviet Union during the Cold War. Clifford Case began in the House in 1954 as an anti-McCarthy Republican and, as a senator, sponsored the Case-Church Amendment to prohibit further military action in Southeast Asia in 1973.

8. More specifically, they are derived using an item response model to estimate the number of substantive dimensions in legislative voting and each legislator's ideal point on these dimensions. DW-NOMINATE scores are based on a wider set of votes than party unity scores. The former includes all nonunanimous votes, including votes on which a majority of both parties votes against a minority of one party, or a bipartisan minority coalition.

9. Since we are only interested in incumbents running for reelection, there is no loss of cases by including this lagged variable for the House. Given concerns about the consequences to inference of including a lagged endogenous variable (Achen 2000), this variable does not appear in all of our House models.

10. Presidential approval is scored as the raw approval number minus 50 percent and multiplied by −1 for members not of the president's party. Change in real

disposable income is taken from the third quarter of the election year and is multiplied by −1 for members of the out-party.

11. Specifically, we use XTIVREG commands in Stata 12, a generalized two-stage least-squares panel data estimator with fixed effects and instrumental variables (Baltagi 2005). We also estimated our models using random effects and random coefficient models. In every case, our findings were nearly identical. We present the fixed effects models due to their ease of interpretation—the coefficients are the within-year effects on the dependent variable due to a one-unit increase in the independent variable of interest. Note that low values of ρ in the tables indicate that the vast majority of unexplained variance is going on within years rather than between years, thus making the results of the various approaches quite similar.

12. Our study is the first to apply a two-stage approach to electoral outcomes, but Canes-Wrone, Rabinovich, and Volden (2007) use a two-stage model to explain ideological extremity in legislative voting.

13. When we use party unity as an endogenous variable and revealed preferences as an instrument in a first-stage equation, our instrument tests can tell us if preferences predict unity but not incumbent vote share. If preferences are not a good instrument, they belong in the second-stage equation as a direct predictor of incumbent vote share.

14. However, this costs us cases. It is left out of the Senate models to conserve cases. Since the first stage involves using the lag of party unity, for freshmen we use the value of party unity of the previous person to hold the seat. This is justifiable in that we expect similar patterns of unity based on the type of district. Doing so allows us to keep freshmen in the sample. When we leave freshmen out, the results are somewhat stronger.

15. For comparisons when not accounting for electoral security, *Incumbent Vote*$_{t-1}$ is left out of model 1 of table 4.1. Throughout, identification is helped by having at least two instruments that are uncorrelated with the second-stage errors (see Wooldridge 2002, 90).

16. Random effects models give very similar results to these fixed effects models, and Hausman tests establish that there are no distinguishable differences in our coefficient estimates.

17. It does, however, prove to be a useful instrumental variable as a predictor of party unity with *z* statistics of 15.82 and 14.74 in the first stage of the two models.

18. These are abbreviated results of models where we move extremity from the first stage to the second stage. Our instrument tests suggest that models 1b and 2b are misspecified (and may suffer from the endogeneity bias that partially motivates our two-stage approach), but they do allow *Extremity* to predict *Voteshare* side-by-side with predicted values of *Party Unity*. Thus our assertions in support of *Party Unity* do not rest only on our two-stage modeling strategy. For the complete results of these models, see the online appendix.

19. It might seem plausible that an incumbent's *Voteshare* would depend on a longer voting history so that *Unity$_{t-1}$* might belong in the second stage of the equation. The instrument tests including the Hansen-Sargan results indicate this is not a problem. What useful information might be present in *Unity$_{t-1}$* to predict *Voteshare$_t$* is accounted for by incumbents' most recent voting record.

20. The Hansen-Sargan χ^2 test easily shows that extremity is properly excluded from the second-stage equation ($p = 0.84$).

21. *Voteshare* values are predicted in a first-stage equation that uses challenger quality, spending gap, lagged values of incumbent vote share, freshman status, change in income growth, and presidential approval as instruments. These are all excluded from the second stage of the estimation. All but income growth are instruments for the Senate.

22. Note that all these results hold when we move *Extremity* alongside *Unity* and use a single-stage approach. Also see Carson, Koger, Lebo, and Young (2010) for additional analyses of non-Southern states as well as interactive relationships between *District Partisanship* and *Party Unity, Change in Personal Income* and *Party Unity*, and *Presidential Approval* and *Party Unity*.

23. We treat Δ*Party Unity* as an endogenous variable and use Δ*Extremity* and *Party Unity$_{t-1}$* as instruments. Δ*Party Unity* and *Party Unity$_{t-1}$* are strongly and negatively correlated, since our instrument accounts for a natural tendency of *Party Unity* to regress to its mean. That is, holding all else equal, when *Party Unity* at *t–1* is high (or low), it moves lower (or higher) as it changes in the next period. *Party Unity$_{t-1}$* is properly excluded in the second stage, since it has no direct effect on Δ*Voteshare$_t$*.

24. The ideal points of legislators can change slightly between congresses as a result of additional votes being added to the roll call matrix (Poole and Rosenthal 2007).

25. CQ "key votes" are about twenty votes a year in each chamber that CQ considered salient and important. We exclude key votes on which a majority of both party voted the same way.

26. The first stage equation is <u>Party Unity</u> = β_9 + β_{10}(Blue Dog) + β_{11}(Progressive) + β_{12}(RSC) + [all second-stage variables] + ξ. The second stage is <u>Incumbent Vote Share</u> = β_0 + β_1(Party Unity) + β_2(Democrat) + β_3(2008 Presidential Vote) + β_4(Pork Projects) + β_5(Dem. Pork Projects) + β_5(Spending Gap) + β_6(Freshman) + β_7(New Democratic Coalition) + β_8(GOP Main Street) + ε. The NDC and GOP Main Street members are included in the second stage because preliminary regressions (and Sargan statistical tests) suggested that membership in these caucuses was correlated with both party unity and electoral vote share. We also estimated our equations using DW-NOMINATE first-dimension scores together with caucus membership as instruments. This gave a slight improvement in instruments' R^2 but no substantive change in our findings.

27. The Hansen-Sargan χ^2 test shows that extremity is properly excluded from

the second-stage equation for the first two models ($p = 0.3645$ and $p = 0.1886$). For the presidential support analysis, the test does not apply to the Republican model (column 3) because there is only one instrument. The test raises warnings about our analysis of Democratic presidential support. Here we use the same model for comparability. In a model that uses Progressive caucus membership as a second-stage predictor of incumbent vote share, Progressive caucus membership is correlated with a −2.1 percent loss ($p = 0.032$).

28. For the presidential support results, the R^2 of the excluded instruments is a bit low for the Republicans. In a separate result, we recalculated this equation adding pork projects as an instrument. This increased the R^2 without raising endogeneity problems. The results for other variables in both stages were essentially the same. Here we display the initial results to maintain consistency across models and to demonstrate that pork projects are not directly related to electoral success.

29. This is the number of fiscal year 2010 pork projects that Citizens Against Government Waste attributed to each member (see http://www.cagw.org/). For projects with multiple sponsors, each sponsor received full credit. The mean and standard deviation for Republicans were 15.8 and 15.3, respectively. For Democrats, the mean was 23.6 projects with a standard deviation of 13.8. Overall, the mean was 20.4 with a standard deviation of 14.9.

30. This is an imperfect approach. Like overall *Party Unity*, we would expect these votes to be endogenous; vulnerable members avoid voting for controversial measures.

Chapter Five

1. One extension of this work is to test whether members choose party leaders and party rules to advance electoral goals. Gamm and Smith (2006), for example, stress that electoral considerations motivate innovation in party structure and that Senate party leaders are expected to advance senators' electoral interests and the party's public reputation.

2. Our sample here is the first 111 congresses. Yearly variables are averaged over each Congress. We use fractional differencing to control for nonstationarity.

3. For the Thirty-Fourth House (1855–57), we use the final vote for Speaker (pro-Banks = Republican) to define coalitions. Party factions—for example, Van Buren Democrats—are reunited with their parent parties for our analyses. Independents and members of third parties are dropped from the analyses, except in recent years. "Independent" legislators such as Bernie Sanders (I/D-VT) are coded with a major party if they attend its meetings or obtain committee assignments from the party.

4. By using the win rate on all party votes, we combine salient image-defining votes with less important votes that also divided the parties.

5. These are calculated by Ornstein, Mann, and Malbin (2008) from analysis of CQ Weekly Reports. They divide the number of votes supporting the president's stated position by the total number of votes on which he took a position. To account for the fact that our dependent variable is Democratic chamber share, we take the raw proportion of presidential wins and subtract the average proportion (0.684 in the House and 0.576 in the Senate) and then multiply values by −1 during Republican presidencies.

6. While other variables such as economic conditions and campaign financing may be important, it is impossible to collect such data for long enough to make our time series analyses useful.

7. From 1953 to September 1981, the question read, "Do you approve or disapprove of the way [president's last name] is handling his job as President?" Between October 1981 and 2000, the question read, "Do you approve or disapprove of the way [president's first and last name] is handling his job as President?"

8. For tests of this assumption, see chapter 7.

9. For the full results of these models, see online appendix tables A.5.1 and A.5.2.

10. In addition to control variables for midterm and presidential swings, our Senate election analysis accounts for variation in the set of senators up for election each year. Since shifts in party composition in one election may be due to exposure (the party balance of senators up for reelection) rather than partisan behavior, we include the value of the dependent variable (again, *change* in party composition) from six years prior as a predictor variable. The negative coefficient shows that a party's success in one election increases exposure and costs them seats in the election six years later. Note, however, that this is only true in the modern era.

11. Gailmard and Jenkins (2009) similarly find that senators were more responsive to their state's voters after the adoption of the Seventeenth Amendment. They find that the DW-NOMINATE scores of senators from the same state tended to deviate more from each other after the adoption of direct elections, suggesting that legislators have increased discretion in voting.

12. "What Americans Know, 1989–2007." Pew Research Center. Downloaded April 12, 2010, from http://people-press.org/report/319/public-knowledge-of-current-affairs-little-changed-by-news-and-information-revolutions.

13. One member is equal to just under 0.23 percent of the chamber in a 435-seat House. Over the period of table 5.2, the average win rate for a president was 61.2 percent. An example of the effect is the Republicans' loss of 11.3 percent of the share of the House in the 1974 elections after President Nixon's win rate fell from 83.55 percent to 55.80 percent from the Ninety-Second to Ninety-Third Congress (Lebo and O'Geen 2011).

14. See the online appendix for explanation of the variables and table A.5.3 for full results.

Chapter Six

1. Using sessions would give too much weight to special sessions. Studying the 111 congresses would halve our sample and eliminate interesting within-Congress variation. Votes were excluded if most of one party voted while most of the other party did not, suggesting the strategic use of abstention—a form of filibustering known as a "disappearing quorum" (Koger 2010).

2. Of course, the "Democratic" and "Republican" labels were not used throughout the 1789–2010 time-span. By "Democratic," we mean opponents of the Washington administration, the (Jeffersonian) Republican Party, supporters of Andrew Jackson, and members labeled "Democrat" or "Independent Democrat," all identified using Kenneth Martis's (1989) party affiliation coding. By "Republican," we mean supporters of the Washington administration, Federalists, pro-Adams and anti-Jackson factions, Whigs, and members labeled "Republicans" and "Independent Republicans." For the thirty-fourth House (1855–57), we use the final vote for Speaker (pro-Banks = Republican) to define coalitions. Party factions—for example, Van Buren Democrats—are reunited with their parent parties for our analyses. Independents and members of third parties are dropped from the analyses. We do not imply that these labels signify two constant coalitions. Rather, we merely assume that the coalitions we identify are similar to the group of legislators with the same label in adjacent years. Basically, we are interested in explaining how parties respond to their opponents, and we expect similar behavior from the modern Democrats facing the Republicans as we do from the nineteenth-century Democrats facing the Whigs.

3. This was first described by Granger (1981) and Engle and Granger (1987) and was used to describe close relationships between macroeconomic variables. For example, income and consumption at the national level (or even at the personal level) are in such an equilibrium relationship. Country-level income is strongly enough related to how much its people spend that if earnings and spending move too far apart, they each adjust to the other and reequilibrate.

4. The level of aggregation plays a role here as well. Parties may respond to each other sequentially, but the yearly aggregation makes such moves appear contemporaneous.

5. Also, it meant that the bill that passed was more liberal than a version that could have gained unanimous Democratic support. Each vote beyond 219 would have pushed the content of the bill further to the right.

6. Scores are by Congress, so these series change only every other year.

7. We agree with Cooper and Young (2002) that DW-NOMINATE scores may not accurately represent *party* voting behavior, since differences in DW-NOMINATE party medians between congresses are often unrelated to differences in unity over the same period. Further, the methods used to compare member behavior over time often involve using data from previous congresses to

explain behavior in current periods, "with the result that votes in a particular Congress are discounted if they do not meet certain parameters. Hence, the full impact of party in structuring voting patterns in particular Congresses may not be captured" (Schickler 2000).

8. In a wider analysis of various ideological measures, Bishin (2004) states, "Examination of general ideological trends in Congress are best described using NOMINATE scores."

9. We follow fractional integration techniques set out in Box-Steffensmeier and Smith (1996), Lebo, Walker, and Clarke (2000), and Clarke and Lebo (2003). See the online appendix for details and tests on the stationarity of our data.

10. See the online appendix for a discussion of cointegration and fractional cointegration.

11. See the online appendix for a discussion of our three-stage least-squares approach (Kmenta 1997).

12. See the online appendix and table A.7.1 for discussion, descriptive statistics, and estimates of d.

13. See the online appendix for a discussion of our ECM approach.

14. Lags of right-hand-side variables are included where significant and of left-hand-side variables to account for autocorrelation still present after differencing.

15. This was tried in every equation for both NOMINATE dimensions and was dropped when not significant. Substantively, it means that unity rises when opposition cohesion rises.

16. For each chamber, combining Democratic Unity, Republican Unity, and Democratic Size yields a series with a lower d—faster mean reversion—than any of the three variables.

17. Having the fastest mean reversion ($d = 0.38$) for the Senate Democrats' ECM shows this, too.

18. The Senate's election of only a third of its members per Congress may be the cause of this effect occurring with a lag, as it takes time for changes in delegations to affect voting behavior.

19. In addition, the forecast root MSE is improved in each case when we go from forecasts estimated using the CPG model to those estimated using the SPG model. For example, using the House data, the equations of Democratic and Republican unity have root MSEs of 8.51 and 7.91, respectively, when the SPG variables are excluded. Once SPG variables are included, these errors drop to 8.03 and 7.55. We performed several other diagnostic tests. Durbin-Watson statistics indicate that our methods have done a good job of controlling for autocorrelation, and tests of the residuals indicate they are white noise. Lastly, our Hausman specification tests all indicate a well-specified model with no evidence of omitted variables or endogeneity.

20. Our analysis explains a substantial portion of the variance in our dependent variable with R^2 between .35 and .45 for our four equations.

21. The figure is based on data in a single equation model. We also used Tse's (2000) test of constant correlations between the unity levels of the two parties in each of the chambers and were unable to reject the null hypothesis that the correlations between the variables are constant over our sample period ($p = 0.18$ for the House and $p = 0.19$ for the Senate). Koger and Lebo (2006) apply Engle's (2002) dynamic conditional correlation estimator to these data and find that while the strategic behavior of parties in Congress has always been present, it has fluctuated in its strength over time. See tables A.7.2 and A.7.3 of the online appendix for complete models estimated in each of four separate periods: 1792–1824, 1825–60, 1861–1932, and 1933–2010. In each period, we find strong support for hypotheses 7.1, 7.2, and 7.3.

22. A full exposition of this period would trace every reform in chamber rules and party rules, every leadership contest, and collective shifts in party voting. This has been the subject of much recent research (e.g., Binder 1997; Lee 2009; Schickler 2001; Zelizer 2004), which we draw upon for this section.

23. On January 16, 1975, the caucus's power over committee chairmen claimed its first victim when F. Edward Hebert was defeated in his bid to hold on to the chairmanship of the Committee on Armed Services. Hebert, a Louisiana member of the House since his election in 1940, had been criticized for being too easy on the Republican administration overseeing the Vietnam War—for example, refusing to hold hearings on the bombing of Cambodia. His ousting was called by the *Washington Post* "a stunning abandonment of tradition . . . the first occasion in modern times that a party caucus had abandoned the seniority system to remove a chairman" (Farrell 2002, 401). The removal of Hebert, who declined to run for reelection in 1976, also served to break the hold of Southerners in the power structure of the Democratic Caucus.

24. The Utah Republicans used a two-stage nomination process in which a candidate could win the nomination by obtaining the support of a majority of delegates at a state party convention. If not, the top two convention candidates would face off in a statewide primary. Bennett came in third at the 2010 convention behind Mike Lee and Tim Bridgewater (Hohmann 2010).

25. It is worth stressing that these were the largest majorities in the House and Senate since 1994 and 1980, respectively. Some scholars argue that narrow majority margins are a contributing factor to congressional partisanship by giving hope to the minority party that they are just an election away from majority status. By this logic, the Republicans should have abandoned hope and bargained for favorable legislative compromises in 2009–10.

26. Formally, a cloture vote imposes a thirty-hour limit on debate of bills and major nominations. In practice, senators recognize these votes as the de facto test of whether a bill has enough support to pass. For more on filibustering and cloture, see Koger (2010), Krehbiel (1998), and Sinclair (2002). Two landmark bills—the 2009 stimulus bill and the 2010 Dodd-Frank financial reform bill—cleared this

hurdle with a few Republican supporters. A third—the Affordable Care Act, or "Obamacare"—passed the Senate with sixty Democratic votes and was subsequently amended using the budget reconciliation process, which cannot be filibustered.

27. A "generic ballot" poll asks some version of the question, "This November, do you plan to vote for a Democratic or a Republican candidate in your Congressional district?"

Chapter Seven

1. Again, there are dozens of other interesting cases. The 2003 Medicare Modernization Act, which added prescription drug coverage to Medicare without offsetting revenue increases or entitlement reductions, is an especially good example; Mann and Ornstein (2006) begin their book using this bill as an example. From our perspective, the extraordinary efforts employed by Republican leaders to pass this bill are all the more remarkable because the bill was, on its face, the *opposite* of the small-government, antispending, budget-balancing ideology espoused by most Republican members of Congress.

2. As a "revenue" measure, the Senate cannot act first on trade bills. In this case, the Senate passed its own bill as a signal of encouragement but then had to wait for the House to pass its own measure.

3. This is identical to Sarah Binder's (1997) "partisan capacity." We use a different term that is less specific to the context of institutional change.

4. For the sake of thoroughness, we also tested the relationship between majority-party unity and size at the level of individual votes with a probit regression. Both variables are extremely related to majority roll rates in a pooled analysis of each chamber.

5. In addition, there are previous studies finding a relationship between majority-party influence and policy outcomes. Cox and McCubbins (2005; see also Covington and Bargen 2004) estimate that from 1877 to 1999, about 90 percent of all policy change culminating from a House party "roll" is in the direction of the majority party, while only about 8 percent shifts policy toward the minority party (see also Covington and Bargen 2004; Lawrence et al. 2006). We explored the predictors of party loss rates over a limited range of time and found few consistent relationships among party size, constituency diversity, procedural partisanship, and minority loss rates on bills or amendments. Results of these analyses are available from the authors.

6. For the Thirty-Fourth House (1855–57), we use the final vote for Speaker (pro-Banks = Republican) to define coalitions. Party factions—for example, Van Buren Democrats—are reunited with their parent parties for our analyses. Independents and members of third parties are dropped from the analyses.

7. In a related work, Lindstädt and Vander Wielen (2014) analyze the partisanship of individual legislators over the course of a two-year Congress, finding that partisanship decreases as elections draw near.

8. Voters may punish recent partisanship because they are more likely to pay attention to MC behavior as elections draw near or because they weight recent behavior more heavily when making inferences about MCs' future behavior. See Lindstädt and Vander Wielen (2011).

9. Specifically, we use Koger's (2010) definition of a minority-party disappearing quorum: more than half the majority party participates, less than half the minority party votes, and there is less than a 0.1 percent chance that this difference is random.

10. Standard pooled cross-sectional time-series methods are not appropriate, since these are not panel data. That is, we do not observe the same units repeatedly as we would if we had information on persons, states, or countries for multiple periods of time.

11. In terms of assumptions for ordinary least-squares regression, data nested in time violate the assumption of an independent and identically distributed error structure. A multilevel model is best able to overcome this violation. We use a double-filtering ARFIMA-MLM approach.

12. Complete results from the pooled model are available in the online appendix accompanying this chapter.

References

Abramowitz, Alan I. 2010. *The Disappearing Center*. New Haven: Yale University Press.

Achen, Christopher H. 1975. "Mass Political Attitudes and the Survey Response." *American Political Science Review* 69, no. 4: 1218–31.

———. 2000. "Why Lagged Dependent Variables Can Suppress the Explanatory Power of Other Independent Variables." Working Paper. https://www.princeton.edu/csdp/events/Achen121201/achen.pdf.

Adler, E. Scott. 2000. "Constituency Characteristics and the 'Guardian' Model of Appropriations Subcommittees, 1959–1998." *American Journal of Political Science* 44, no. 1: 104–14.

Adler, E. Scott, and John S. Lapinski. 1997. "Demand-Side Theory and Congressional Committee Composition: A Constituency Characteristics Approach." *American Journal of Political Science* 41, no. 3: 895–918.

Adler, E. Scott, and John D. Wilkerson. 2013. *Congress and the Politics of Problem Solving*. New York: Cambridge University Press.

Aldrich, John H. 1983. "A Downsian Spatial Model with Party Activism." *American Political Science Review* 77:974–90.

———. 1995. *Why Parties?* Chicago: University of Chicago Press.

———. *Why Parties?: A Second Look*. Chicago: University of Chicago Press.

Aldrich, John H., Mark M. Berger, and David W. Rohde. 2002. "The Historical Variability in Conditional Party Government, 1877–1994." In *Party, Process, and Political Change in Congress: New Perspectives on the History of Congress*, Vol. 1, edited by David W. Brady and Mathew D. McCubbins, 17–35. Stanford: Stanford University Press.

Aldrich, John H., and David W. Rohde. 1997–98. "The Transition to Republican Rule in the House: Implications for Theories of Congressional Politics." *Political Science Quarterly* 112 (Winter): 541–67.

———. 2000a. "The Consequences of Party Organization in the House: The Role of the Majority and Minority Parties in Conditional Party Government." In *Po-*

larized Politics: Congress and the President in a Partisan Era, edited by Jon R. Bond and Richard Fleisher, 31–72. Washington, DC: CQ Press.

———. 2000b. "The Republican Revolution and the House Appropriations Committee." *Journal of Politics* 62, no. 1: 1–33.

———. 2001. "The Logic of Conditional Party Government." In *Congress Reconsidered*, 7th ed., edited by Lawrence C. Dodd and Bruce I. Oppenheimer, 269–92. Washington, DC: Congressional Quarterly Press.

Aldrich, John H., David W. Rohde, and Michael W. Tofias. 2007. "One D Is Not Enough: Measuring Conditional Party Government, 1887–2002." In *Party, Process, and Policy Making: Further New Perspectives on the History of Congress*, Vol. 2, edited by David W. Brady and Mathew D. McCubbins, 102–12. Stanford: Stanford University Press.

Anderson, William D., Janet M. Box-Steffensmeier, and Valeria Sinclair-Chapman. 2003. "The Keys to Legislative Success in the U.S. House of Representatives." *Legislative Studies Quarterly* 28:357–86.

Ansolabehere, Stephen, James M. Snyder, and Charles Stewart III. 2001. "The Effects of Party and Preferences on Congressional Roll-Call Voting." *Legislative Studies Quarterly* 26, no. 4: 533–72.

APSA Committee on Political Parties. 1950. "Toward a More Responsible Two-Party System." *American Political Science Review* 44 (Supplement): i–xi, 1–100.

Arceneaux, Kevin, and Martin Johnson. 2013. *Changing Minds or Changing Channels? Partisan News in an Age of Choice*. Chicago: University of Chicago Press.

Arnold, R. Douglas. 1990. *The Logic of Congressional Action*. New Haven: Yale University Press.

Arrow, Kenneth J. 1950. "A Difficulty in the Concept of Social Welfare." *Journal of Political Economy* 58:328–46.

Avlon, John. 2010. "Today's Holiday of Hate." *Daily Beast*, April 18. http://www.thedailybeast.com/articles/2010/04/19/todays-holiday-of-hate.html.

Axelrod, Robert. 1972. "Where the Votes Come From: An Analysis of Electoral Coalitions, 1952–1968." *American Political Science Review* 66, no. 1: 11–20.

Bachrach, Peter, and Morton S. Baratz. 1962. "Two Faces of Power." *American Political Science Review* 56, no. 4: 947–52.

Bafumi, Joseph, and Michael C. Herron. 2010. "Leapfrog Representation and Extremism: A Study of American Voters and Their Members in Congress." *American Political Science Review* 104:519–42.

Bafumi, Joseph, and Joseph M. Parent. 2012. "International Polarity and America's Polarization." *International Politics* 49:1–35.

Bailey, Michael A., Jonathan Mummolo, and Hans Noel. 2012. "Tea Party Influence: A Story of Activists and Elites." *American Politics Research* 40:769–804.

Baltagi, Badi H. 2005. *Econometric Analysis of Panel Data*, 3rd ed. West Sussex: John Wiley & Sons.

Banerjee, Aninyda, Juan Dolado, John W. Galbraith, and David F. Hendry.

1993. *Cointegration, Error Correction, and the Econometric Analysis of Non-Stationary Data.* New York: Oxford University Press.

Barrett, Andrew W., and Matthew Eshbaugh-Soha. 2007. "Presidential Success on the Substance of Legislation." *Political Research Quarterly* 60, no. 1: 100–112.

Bartels, Larry M. 2000. "Partisanship and Voting Behavior, 1952–1996." *American Journal of Political Science* 44, no. 1: 35–50.

Bawn, Kathleen. 1998. "Congressional Party Leadership: Utilitarian versus Majoritarian Incentives." *Legislative Studies Quarterly* 23, no. 2: 219–43.

Bennett, Stephen Earl. 1988. "Know-Nothings Revisited: The Meaning of Political Ignorance Today." *Social Science Quarterly* 69, no. 2: 476–90.

Bernstein, Jeffrey L. 1989. "Linking Presidential and Congressional Approval during Unified and Divided Governments." In *What Is It about Government That Americans Dislike?*, edited by John R. Hibbing and Elizabeth Theiss-Morse, 98–117. New York: Cambridge University Press.

Berry, Christopher R., Barry C. Burden, and William G. Howell. 2010. "The President and the Distribution of Federal Spending." *American Political Science Review* 104, no. 4: 783–99.

Bianco, William T., David B. Spence, and John D. Wilkerson. 1996. "The Electoral Connection in the Early Congress: The Case of the Compensation Act of 1816." *American Journal of Political Science* 40, no. 1: 145–71.

Billings, Erin P. 2005. "Pelosi Calls Steering Meeting to Review Defectors' Votes for CAFTA." *Roll Call*, July 28. http://www.citizen.org/documents/Roll_Call_Meeks_Pelosi_Meeting.pdf.

Binder, Sarah. 1997. *Minority Rights, Majority Rule: Partisanship and the Development of Congress.* New York: Cambridge University Press.

———. 2003. *Stalemate: Causes and Consequences of Legislative Gridlock.* Washington, DC: Brookings Institution Press.

Binder, Sarah A., and Steven S. Smith. 1997. *Politics or Principle? Filibustering in the United Senate.* Washington, DC: Brookings Institution Press.

Bishin, Benjamin G. 2000. "Constituency Influence in Congress: Does Subconstituency Matter?" *Legislative Studies Quarterly* 25, no. 3: 389–415.

———. 2004. "The Validity and Accuracy of Commonly Used Ideology Measures: A Consumer's Guide." *American Review of Politics* 25, no. 3: 201–20.

———. 2009. *Tyranny of the Minority: The Subconstituency Politics Theory Representation.* Philadelphia: Temple University Press.

Black, Duncan. 1948. "On the Rationale of Group Decision-Making." *Journal of Political Economy* 56, no. 1: 23–34.

Blake, Aaron. 2013. "Pelosi: Health-Care Vote Didn't Cost Democrats the House." *Washington Post*, October 23. http://www.washingtonpost.com/blogs/post-politics/wp/2013/10/23/pelosi-health-care-vote-didnt-cost-democrats-the-house/.

Boaz, David. 2014. "Worst Congress Ever? You Must Be Kidding." *Cato at Lib-

erty, December 21. http://www.cato.org/blog/worst-Congress-ever-you-must-be
-kidding.

Bolton, Alexander. 2014. "Worst Congress Ever?" *The Hill*, March 10. http://thehill
.com/homenews/senate/200295-worst-congress-ever.

Bond, Jon R., and Richard Fleisher. 1990. *The President in the Legislative Arena*.
Chicago: University of Chicago Press.

Bond, Jon R., Richard Fleisher, and B. Dan Wood. 2003. "The Marginal and Time-
Varying Effect of Public Approval on Presidential Success in Congress." *Journal of Politics* 65, no. 1: 92–110.

Bovitz, Gregory L., and Jamie L. Carson. 2006. "Position Taking and Electoral Accountability in the U.S. House of Representatives." *Political Research Quarterly*
59, no. 2: 297–312.

Box-Steffensmeier, Janet M. 1996. "A Dynamic Analysis of the Role of War Chests
in Campaign Strategy." *American Journal of Political Science* 40, no. 2: 352–71.

Box-Steffensmeier, Janet M., and Renee M. Smith. 1996. "The Dynamics of Aggregate Partisanship." *American Political Science Review* 90, no. 3: 567–80.

———. 1998. "Investigating Political Dynamics Using Fractional Integration
Methods." *American Journal of Political Science* 42, no. 2: 661–89.

Brooks, David. 2011. "A Most Valuable Democrat." *New York Times*, January 21.
Accessed April 18, 2011. http://www.nytimes.com/2011/01/21/opinion/21brooks
.html.

Burden, Barry C., and Tammy M. Frisby. 2004. "Preferences, Partisanship, and
Whip Activity in the U.S. House of Representatives." *Legislative Studies Quarterly* 29, no. 4: 569–90.

Butler, Daniel M., and Eleanor N. Powell. 2014. "Understanding the Party Brand:
Experimental Evidence on the Role of Valence." *Journal of Politics*, 76:492–505.

Campbell, A., P. E. Converse, W. E. Miller, and D. E. Stokes. 1960. *The American
Voter*. Chicago: University of Chicago Press.

Campbell, Andrea, Gary W. Cox, and Mathew D. McCubbins. 2002. "Agenda Power
in the U.S. Senate, 1877 to 1986." In *Party, Process, and Political Change in Congress: New Perspectives on the History of Congress*, Vol. 1, edited by David W.
Brady and Mathew D. McCubbins, 146–65. Stanford: Stanford University Press.

Canes-Wrone, Brandice. 2001. "The President's Legislative Influence from Public
Appeals." *American Journal of Political Science* 45, no. 2: 313–29.

Canes-Wrone, Brandice, David W. Brady, and John F. Cogan. 2002. "Out of
Step, Out of Office: Electoral Accountability and House Members' Voting."
American Political Science Review 96, no. 1: 127–40.

Canes-Wrone, Brandice, and Scott de Marchi. 2002. "Presidential Approval and
Legislative Success." *Journal of Politics* 64, no. 2: 491–509.

Canes-Wrone, Brandice, William Minozzi, and Jessica Bonney Reveley. 2011.
"Issue Accountability and the Mass Public." *Legislative Studies Quarterly* 36,
no. 1: 5–35.

Canes-Wrone, Brandice, Julia Rabinovich, and Craig Volden. 2007. "Who Parties? Floor Voting, District Ideology, and Electoral Margins." In *Party, Process, and Political Change in Congress: Further New Perspectives on the History of Congress*, Vol. 2, edited by David W. Brady and Mathew D. McCubbins, 113–25. Stanford: Stanford University Press.

Cann, Damon M. 2008. *Sharing the Wealth: Member Contributions and the Exchange Theory of Party Influence in the U.S. House of Representatives*. Albany: SUNY Press.

Canon, David T. 1990. *Actors, Athletes, and Astronauts: Political Amateurs in the United States Congress*. Chicago: University of Chicago Press.

Carmines, Edward G., and James A. Stimson. 1989. *Issue Evolution: Race and the Transformation of American Politics*. Princeton: Princeton University Press.

Carney, Eliza Newlin. 2013. "Once More unto the Brink." *CQ Weekly*, September 30.

Caro, Robert A. 2002. *Master of the Senate*. New York: Random House.

Carson, Jamie L. 2005. "Strategy, Selection, and Candidate Competition in U.S. House and Senate Elections." *Journal of Politics* 67, no. 1: 1–28.

Carson, Jamie L., and Michael H. Crespin. 2004. "The Effect of State Redistricting Methods on Electoral Competition in United States House of Representatives Races." *State Politics & Policy Quarterly* 4, no. 4: 455–69.

Carson, Jamie L., Michael H. Crespin, Charles J. Finocchiaro, and David W. Rohde. 2007. "Representatives Redistricting and Party Polarization in the U.S. House of Representatives." *American Politics Research* 35, no. 6: 878–904.

Carson, Jamie L., Gregory Koger, Matthew J. Lebo, and Everett Young. 2010. "The Electoral Costs of Party Loyalty in Congress." *American Journal of Political Science* 54, no. 3: 598–616.

Carson, Jamie L., and Jason Matthew Roberts. 2013. *Ambition, Competition, and Electoral Reform: The Politics of Congressional Elections across Time*. Ann Arbor: University of Michigan Press.

Carter, Jennifer, and John W. Patty. 2015. "Valence and Campaigns." *American Journal of Political Science*. Published online February 6, 2015.

Catalini, Michael. 2013. "Can Reid's Shutdown Strategy Hold?" *National Journal Daily*, October 1. http://www.nationaljournal.com/daily/can-reid-s-shutdown-strategy-hold-20131001.

Chinni, Dante, and James Gimpel. 2011. *Our Patchwork Nation: The Surprising Truth about the "Real" America*. New York: Penguin.

Chiu, Chang-Wei. 1928. *The Speaker of the House of Representatives since 1896*. New York: Columbia University Press.

Clarke, Harold D., and Matthew J. Lebo. 2003. "Fractional (Co)integration and Governing Party Support in Britain." *British Journal of Political Science* 33, no. 2: 283–301.

Clarke, Harold D., and Marianne C. Stewart. 1994. "Prospections, Retrospections, and Rationality: The 'Bankers' Model of Presidential Approval Reconsidered." *American Journal of Political Science* 38, no. 4: 1104–23.

Clausen, Aage, and Clyde Wilcox. 1987. "Policy Partisanship in Legislative Recruitment and Behavior." *Legislative Studies Quarterly* 12, no. 2: 243–63.

Cohen, Jeffrey. 2002. *The Presidency in the Era of 24-Hour News*. Princeton: Princeton University Press.

Coker, David C., and W. Mark Crain. 1994. "Legislative Committees as Loyalty-Generating Institutions." *Public Choice* 81, no. 3–4: 195–221.

Converse, Philip E. 1964. "The Nature of Belief Systems in Mass Publics." In *Ideology and Discontent*, edited by David Ernest Apter, 206–61. London: Free Press of Glencoe.

Cooke, Charles C. 2015. "The Historical Idiocy of Complaining about the Worst Congress Ever." *National Review*, January 6. http://www.nationalreview.com /article/395824/historical-idiocy-complaining-about-worst-congress-ever -charles-c-w-cooke.

Cooper, Joseph. 1970. *The Origins of the Standing Committees and the Development of the Modern House*. Rice University Studies 56, no. 3. Houston: Rice University.

Cooper, Joseph, and David W. Brady. 1981. "Institutional Context and Leadership Style: The House from Cannon to Rayburn." *American Political Science Review* 75, no. 2: 411–25.

Cooper, Joseph, and Garry Young. 2002. "Party and Preference in Congressional Decision Making: Roll Call Voting in the House of Representatives, 1889–1999." In *Party, Process, and Political Change in Congress: New Perspectives on the History of Congress*, Vol. 1, edited by David W. Brady and Mathew D. McCubbins, 64–106. Stanford: Stanford University Press.

Covington, Cary R., and Andrew A. Bargen. 2004. "Comparing Floor-Dominated and Party-Dominated Explanations of Policy Change in the House of Representatives." *Journal of Politics* 66, no. 4: 1069–88.

Cox, Gary W. 1987. *The Efficient Secret: The Cabinet and the Development of Political Parties in Victorian England*. New York: Cambridge University Press.

Cox, Gary W., and Jonathan N. Katz. 1996. "Why Did the Incumbency Advantage in U.S. House Elections Grow?" *American Journal of Political Science* 40, no. 2: 478–97.

———. 2002. *Elbridge Gerry's Salamander: The Electoral Consequences of the Reapportionment Revolution*. New York: Cambridge University Press.

Cox, Gary W., and Eric Magar. 1999. "How Much Is Majority Status in the U.S. Congress Worth?" *American Political Science Review* 93, no. 2: 299–309.

Cox, Gary W., and Mathew D. McCubbins. 1993. *Legislative Leviathan: Party Government in the House*. Berkeley: University of California Press.

———. 1994. "Bonding, Structure, and the Stability of Political Parties: Party Government in the House." *Legislative Studies Quarterly* 19, no. 2: 215–31.

———. 2005. *Setting the Agenda: Responsible Party Government in the US House of Representatives*. New York: Cambridge University Press.

———. 2007. *Legislative Leviathan: Party Government in the House*, 2nd ed. New York: Cambridge University Press.

Cox, Gary W., and Keith T. Poole. 2002. "On Measuring Partisanship in Roll Call Voting: The U.S. House of Representatives 1877–1999." *American Journal of Political Science* 46, no. 3:477–89.

Crabtree, Susan. 2002. "GOP Whip Team Goes into Overtime." *Roll Call*, July 1.

Crespin, Michael H., and Charles J. Finocchiaro. 2008. "Distributive and Partisan Politics in the US Senate: An Exploration of Earmarks." In *Why Not Parties? Party Effects in the United States Senate*, edited by Nathan W. Monroe, Jason M. Roberts, and David W. Rhode, 229–51. Chicago: University of Chicago Press.

Currinder, Marian L. 2003. "Leadership PAC Contribution Strategies and House Member Ambitions." *Legislative Studies Quarterly* 28, no. 4: 551–77.

Davidson, Roger H. 1989. "The Senate: If Everyone Leads, Who Follows?" In *Congress Reconsidered*, 4th ed., edited by Lawrence C. Dodd and Bruce I. Oppenheimer, 275–305. Washington, DC: Congressional Quarterly Press.

Davidson, Russell, and James G. MacKinnon. 1993. *Estimation and Inference in Econometrics*. New York: Oxford University Press.

Davidson, Paul. 2013. "Political Uncertainty Keeps Slowing Economy's Rise." *USA Today*, October 17. Accessed October 30, 2013. http://www.usatoday.com/story/money/business/2013/10/16/political-uncertainty-effects-economy/2995829/.

Deering, Christopher J., and Paul J. Wahlbeck. 2006. "U.S. House Committee Chair Selection: Republicans Play Musical Chairs in the 107th Congress." *American Politics Research* 34, no. 2: 223–42.

Den Hartog, Chris, and Nate Monroe. 2008. "The Value of Majority Status: The Effect of Jeffords's Switch on Asset Prices of Republican and Democrat Firms." *Legislative Studies Quarterly* 33, no. 1: 63–84.

———. 2011. *Agenda Setting in the US Senate: Costly Consideration and Majority Party Advantage*. New York: Cambridge University Press.

Dion, Douglas. 1997. *Turing the Legislative Thumbscrew: Minority Rights and Procedural Changes in Legislative Politics*. Ann Arbor: University of Michigan Press.

Dixit, Avinash, and John Londregan. 1996. "The Determinants of Success of Special Interests in Redistributive Politics." *Journal of Politics* 58, no. 4: 1132–55.

Doherty, Brendan J. 2010. "Polls and Elections: Hail to the Fundraiser in Chief: The Evolution of Presidential Fundraising Travel, 1977–2004." *Presidential Studies Quarterly* 40, no. 1: 159–70.

Donnelly, John M. 2010. "Authorization, 'Don't Ask' Repeal Blocked." *CQ Weekly*, September 27, 2232.

Downs, Anthony. 1957. *An Economic Theory of Democracy*. New York: Harper and Row.

Draper, Robert. 2012. *Do Not Ask What Good We Do: Inside the U.S. House of Representatives*. New York: Simon and Schuster.

Drutman, Lee. 2012. "Ways and Means, Financial Services, and Energy and Commerce Are Top House Fundraising Committees." *The Sunlight Foundation Blog*, April 2. https://sunlightfoundation.com/blog/2012/04/02/housecommittees.

Duverger, Maurice. 1963. *Political Parties: Their Organization and Activity in the Modern State*. Vol. 22865 of Science Editions, 1959. Reprint, Hoboken: Wiley.

Egan, Patrick J. 2013. *Partisan Priorities: How Issue Ownership Drives and Distorts American Politics*. New York: Cambridge University Press.

Enelow, James M., and Melvin J. Hinich. 1984. *The Spatial Theory of Voting: An Introduction*. New York: Cambridge University Press.

Engle, Robert F. 2002. "Dynamic Conditional Correlation: A Simple Class of Multivariate GARCH Models." *Journal of Business and Economics Statistics* 17, no. 3: 425–46.

Engle, Robert F., and Clive W. J. Granger. 1987. "Co-integration and Error Correction: Representation, Estimation, and Testing." *Econometrica: Journal of the Econometric Society* 55, no. 2: 251–76.

Ensley, Michael J. 2009. "Individual Campaign Contributions and Candidate Ideology." *Public Choice* 138, no. 1–2: 221–38.

Erikson, Robert S. 1971. "The Electoral Impact of Congressional Roll Call Voting." *American Political Science Review* 65, no. 3: 1018–32.

Erikson, Robert S., Michael B. MacKuen, and James A. Stimson. 2002. *The Macro Polity*. New York: Cambridge University Press.

Erikson, Robert S., and Gerald C. Wright. 2001. "Voters, Candidates, and Issues in Congressional Elections." In *Congress Reconsidered*, 7th ed., edited by Lawrence C. Dodd and Bruce I. Oppenheimer, 77–134. Washington, DC: Congressional Quarterly Press.

Eshbaugh-Soha, Matthew. 2005. "The Politics of Presidential Agendas." *Political Research Quarterly* 58, no. 2: 257–68.

Evans, C. Lawrence, and Claire E. Grady. 2009. "The Whip System of Congress." In *Congress Reconsidered*, 9th ed., edited by Lawrence C. Dodd and Bruce I. Oppenheimer, 189–215. Washington, DC: Congressional Quarterly Press.

Farrell, John A. 2002. *Tip O'Neill and the Democratic Century*. Boston: Back Bay Books.

Federico, Christopher M., and Monica C. Schneider. 2007. "Political Expertise and the Use of Ideology: Moderating Effects of Evaluative Motivation." *Public Opinion Quarterly* 71, no. 2: 221–52.

Fenno, Richard F. 1973. *Congressmen in Committees*. Boston: Little, Brown.

———. 1997. *Learning to Govern: An Institutional View of the 104th Congress*. Washington, DC: Brookings Institution Press.

———. 2000. *Congress at the Grassroots*. Chapel Hill: University of North Carolina.

———. 2008. *Home Style: House Members in Their Districts*. Reprint, New York: Longman.

Finocchiaro, Charles J., and David W. Rhode. 2008. "War and the Floor: Partisan Theory and Agenda Control in the U.S. House of Representatives." *Legislative Studies Quarterly* 33, no. 1: 35–61.

Fiorina, Morris P. 2002. "Parties and Partisanship: A 40-year Retrospective." *Political Behavior* 24, no. 2: 93–115.

"Fiscal Crisis Watch, Week 1: Timeline." 2013. *CQ Weekly*, October 7. http://iiiprxy .library.miami.edu:2346/cqweekly/weeklyreport113-000004357278.

Follett, Mary P. 1974. *The Speaker of the House of Representatives*. 1896. Reprint, New York: Burt Franklin Reprints.

Forgette, Richard. 2004. "Party Caucuses and Coordination: Assessing Caucus Activity and Party Effects." *Legislative Studies Quarterly* 29, no. 3: 407–30.

Fowler, James H., and Oleg Smirnov. 2007. *Mandates, Parties, and Voters: How Elections Shape the Future*. Philadelphia: Temple University Press.

Franklin, Charles H. 1984. "Issue Preferences, Socialization, and the Evolution of Party Identification." *American Journal of Political Science* 28, no. 3: 459–78.

Frisch, Scott A., and Sean Q. Kelly. 2006. *Committee Assignment Politics in the U.S. House of Representatives*. Congressional Studies Series 5. Norman: University of Oklahoma Press.

———. 2008. "Leading the Senate in the 110th Congress." *P.S. Political Science and Policy* 41, no. 1: 69–75.

Froman, Lewis A., and Randall B. Ripley. 1965. "Conditions for Party Leadership: The Case of the House Democrats." *American Political Science Review* 59, no. 1: 52–63.

Frymer, Paul. 1999. *Uneasy Alliances: Race and Party Competition in America*. Princeton: Princeton University Press.

Fulton, Sarah A. 2012. "Running Backwards and in High Heels: The Gendered Quality Gap and Incumbent Electoral Success." *Political Research Quarterly* 65:303–14.

Gailmard, Sean, and Jeffery A. Jenkins. 2007. "Negative Agenda Control in the Senate and House: Fingerprints of Majority Party Power." *Journal of Politics* 69, no. 3: 689–700.

———. 2009. "Agency Problems, the 17th Amendment, and Representation in the Senate." *American Journal of Political Science* 53:324–42.

Gaines, Brian J., James H. Kuklinski, Paul J. Quirk, Buddy Peyton, and Jay Verkuilen. 2007. "Same Facts, Different Interpretations: Partisan Motivation and Opinion on Iraq." *Journal of Politics* 69, no. 4: 957–74.

Galvin, Daniel. 2010. *Presidential Party Building: Dwight D. Eisenhower to George W. Bush*. Princeton: Princeton University Press.

Gamm, Gerald, and Steven S. Smith. 2000. "Last among Equals: The Presiding Officer of the Senate." In *Esteemed Colleagues: Civility and Deliberation in United States Senate*, edited by B. Loomis, 105–36. Washington, DC: Brookings Institution Press.

———. 2002a. "The Emergence of Senate Party Leadership." In *Senate Exceptionalism*, edited by B. Oppenheimer, 212–40. Columbus: Ohio University Press.

———. 2002b. "Policy Leadership and the Development of the Modern Senate." In *Party, Process, and Political Change in Congress: New Perspectives on the History of Congress*, Vol. 1, edited by David W. Brady and Mathew D. McCubbins, 287–311. Stanford: Stanford University Press.

———. 2006. "The Rise of Floor Leaders in the United States Senate, 1890–1915." Paper presented at the 2006 Party Effects in the Senate Conference, Durham, Duke University, April 7–8.

Gelman, Andrew, and Gary King. 1990. "Estimating Incumbency Advantage without Bias." *American Journal of Political Science* 34, no. 4: 1142–64.

———. 1994. "Enhancing Democracy through Legislative Redistricting." *American Political Science Review* 88, no. 3: 541–59.

Gilmour, John B. 1995. *Strategic Disagreement: Stalemate in American Politics*. Pittsburgh: University of Pittsburgh Press.

Gimpel, James G., Frances E. Lee, and Shanna Pearson-Merkowitz. 2008. "The Check Is in the Mail: Interdistrict Funding Flows in Congressional Elections." *American Journal of Political Science* 52, no. 2: 373–94.

Gimpel, James, and Jason E. Schuknecht. 2004. *Patchwork Nation: Sectionalism and Political Change in American Politics*. Ann Arbor: University of Michigan Press.

Goldfarb, Zachary A., David Cho, and Binyamin Appelbaum. 2008. "Regulators Seek to Keep Firms' Troubles from Setting Off Wave of Bank Failures." *Washington Post*, September 7.

Goodwin, Doris Kearns. 1991. *Lyndon Johnson and the American Dream*. New York: Macmillan.

Goren, Paul. 2005. "Party Identification and Core Political Values." *American Journal of Political Science* 49, no. 4: 881–96.

Granger, Clive W. J. 1981. "Some Properties of Time Series Data and Their Use in Econometric Model Specification." *Journal of Econometrics* 16, no. 1: 121–30.

Green, Donald P., and Jonathan S. Krasno. 1990. "Rebuttal to Jacobson's 'New Evidence for Old Arguments.'" *American Journal of Political Science* 34, no. 2: 363–72.

Green, Donald P., and Bradley Palmquist. 1990. "Of Artifacts and Partisan Instability." *American Journal of Political Science* 34, no. 3: 872–902.

Green, Donald P., Bradley Palmquist, and Eric Schickler. 2002. *Partisan Hearts and Minds: Political Parties and the Social Identities of Voters*. New Haven: Yale University Press.

Green, Matthew N. 2008. "The 2006 Race for Democratic Majority Leader: Money, Policy, and Personal Loyalty." *PS: Political Science and Politics* 41, no. 1: 63–67.

———. 2010. *The Speaker of the House: A Study of Leadership*. New Haven: Yale University Press.

Green, Matthew N., and Douglas B. Harris. 2007. "Goal Salience and the 2006 Race for House Majority Leader." *Political Research Quarterly* 60, no. 4: 618–30.

Greene, Stephen. 1999. "Understanding Partisan Identification: A Social Identity Approach." *Political Psychology* 20, no. 2: 393:403.

Greenstein, Fred I. 1965. *Children and Politics.* New Haven: Yale University Press.

Grofman, Bernard, William Koetzle, and Anthony J. McGann. 2002. "Congressional Leadership 1965–96: A New Look at the Extremism versus Centrality Debate." *Legislative Studies Quarterly* 27, no. 1: 87–105.

Gronke, Paul, Jeffrey Koch, and J. Matthew Wilson. 2003. "Follow the Leader? Presidential Approval, Presidential Support, and Representatives' Electoral Fortunes." *Journal of Politics* 65, no. 3: 785–808.

Groseclose, Tim, and Nolan McCarty. 2001. "The Politics of Blame: Bargaining before an Audience." *American Journal of Political Science* 45, no. 1: 100–19.

Groseclose, Tim, and James M. Snyder. 1996. "Buying Supermajorities." *American Political Science Review* 90, no. 2: 303–15.

Grynaviski, Jeffrey D. 2010. *Partisan Bonds: Political Reputations and Legislative Accountability.* New York: Cambridge University Press.

Hanson, Peter C. 2014. *Too Weak to Govern: Majority Party Power and Appropriations in the U.S. Senate.* New York: Cambridge University Press.

Harbridge, Laurel. 2015. *Is Bipartisanship Dead? Policy Agreement in the Face of Partisan Agenda-Setting in the House of Representatives.* New York: Cambridge University Press.

Harbridge, Laurel, and Neil Malholtra. 2011. "Electoral Incentives and Partisan Conflict in Congress: Evidence from Survey Experiments." *American Journal of Political Science* 55, no. 3: 494–510.

Harris, Douglas B., and Garrison Nelson. 2008. "Middlemen No More? Emergent Patterns in Congressional Leadership Selection." *PS: Political Science and Politics* 41, no. 1: 49–55.

Hasecke, Edward B., and Jason D. Mycoff. 2007. "Party Loyalty and Legislative Success: Are Loyal Majority Party Members More Successful in the U.S. House of Representatives?" *Political Research Quarterly* 60, no. 4: 607–17.

Hawkings, David. 2013. "Sending Messages with Doomed Bills." *CQ Weekly*, September 2. http://iiiprxy.library.miami.edu:2346/cqweekly/weeklyreport113 -000004337271.

Heberlig, Eric S. 2003. "Congressional Parties, Fundraising, and Committee Ambition." *Political Research Quarterly* 56, no. 2: 151–61.

Heberlig, Eric, Marc Hetherington, and Bruce Larson. 2006. "The Price of Leadership: Campaign Money and the Polarization of Congressional Parties." *Journal of Politics* 68, no. 4: 992–1005.

Heberlig, Eric S., and Bruce A. Larson. 2005. "Redistributing Campaign Funds by U.S. House Members: The Spiraling Costs of the Permanent Campaign." *Legislative Studies Quarterly* 30, no. 4: 597–624.

Herrnson, Paul S. 2009. "The Roles of Party Organizations, Party-Connected Committees, and Party Allies in Elections." *Journal of Politics* 71, no. 4: 1207–24.

Hess, Robert D., and Judith V. Torney. 1965. *The Development of Basic Attitudes and Values toward Government and Citizenship during the Elementary School Years*, Part I. Chicago: University of Chicago Press.

Hetherington, Marc J. 2001. "Resurgent Mass Partisanship: The Role of Elite Polarization." *American Political Science Review* 95, no. 3: 619–31.

Hibbing, John R., and Elizabeth Theiss-Morse. 2001. *What Is It about Government That Americans Dislike?* New York: Cambridge University Press.

Hill, Kim Quaile. 2012. "In Search of General Theory." *Journal of Politics* 74:917–31.

Hirsh, Michael. 2013. "George W. Bush: He Gave Rise to the Tea Party." *National Journal*, October 3. Accessed April 19, 2014. http://www.nationaljournal.com/who-brokewashington/george-w-bush-he-gave-rise-to-the-tea-party-20131003.

Hofstadter, Richard. 1969. *The Idea of a Party System: The Rise of Legitimate Opposition in the United States, 1780–1840*. Jefferson Memorial Lecture Series 2. Berkeley: University of California Press.

Hohmann, James. 2010. "TARP Traps GOP Incumbents." *Politico*, May 14. http://www.politico.com/news/stories/0510/37228.html.

"House Votes Violating the 'Hastert Rule.'" 2014. *New York Times*. Accessed April 9. https://politics.nytimes.com/congress/votes/house/hastert-rule.

Huckfeldt, Robert, Jeffrey Levine, William Morgan, and John Sprague. 1999. "Accessibility and the Political Utility of Partisan and Ideological Orientations." *American Journal of Political Science* 43, no. 3: 888–911.

Hulse, Carl, and David M. Herszenhorn. 2008. "Defiant House Rejects Huge Bailout; Next Step Is Uncertain." *New York Times*, September 29. http://www.nytimes.com/2008/09/30/business/30cong.html.

Hulse, Carl, and Adam Nagourney. 2010. "Senate G.O.P. Leader Finds Weapon in Unity." *New York Times*, March 16. http://www.nytimes.com/2010/03/17/us/politics/17mcconnell.html?pagewanted=all.

Hyman, Herbert. 1959. *Political Socialization*. New York: Free Press.

Inter-university Consortium for Political and Social Research, and Congressional Quarterly, Inc. 1998. *United States Congressional Roll Call Voting Records, 1789–1996 (ICPSR 0004)*. Ann Arbor, MI: ICPSR.

Intriligator, Michael D., and D. L. Brito. 1976. "Formal Models of Arms Races." *Conflict Management and Peace Science* 2:77–88.

Jacobson, Gary C. 1980. *Money in Congressional Elections*. New Haven: Yale University Press.

———. 1987. "The Marginals Never Vanished: Incumbency and Competition in Elections to the US House of Representatives, 1952–82." *American Journal of Political Science* 31, no. 1: 126–41.

———. 1993. "Deficit-Cutting Politics and Congressional Elections." *Political Science Quarterly* 108, no. 3: 375–402.

———. 1996. "The 1994 House Elections in Perspective." *Political Science Quarterly* 111, no. 2: 202–23.

———. 2000. "Party Polarization in National Politics: The Electoral Connection." In *Polarized Politics: Congress and the President in a Partisan Era*, edited by Jon R. Bond and Richard Fleisher, 9–30. Washington, DC: CQ Press.

———. 2007. "Explaining the Ideological Polarization of the Congressional Parties since the 1970s." In *Party, Process, and Political Change in Congress: Further New Perspectives on the History of Congress*, Vol. 2, edited by David W. Brady and Mathew D. McCubbins, 91–101. Stanford: Stanford University Press.

———. 2008. *A Divider, Not a Uniter: George W. Bush and the American People*. Boston: Longman.

———. 2009. *The Politics of Congressional Elections*, 7th ed. New York: Pearson.

———. 2011. "The Republican Resurgence in 2010." *Political Science Quarterly* 127, no. 1: 27–52.

James, Scott. 2000. *Presidents, Parties, and the State: A Party System Perspective on Democratic Regulatory Choice, 1884–1936*. New York: Cambridge University Press.

———. 2006. "Patronage Regimes and American Party Development from 'The Age of Jackson' to the Progressive Era." *British Journal of Political Science* 36, no. 1: 39–60.

Jenkins, Jeffery A., and Timothy P. Nokken. 2000. "The Institutional Origins of the Republican Party: Spatial Voting and the House Speakership Election of 1855–56." *Legislative Studies Quarterly* 25, no. 1: 101–30.

Jenkins, Jeffery A., and Charles Stewart III. 2003. "Out in the Open: The Emergence of Viva Voce Voting in House Speakership Elections." *Legislative Studies Quarterly* 28, no. 4: 481–508.

———. 2012. *Fighting for the Speakership: The House and the Rise of Party Government*. Princeton: Princeton University Press.

Jessee, Stephan, and Neil Malhotra. 2010. "Are Congressional Leaders Middlepersons or Extremists? Yes." *Legislative Studies Quarterly* 35, no. 3: 361–92.

Jones, David R., and Monika L. McDermott. 2010. *Americans, Congress, and Democratic Responsiveness: Public Evaluations of Congress and Electoral Consequences*. Ann Arbor: University of Michigan Press.

Judd, Charles M., and Jon A. Krosnick. 1989. "The Structural Bases of Consistency among Political Attitudes: Effects of Expertise and Attitude Importance." In *Attitude Structure and Function*, edited by Anthony R. Pratkanis, Steven J. Breckler, and Anthony G. Greenwald, 99–128. Hillsdale: Erlbaum.

Kanthak, Kris. 2007. "Crystal Elephants and Committee Chairs: Campaign Contributions and Leadership Races in the U.S. House of Representatives." *American Politics Research* 35, no. 3: 389–406.

Karol, David. 2009. *Party Position Change in American Politics: Coalition Management*. Cambridge: Cambridge University Press.

Kernell, Samuel. 2006. *Going Public: New Strategies of Presidential Leadership*. Washington, D.C.: CQ Press.

Kiewiet, D. Roderick, and Mathew D. McCubbins. 1991. *The Logic of Delegation.* Chicago: University of Chicago Press.

Kinder, Donald. 1998. "Opinion and Action in the Realm of Politics." In *The Handbook of Social Psychology*, 4th ed., edited by Daniel T. Gilbert, Susan T. Fiske, and Gardner Lindzey, 778–867. New York: McGraw-Hill.

King, David C., and Richard J. Zeckhauser. 2003. "Congressional Vote Options." *Legislative Studies Quarterly* 28, no. 3: 387–411.

Kingdon, John W. 1989. *Congressmen's Voting Decisions.* Ann Arbor: University of Michigan Press.

Klein, Ezra. 2012. "14 Reasons Why This Is the Worst Congress Ever." *Washington Post*, July 13. https://www.washingtonpost.com/blogs/ezra-klein/wp/2012/07/13/13-reasons-why-this-is-the-worst-congress-ever.

Kmenta, Jan. 1997. *Elements of Econometrics*, 2nd ed. Ann Arbor: University of Michigan Press.

Koger, Gregory. 2003. "Position-Taking and Cosponsorship in the U.S. House." *Legislative Studies Quarterly* 28, no. 2: 225–46.

———. 2009. "Making Change: A Six-Month Review." *The Forum: A Journal of Applied Research in Contemporary Politics* 7, no. 3. doi:10.2202/1540-8884.1314.

———. 2010. *Filibustering: A Political History of Obstruction in the House and Senate.* Chicago: University of Chicago Press.

Koger, Gregory, and Sergio Campos. 2014. "The Conventional Option." *Washington University Law Review* 91:867–909.

Koger, Gregory, and Matthew J. Lebo. 2006. "Dynamic Error Correction." Paper presented at the annual meeting of the American Political Science Association, Philadelphia, PA, August 31–September 3.

———. 2012. "Strategic Party Government and the 2010 Elections." *American Politics Research* 40, no. 5: 927–45.

Koger, Gregory, Seth Masket, and Hans Noel. 2009. "Partisan Webs: Information Exchange and Party Networks." *British Journal of Political Science* 39:633–53.

———. 2010. "Cooperative Party Factions in American Politics." *American Politics Research* 38:33–53.

Koger, Gregory, and Jennifer Victor. 2009. "Polarized Agents: Campaign Contributions by Lobbyists." *PS: Political Science and Politics* 42, no. 3: 485–88.

Kolodny, Robin. 1998. *Pursuing Majorities: Congressional Campaign Committees in American Politics.* Norman: University of Oklahoma Press.

Krehbiel, Keith. 1991. *Information and Legislative Organization.* Ann Arbor: University of Michigan Press.

———. 1993. "Where's the Party?" *British Journal of Political Science* 23, no. 2: 235–66.

———. 1998. *Pivotal Politics: A Theory of U.S. Lawmaking.* Chicago: University of Chicago Press.

———. 1999. "Paradoxes of Parties in Congress." *Legislative Studies Quarterly* 24, no. 1: 31–64.

———. 2000. "Party Discipline and Measures of Partisanship." *American Journal of Political Science* 44, no. 2: 212–27.

Krehbiel, Keith, Adam Meirowitz, and Alan E. Wiseman. 2013. "A Theory of Competitive Partisan Lawmaking." *Center for the Study of Democratic Institutions.* Working Paper.

Krutz, Glen. 2005. "Issues and Institutions: 'Winnowing' in the U.S. Congress." *American Journal of Political Science* 49:313–26.

Kuklinski, James H., and Paul J. Quirk. 2000. "Reconsidering the Rational Public: Cognition, Heuristics, and Mass Opinion." In *Elements of Reason*, edited by Arthur Lupia, Mathew D. McCubbins, and Samuel L. Popkin, 153–82. New York: Cambridge University Press.

Kydd, Andrew. 2000. "Arms Races and Arms Control: Modeling the Hawk Perspective." *American Journal of Political Science* 44:228–44.

Laracey, Mel. 1998. "The Presidential Newspaper: The Forgotten Way of Going Public." In *Speaking to the People: The Rhetorical Presidency in Historical Perspective*, edited by Richard J. Ellis, 66–86. Amherst: University of Massachusetts Press.

"Last-Minute Deal Averts Fiscal Cliff, Punts Big Issues to New Congress." 2013. In *CQ Almanac 2012*, 68th ed., 7-3 to 7-7. Washington, DC: CQ-Roll Call Group.

Lau, Richard R., and David P. Redlawsk. 2001. "Advantages and Disadvantages of Cognitive Heuristics in Political Decision Making." *American Journal of Political Science* 45, no. 4: 951–71.

Lavine, Howard G., Christopher D. Johnston, and Marco R. Steenbergen. 2012. *The Ambivalent Partisan: How Critical Loyalty Promotes Democracy.* New York: Oxford University Press.

Lawless, Jennifer L., and Kathryn Pearson. 2008. "The Primary Reason for Women's Underrepresentation? Reevaluating the Conventional Wisdom." *Journal of Politics* 70:67–82.

Lawrence, Eric D., Forrest Maltzman, and Steven S. Smith. 2006. "Who Wins? Party Effects in Legislative Voting." *Legislative Studies Quarterly* 31, no. 1: 33–69.

Lawrence, Evans C., and Claire Grandy. 2009. "The Whip Systems of Congress." In *Congress Reconsidered*, 9th ed., edited by Lawrence C. Dodd and Bruce I. Oppenheimer, 189–216. Washington, DC: Congressional Quarterly Press.

Lazarus, Jeffrey. 2010. "Giving the People What They Want? The Distribution of Earmarks in the U.S. House of Representatives." *American Journal of Political Science* 54, no. 2: 338–53.

Lazarus, Jeffrey, Jeffrey Glas, and Kyle T. Barbieri. 2012. "Earmarks and Elections to the U.S. House of Representatives." *Congress and the Presidency* 39, no. 3: 254–69.

Lazarus, Jeffrey, and Shauna Reilly. 2010. "The Electoral Benefits of Distributive Spending." *Political Research Quarterly* 63, no. 2: 343–55.

Lazarus, Jeffrey, and Amy Steigerwalt. 2009. "Different Houses: The Distribution of Earmarks in the U.S. House and Senate." *Legislative Studies Quarterly* 34, no. 3: 347–73.

Leavitt, Stephen D., and Catherine D. Wolfram. 1997. "Decomposing the Sources of Incumbency Advantage in the U.S. House." *Legislative Studies Quarterly* 22, no. 1: 45–60.

Lebo, Matthew J. 2008. "Divided Government, United Approval: The Dynamics of Congressional and Presidential Approval." *Congress and the Presidency* 35, no. 2: 1–16.

Lebo, Matthew J., and Daniel Cassino. 2007. "The Aggregated Consequences of Motivated Reasoning and the Dynamics of Partisan Presidential Approval." *Political Psychology* 28, no. 6: 719–46.

Lebo, Matthew J., Adam J. McGlynn, and Greg Koger. 2007. "Strategic Party Government: Party Influence in Congress, 1789–2000." *American Journal of Political Science* 51, no. 3: 464–81.

Lebo, Matthew J., and Will H. Moore. 2003. "Dynamic Foreign Policy." *Journal of Conflict Resolution* 47, no. 1: 13–32.

Lebo, Matthew J., and Andrew J. O'Geen. 2011. "The President's Role in the Partisan Congressional Arena." *Journal of Politics* 73, no. 3: 718–34.

Lebo, Matthew J., Robert W. Walker, and Harold D. Clarke. 2000. "You Must Remember This: Dealing with Long Memory in Political Analyses." *Electoral Studies* 19, no. 1: 31–48.

Lebo, Matthew J., and Christopher Weber. 2015. "An Effective Approach to the Repeated Cross-Sectional Design." *American Journal of Political Science* 59, no. 1: 242–58.

Lee, Frances E. 2009. *Beyond Ideology: Politics, Principles, and Partisanship in the U.S. Senate*. Chicago: University of Chicago Press.

Leighton, Wayne A., and Edward J. Lopez. 2002. "Committee Assignments and the Cost of Party Loyalty." *Political Research Quarterly* 55, no. 1: 59–90.

Levendusky, Matthew. 2009. *The Partisan Sort: How Liberals Became Democrats and Conservatives Became Republicans*. Chicago: University of Chicago Press.

———. 2013. *How Partisan Media Polarize America*. Chicago: University of Chicago Press.

Lewis-Beck, Michael S., and Tom W. Rice. 1984. "Forecasting U.S. House Elections." *Legislative Studies Quarterly* 9, no. 3: 475–86.

Light, Paul. 1998. *The President's Agenda: Domestic Policy Choice from Kennedy to Clinton*, 3rd ed. Baltimore: Johns Hopkins University Press.

Lindstädt, Rene, and Ryan Vander Wielen. 2011. "Timely Shirking: Time Dependent Monitoring and its Effects on Legislative Behavior in the U.S. Senate." *Public Choice* 148, no. 1–2: 119–48.

———. 2014. "Dynamic Elite Partisanship: Party Loyalty and Agenda Setting in the US House." *British Journal of Political Science* 44:741–72.

Londregan, John B. 2000. "Estimating Legislators Preferred Points." *Political Analysis* 8, no. 1: 35–56.

Lowell, Abbott Lawrence. 1902. "The Influence of Party upon Legislation in England and America." *Annual Report of the American Historical Association for 1901* 1:319–542.

Lupia, Arthur. 1994. "Shortcuts versus Encyclopedias: Information and Voting Behavior in California Insurance Reform Elections." *American Political Science Review* 88, no. 1: 63–76.

Lupia, Arthur, and Mathew D. McCubbins. 1998. *The Democratic Dilemma: Can Citizens Learn What They Need to Know?* New York: Cambridge University Press.

Mael, Fred A., and Lois Tetrick. 1992. "Identifying Organizational Identification." *Educational and Psychological Measurement* 54, no. 4: 813–24.

Maltzman, Forrest. 1997. *Competing Principles: Committees, Parties, and the Organization of Congress.* Ann Arbor: University of Michigan Press.

Mann, Robert. 1996. *The Walls of Jericho: Lyndon Johnson, Hubert Humphrey, Richard Russell, and the Struggle for Civil Rights.* New York: Harcourt Brace.

Mann, Thomas E., and Norman J. Ornstein. 2006. *The Broken Branch: How Congress Is Failing America and How to Get It Back on Track.* New York: Oxford University Press.

———. 2012. *It's Even Worse than It Looks: How the American Constitutional System Collided with the New Politics of Extremism.* New York: Basic Books.

Mann, Thomas E., and Raymond E. Wolfinger. 1980. "Candidates and Parties in Congressional Elections." *American Political Science Review* 74, no. 3: 617–32.

Mansbridge, Jane, and Cathie Jo Martin. 2013. "Negotiating Agreement in Politics: Report of the Task force on Negotiating Agreement in Politics." Washington, DC: American Political Science Association.

Marcos, Cristina, and Ramsey Cox. 2014. "Historically Unproductive Congress Ends." *The Hill*, December 16. http://thehill.com/blogs/floor-action/senate/227365-historically-unproductive-congress-ends.

Marshall, Bryan W. 2002. "Explaining the Role of Restrictive Rules in the Postreform House." *Legislative Studies Quarterly* 27, no. 1: 61–85.

Martis, Kenneth C. 1989. *The Historical Atlas of Political Parties in the United States Congress: 1789–1989.* New York: Macmillan.

Masket, Seth. 2013. "Can Polarization Be 'Fixed'? California's Experiment with the Top-Two Primary." In *Politics to the Extreme: American Political Institutions in the Twenty-First Century*, edited by Scott Frisch and Sean Kelley, 205–19. New York: Palgrave Macmillan.

Mayhew, David. 1974a. "The Case of the Vanishing Marginals." *Polity* 6:295–317.

———. 1974b. *Congress: The Electoral Connection.* New Haven: Yale University Press.

————. 2002. *Divided We Govern: Party Control, Lawmaking, and Investigations, 1946–2002*, 2nd ed. New Haven: Yale University Press.

McCarty, Nolan, Keith T. Poole, and Howard Rosenthal. 2006. *Polarized America: The Dance of Ideology and Unequal Riches*. Cambridge, MA: MIT Press.

McCormick, Richard L. 1982. "The Realignment Synthesis in American History." *Journal of Interdisciplinary History* 13, no. 1: 85–105.

McCown, Ada C. 1927. *The Congressional Conference Committee*. New York: Cambridge University Press.

McDonald, Michael P. 2004. "A Comparative Analysis of Redistricting Institutions in the United States, 2001–02." *State Politics & Policy Quarterly* 4, no. 4: 371–95.

McGhee, Eric, Seth Masket, Boris Shor, Steven Rogers, and Nolan McCarty. 2014. "A Primary Cause of Partisanship? Nomination Systems and Legislator Ideology." *American Journal of Political Science* 58, no. 2: 337–51.

McKelvey, Richard. 1976. "Intransitivities in Multidimensional Voting Models and Some Implications for Agenda Control." *Journal of Economic Theory* 12:471–82.

Milbank, Dana. 2014. "Good Riddance to the Worst Congress Ever." *Washington Post*, December 19. http://wpo.st/Fhxt0.

Miller, Gary, and Norman Schofield. 2003. "Activism and Partisan Realignment in the United States." *American Political Science Review* 97:245–60.

Miller, Warren E., and Donald E. Stokes. 1963. "Constituency Influence in Congress." *American Political Science Review* 57:45–56.

"Minutes of the Democratic Conference, May 20, 1969." Series 22, Box 90, Folder 10. Mike Mansfield Archives, K. Ross Toole Archives, University of Montana.

Montgomery, Lori, and Rosalind S. Helderman. 2012. "Boehner Abandons Plan to Avoid 'Fiscal Cliff.'" *Washington Post*, December 20. Accessed April 11, 2014. http://www.washingtonpost.com/politics/cliff-standoff-boehner-works-to -wrangle-votes-for-plan-b-obama-threatens-veto/2012/12/20/d37cd8c6-4aa5 -11e2-9a42d1ce6d0ed278_story.html.

Murray, Michael P. 1994. "A Drunk and Her Dog: An Illustration of Cointegration and Error Correction." *The American Statistician* 48, no. 1: 37–39.

Nelson, Garrison, and Clark Hamilton Benson. 1993. *Committees in the U.S. Congress, 1947–1992, Vol. 2, Committee Histories and Member Assignments*. Washington, DC: Congressional Quarterly Press.

Nie, Norman, Sidney Verba, and John R. Petrocik. 1978. *The Changing American Voter*. Cambridge, MA: Harvard University Press.

Noel, Hans. 2014. *Political Ideologies and Political Parties in America*. New York: Cambridge University Press.

Norton, Stephen J. 2005a. "CAFTA Squeaks through in House Vote." *CQ Weekly*, August 1, 2111–13.

————. 2005b. "Central America Accord Gropes for Hill Support." *CQ Weekly*, April 25, 1063–64.

————. "House Primed for Vote on CAFTA." *CQ Weekly*, July 25, 2047.

Nyhan, Brendan, Eric McGhee, John Sides, Seth Masket, and Steven Greene. 2012. "One Vote Out of Step? The Effects of Salient Roll Call Votes in the 2010 Election." *American Politics Research* 40, no. 5: 844–79.

O'Connor, Patrick. 2005a. "Anatomy of a Vote: How Blunt Whipped CAFTA." *The Hill*, September 6.

———. 2005b. "CAFTA: The Night of the Vote." *The Hill*, September 8.

———. 2005c. "Marshalling K Street's Battalions for CAFTA." *The Hill*, September 7.

O'Keefe, Ed. 2014. "The House Has Voted 54 Times in Four Years on Obamacare. Here's the Full List." *Washington Post*, March 21. Accessed April, 21, 2014. http://www.washingtonpost.com/blogs/the-fix/wp/2014/03/21/the-house-has-voted-54-times-in-four-years-on-obamacare-heres-the-full-list/.

Ornstein, Norman J. 2011. "Worst. Congress. Ever." *Foreign Policy*, July 19. http://foreignpolicy.com/2011/07/19/worst-congress-ever/.

Ornstein, Norman J., Thomas E. Mann, and Michael J. Malbin. 2008. *Vital Statistics on Congress*. Washington, DC: Brookings Institution Press.

Ornstein, Norman J., Thomas E. Mann, Michael J. Malbin, Andrew Rugg, and Raffaela Wakeman. 2013. *Vital Statistics on Congress Data on the U.S. Congress—a Joint Effort from Brookings and the American Enterprise Institute*. Brookings Institution Report, July. http://www.brookings.edu/research/reports/2013/07/vital-statistics-congress-mann-ornstein.

Ota, Alan K. 2005. "Lobbyists Enlisted to Whip the House." *CQ Weekly*, May 2, 1122–23.

Parker, Christopher S., and Matt A. Barreto. 2013. *Change They Can't Believe In*. Princeton: Princeton University Press.

Patty, John W. 2007. "The House Discharge Procedure and Majoritarian Politics." *Journal of Politics* 69, no. 3: 678–88.

———. 2008. "Equilibrium Party Government." *American Journal of Political Science* 52, no. 3: 636–55.

Patty, John, and Elizabeth Maggie Penn. 2008. "The Legislative Calendar." *Mathematical and Computer Modelling* 48:1590–1601, 2008.

Payne, Ethel. 1956. "How Ike Broke Back of South." *Chicago Defender*, November 17.

Peabody, Robert L. 1976. *Leadership in Congress: Stability, Succession and Change*. Boston: Little, Brown.

Pearson, Kathryn, and Eric Schickler. 2009. "Discharge Petitions, Agenda Control, and the Congressional Committee System, 1929–1976." *Journal of Politics* 71, no. 4: 1238–56.

Peterson, Michael B., Rune Slothuus, Rune Stubager, and Lise Togeby. 2011. "Deservingness versus Values in Public Opinion on Welfare: The Automaticity of the Deservingness Heuristic." *European Journal of Political Research* 50, no. 1: 24–52.

Petrocik, John. 1996. "Issue Ownership in Presidential Elections, with a 1980 Case Study." *American Journal of Political Science* 40, no. 3: 825–50.

Pew Research Center. 2010. "What Americans Know, 1989–2007." Accessed April 12. http://people-press.org/report/319/public-knowledge-of-current -affairs-little-changed-by-news-and-information-revolutions.

Plott, Charles. 1967. "A Notion of Equilibrium and Its Possibility under Majority Rule." *American Economic Review* 57:787–806.

Polser, Brian, and Carl Rhodes. 1997. "Pre-leadership Signaling in the U.S. House." *Legislative Studies Quarterly* 22, no. 3: 351–68.

Poole, Keith T., and Howard Rosenthal. 1997. *Congress: A Political Economic History of Roll Call Voting*. New York: Oxford University Press.

———. 2007. *Ideology and Congress*. New Brunswick: Transaction.

Pope, Jeremy C., and Jonathan Woon. 2009. "Measuring Changes in American Party Reputations, 1939–2004." *Political Research Quarterly* 62, no. 4: 653–61.

Popkin, Samuel L. 1991. *The Reasoning Voter: Communication and Persuasion in Presidential Campaigns*. Chicago: University of Chicago Press.

Popkin, Samuel L., and Michael A. Dimock. 2000. "Knowledge, Trust and International Reasoning." In *Elements of Reason*, edited by Arthur Lupia, Mathew D. McCubbins, and Samuel L Popkin, 214–38. New York: Cambridge University Press.

Potoski, Matthew, and Jeffery Talbert. 2000. "The Dimensional Structure of Policy Outputs: Distributive Policy and Roll Call Voting." *Political Research Quarterly* 53, no. 4: 695–710.

Prior, Markus. 2007. *Post-broadcast Democracy: How Media Choice Increases Inequality in Political Involvement and Polarizes Elections*. New York: Cambridge University Press.

Rahn, Wendy M. 1993. "The Role of Partisan Stereotypes in Information Processing about Political Candidates." *American Journal of Political Science* 37, no. 2: 472–96.

"Redistricting Key to House Elections." 2013. In *CQ Almanac 2012*, 68th ed., 12-9 to 12-12. Washington, DC: CQ-Roll Call Group. http://library.cqpress.com /cqalmanac/cqal121531-87299-553372.

Richardson, Lewis F. 1960. *Arms and Insecurity*. Chicago: Boxwood Press.

Roberts, Jason M. 2010. "The Development of Special Orders and Special Rules in the U.S. House, 1881–1937." *Legislative Studies Quarterly* 35:307–36.

Roberts, Jason M., and Steven S. Smith. 2003. "Procedural Contexts, Party Strategy, and Conditional Party Government in the U.S. House of Representatives, 1971–2000." *American Journal of Political Science* 47, no. 2: 305–17.

Robinson, Peter M. 1995. "Gaussian Semiparametric Estimation of Long Range Dependence." *Annals of Statistics* 23, no. 5: 1630–61.

Rogowski, Jon C. 2014. "Electoral Choice, Ideological Conflict, and Political Participation." *American Journal of Political Science* 58:479–94.

Rohde, David W. 1991. *Parties and Leaders in the Post-reform House*. Chicago: University of Chicago Press.

———. 2013. "Reflections on the Practice of Theorizing: Conditional Party Government in the Twenty-First Century." *Journal of Politics* 71, no. 4: 849–64.

Rohde, David W., and Kenneth A. Shepsle. 1973. "Democratic Committee Assignments in the of Representatives: Strategic Aspects of a Social Choice Process." *The American Political Science Review* 67, no. 3: 889–905.

Rothman, David J. 1966. *Politics and Power: The United States Senate, 1869–1901*. Cambridge, MA: Harvard University Press.

Schattschneider, Elmer E. 2003. *Party Government: American Government in Action*. 1942. Reprint, New Brunswick: Transaction.

Schickler, Eric. 2000. "Institutional Change in the House of Representatives, 1867–1998: A Test of Partisan and Ideological Balance Models." *American Political Science Review* 94, no. 2: 269–88.

———. 2001. *Disjointed Pluralism: Institutional Innovation and the Development of the U.S. Congress*. Princeton: Princeton University Press.

Schickler, Eric, Kathryn Pearson, and Brian D. Feinstein. 2010. "Congressional Parties and Civil Rights Politics from 1933 to 1972." *Journal of Politics* 72:672–89.

Sears, David O. 1975. "Political Socialization." In *Handbook of Political Science*, Vol. 2, edited by F. I. Greenstein and N. W. Polsby, 93–153. Reading: Addison-Wesley.

Sears, David O., and Nicholas A. Valentino. 1997. "Politics Matters: Political Events as Catalysts for Pre-adult Socialization." *American Political Science Review* 91, no. 1: 45–65.

Shepsle, Kenneth A. 1978. *The Giant Jigsaw Puzzle: Democratic Committee Assignments in the Modern House*. Chicago: University of Chicago Press.

———. 1979. "Institutional Arrangements and Equilibrium in Multidimensional Voting Models." *American Journal of Political Science* 23, no. 1: 27–59.

Shepsle, Kenneth, Robert Van Houweling, Samuel Abrams, and Peter Hanson. 2009. "The Senate Electoral Cycle and Bicameral Appropriations Politics." *American Journal of Political Science* 53, no. 2: 343–59.

Sherman, Jake. 2015. "Freedom Caucus Suggests House Rules Changes." *Politico*, October 8. http://www.politico.com/blogs/the-gavel/2015/10/house-freedom-caucus-rules-change-214591.

Simaan, M., and J. B. Cruz Jr. 1975. "Nash Equilibrium Strategies for the Problem of Armament Race and Control." *Management Science* 22:96–105.

Sinclair, Barbara. 1983. *Majority Leadership in the U.S. House*. Baltimore: Johns Hopkins University Press.

———. 1994. "House Special Rules and the Institutional Design Controversy." *Legislative Studies Quarterly* 19, no. 4: 477–94.

———. 1995. *Legislators, Leaders and Lawmaking*. Baltimore: Johns Hopkins University Press.

———. 2002a. "Do Parties Matter?" In *Party, Process, and Political Change in Congress: New Perspectives on the History of Congress*, Vol. 1, edited by David W. Brady and Mathew D. McCubbins, 36–63. Palo Alto: Stanford University Press.

———. 2002b. "The Dream Fulfilled? Party Development in Congress, 1950–2000." In *Responsible Partisanship*, edited by John Clifford Green and Paul S. Herrnson, 121–40. Lawrence: University of Kansas Press.

———. 2006. *Party Wars: Polarization and the Politics of National Policy Making.* Norman: University of Oklahoma Press.

Skowronek, Stephen. 1982. *Building a New American State: The Expansion of National Administration Capacities, 1877–1920.* New York: Cambridge University Press.

Smith, Steven. 1989. *Call to Order: Floor Politics in the House and Senate.* Washington, DC: Brookings Institution Press.

———. 2005. "Parties and Leadership in the Senate." In *The Legislative Branch and American Democracy: Institutions and Performance*, edited by Sarah A. Binder and Paul J. Quirk, 255–80. Oxford: Oxford University Press.

———. 2007. *Party Influence in Congress.* New York: Cambridge University Press.

Smith, Steven S., and A. Bruce Ray. 1983. "The Impact of Congressional Reform: House Democratic Committee Assignments." *Congress and the Presidency* 10, no. 2: 219–40.

Sniderman, Paul M., Richard A. Brody, and Phillip E. Tetlock. 1991. *Reasoning and Choice: Explorations in Political Psychology.* New York: Cambridge University Press.

Snyder, James M. 1991. "On Buying Legislatures." *Economics and Politics* 3, no. 2: 93–109.

Snyder, James M., Jr., and Tim Groseclose. 2000. "Estimating Party Influence in Congressional Roll-Call Voting." *American Journal of Political Science* 44, no. 2: 193–211.

Snyder, James M., Jr., and Michael M. Ting. 2002. "An Informational Rationale for Political Parties." *American Journal of Political Science* 46, no. 1: 90–110.

———. 2003. "Roll Calls, Party Labels, and Elections." *Political Analysis* 11, no. 4: 419–44.

Sorkin, Andrew Ross, Diana B. Henriques, Edmund L. Andrews, and Joe Nocera. 2008. "As Credit Crisis Spiraled, Alarm Led to Action." *New York Times*, October 1. http://www.nytimes.com/2008/10/02/business/02crisis.html?pagewanted=all.

Stewart, Charles, III, and Jonathan Woon. 2011. *Congressional Committee Assignments, 103rd to 112th Congresses, 1993–2011: House and Senate.* June 24.

Stone, Walter J., and Simas, Elizabeth N. 2010. "Candidate Valence and Ideological Positions in U.S. House Elections." *American Journal of Political Science* 54:371–88.

Strahan, Randall. 2007. *Leading Representatives: The Agency of Leaders in the Politics of the U.S. House*. Baltimore: Johns Hopkins University Press.

Swift, Elaine K., Robert G. Brookshire, David T. Canon, Evelyn C. Fink, John R. Hibbing, Brian D. Humes, Michael J. Malbin, and Kenneth C. Martis. 2000. *Database of Congressional Historical Statistics*. Distributed by Ann Arbor, MI: Inter-university Consortium for Political and Social Research.

Taber, Charles S., and Milton Lodge. 2006. "Motivated Skepticism in the Evaluation of Political Beliefs." *American Journal of Political Science* 50, no. 3: 755–69.

Tajfel, Henri. 1981. *Human Groups and Social Categories: Studies in Social Psychology*. New York: Cambridge University Press.

Tajfel, Henri, and J. Turner. 1979. "An Integrative Theory of Intergroup Conflict." In *The Social Psychology of Intergroup Relations*, edited by W. G. Austin and S. Worchel, 33–48. Chicago: Nelson-Hall.

Talbert, Jeffery C., and Matthew Potoski. 2002. "Setting the Legislative Agenda: The Dimensional Structure of Bill Cosponsoring and Floor Voting." *Journal of Politics* 64, no. 3: 864–91.

Theriault, Sean M. 2005. *The Power of the People: Congressional Competition, Public Attention, and Voter Retribution*. Columbus: Ohio State University Press.

———. 2008. *Party Polarization in Congress*. New York: Cambridge University Press.

———. 2013. *The Gingrich Senators: The Roots of Partisan Warfare in Congress*. New York: Oxford University Press.

Topaz, Jonathan. 2014. "'Worst Congress Ever,' by the Numbers." *Politico*, December 17. http://www.politico.com/story/2014/12/congress-numbers-113658.

Truman, David Bicknell. 1959. *The Congressional Party: A Case Study*. New York: John Wiley & Sons.

Tse, Y. K. 2000. "A Test for Constant Correlations in a Multivariate GARCH Model." *Journal of Econometrics* 98, no. 1: 107–27.

Valelly, Richard M. 2004. *The Two Reconstructions: The Struggle for Black Enfranchisement*. Chicago: University of Chicago Press.

Valeo, Francis R. 1999. *Mike Mansfield, Majority Leader: A Different Kind of Senate, 1961–1976*. New York: M. E. Sharpe.

Volden, Craig, and Elizabeth Bergman. 2006. "How Strong Should Our Party Be? Party Member Preferences over Party Cohesion." *Legislative Studies Quarterly* 31, no. 1: 71–104.

Wawro, Gregory J., and Eric Schickler. 2006. *Filibuster: Obstruction and Lawmaking in the U.S. Senate*. Princeton, NJ: Princeton University Press.

Weisman, Jonathan. 2005. "CAFTA Reflects Democrats' Shift from Trade Bills." *Washington Post*, July 6. Accessed August 17, 2013. http://www.washingtonpost.com/wpdyn/content/article/2005/07/05/AR2005070501345_pf.html.

Welch, Richard E., Jr. 1965. "The Federal Elections Bill of 1890: Postscripts and Prelude." *The Journal of American History* 3 (Dec): 511–26.

Williamson, Vanessa, Theda Skocpol, and John Coggin. 2013. "The Tea Party and the Remaking of Republican Conservatism." *Perspectives on Politics* 9, no. 1: 25–43.

Wilson, James Q. 1962. *The Amateur Democrat: Club Politics in 3 Cities*. Chicago: University of Chicago Press.

Wilson, Woodrow. 1885. *Congressional Government*. Boston: Houghton Mifflin.

Wooldridge, Jeffrey M. 2002. *Econometric Analysis of Cross Section and Panel Data*. Cambridge, MA: MIT Press.

Woon, Jonathan, and Jeremy C. Pope. 2008. "Made in Congress? Testing the Electoral Implications of Party Ideological Brand Names." *Journal of Politics* 70, no. 3: 823–36.

Wright, Fiona M. 2000. "The Caucus Reelection Requirement and the Transformation of House Committee Chairs, 1959–94." *Legislative Studies Quarterly* 25, no. 3: 469–80.

Wright, John R. 2000. "Interest Groups, Congressional Reform, and Party Government in the United States." *Legislative Studies Quarterly* 25:217–35.

Zaller, John R. 1992. *The Nature and Origins of Mass Opinion*. New York: Cambridge University Press.

Zelizer, Julian E. 2004. *The American Congress: The Building of Democracy*. New York: Houghton Mifflin.

Zernike, Kate. 2010. "Tea Party Set to Win Enough Races for Wide Influence." *New York Times*, October 14. http://www.nytimes.com/2010/10/15/us/politics/15teaparty.html?_r=1&hp.

Index

Chicago Studies in American Politics

A SERIES EDITED BY BENJAMIN I. PAGE, SUSAN HERBST,
LAWRENCE R. JACOBS, AND ADAM J. BERINSKY

Series titles, continued from front matter:

HOW PARTISAN MEDIA POLARIZE AMERICA *by Matthew Levendusky*

THE POLITICS OF BELONGING: RACE, PUBLIC OPINION, AND IMMIGRATION *by Natalie Masuoka and Jane Junn*

POLITICAL TONE: HOW LEADERS TALK AND WHY *by Roderick P. Hart, Jay P. Childers, and Colene J. Lind*

THE TIMELINE OF PRESIDENTIAL ELECTIONS: HOW CAMPAIGNS DO (AND DO NOT) MATTER *by Robert S. Erikson and Christopher Wlezien*

LEARNING WHILE GOVERNING: EXPERTISE AND ACCOUNTABILITY IN THE EXECUTIVE BRANCH *by Sean Gailmard and John W. Patty*

ELECTING JUDGES: THE SURPRISING EFFECTS OF CAMPAIGNING ON JUDICIAL LEGITIMACY *by James L. Gibson*

FOLLOW THE LEADER? HOW VOTERS RESPOND TO POLITICIANS' POLICIES AND PERFORMANCE *by Gabriel S. Lenz*

THE SOCIAL CITIZEN: PEER NETWORKS AND POLITICAL BEHAVIOR *by Betsy Sinclair*

THE SUBMERGED STATE: HOW INVISIBLE GOVERNMENT POLICIES UNDERMINE AMERICAN DEMOCRACY *by Suzanne Mettler*

DISCIPLINING THE POOR: NEOLIBERAL PATERNALISM AND THE PERSISTENT POWER OF RACE *by Joe Soss, Richard C. Fording, and Sanford F. Schram*

WHY PARTIES? A SECOND LOOK *by John H. Aldrich*

NEWS THAT MATTERS: TELEVISION AND AMERICAN OPINION, UPDATED EDITION *by Shanto Iyengar and Donald R. Kinder*

SELLING FEAR: COUNTERTERRORISM, THE MEDIA, AND PUBLIC OPINION *by Brigitte L. Nacos, Yaeli Bloch-Elkon, and Robert Y. Shapiro*

OBAMA'S RACE: THE 2008 ELECTION AND THE DREAM OF A POST-RACIAL AMERICA *by Michael Tesler and David O. Sears*

FILIBUSTERING: A POLITICAL HISTORY OF OBSTRUCTION IN THE HOUSE AND SENATE *by Gregory Koger*

IN TIME OF WAR: UNDERSTANDING AMERICAN PUBLIC OPINION FROM WORLD WAR II TO IRAQ *by Adam J. Berinsky*

US AGAINST THEM: ETHNOCENTRIC FOUNDATIONS OF AMERICAN OPINION *by Donald R. Kinder and Cindy D. Kam*

THE PARTISAN SORT: HOW LIBERALS BECAME DEMOCRATS AND CONSERVATIVES BECAME REPUBLICANS *by Matthew Levendusky*

DEMOCRACY AT RISK: HOW TERRORIST THREATS AFFECT THE PUBLIC *by Jennifer L. Merolla and Elizabeth J. Zechmeister*

AGENDAS AND INSTABILITY IN AMERICAN POLITICS, SECOND EDITION *by Frank R. Baumgartner and Bryan D. Jones*

THE PRIVATE ABUSE OF THE PUBLIC INTEREST *by Lawrence D. Brown and Lawrence R. Jacobs*

THE PARTY DECIDES: PRESIDENTIAL NOMINATIONS BEFORE AND AFTER REFORM *by Marty Cohen, David Karol, Hans Noel, and John Zaller*

SAME SEX, DIFFERENT POLITICS: SUCCESS AND FAILURE IN THE STRUGGLES OVER GAY RIGHTS *by Gary Mucciaroni*